THE O'REILLY factor

ALSO BY BILL O'REILLY

The No Spin Zone:
Confrontations with the Powerful and
Famous in America

THE GOOD, BAD, AND COMPLETELY

RIDICULOUS IN AMERICAN LIFE

BILL O'REILLY

BROADWAY BOOKS | New York

Broadway Books titles may be purchased for business or promotional use or for special sales. For information, please write to: Special Markets Department, Random House, Inc., 1540 Broadway, New York, NY 10036.

PRINTED IN THE UNITED STATES OF AMERICA

BROADWAY BOOKS and its logo, a letter B bisected on the diagonal, are trademarks of Broadway Books, a division of Random House, Inc.

Visit our website at www.broadwaybooks.com

First trade paperback edition published 2002

Designed by Gretchen Achilles

The Library of Congress has cataloged the hardcover edition as:
O'Reilly, Bill.
    The O'Reilly factor / Bill O'Reilly.—1st ed.
      p. cm.
    1. United States—Politics and government—1993– 2. United States—Social conditions—1980– 3. O'Reilly, Bill—Political and social views.

    E885 .O74 2000
    973.929—dc21

                                    00-057892

ISBN 0-7679-0529-6

10 9 8 7 6 5 4 3 2

This book is dedicated to my television agent, CAROLE COOPER, who has watched my back for more than twenty years.

acknowledgments

The following people helped me greatly in writing this book. They are in no particular order: MAUREEN, MADELINE, AND ANN O'REILLY, CHARLES FLOWERS, ROGER AILES, CHET COLLIER, MAKEDA WUBNEH, DAVID CHALFANT, GAETON FONZI, LUKE DEMPSEY, ROBERT ASAHINA, BRUCE BORTZ, WALTER ANDERSON, LEE KRAVITZ, ABYNA ZIMMERMAN.

contents

Livin' in America
So nice, with your bad self
Livin' in America,
I feel good.
—JAMES BROWN

INTRODUCTION

If you know who I am, you know why I get letters like this one from a certain Linden S., who lives in Rochester, New York:

> O'Reilly, dislike and contempt dominate your thoughts. So highly charged is your bias that it is a constant astonishment to realize that you are unaware of the effect of your own thinking. A thoughtful, deliberative person doesn't stand a chance with you.

That's only one letter, selected at random. They come in bushels every day. Something about me and my nightly news analysis program, *The O'Reilly Factor*, drives some people up the wall.

But, hey, I'm used to it. I didn't even have to have the top-rated cable news program to get the same response from my first-grade teacher. I was controversial in the first grade, Linden! I come by it honestly!

It took Sister Mary Claudia only to the second day of first grade at St. Brigid's School in Westbury, New York, to get my number. When she ordered our class of sixty six-year-olds to open our *Think and Do* books, I slumped in my seat and let loose a deep sigh. See, I have always had a thing about lies, lying, and liars—and this book was pure propaganda. The illustrations of kids smiling while doing math problems was a major lie. I knew that at six years old.

But Sister Mary Claudia didn't care and leapt on me like a mongoose. "William," she shouted. "You are a bold, fresh piece of humanity! You will open your book and close your mouth. You are bold!"

Thus was laid down the course of my life and career, as writers of another age might put it. Ever since, I have starred in a series of confrontations with overreaching authority figures. Sometimes I was just being a pain in the rear. (Hey, you have to practice these things!) But a lot of the time I was challenging the prevailing wisdom because my sense of justice or truth was outraged. That outrage became my passion . . . and my vocation. Today I get paid a healthy sum for pursuing that passion on national television in prime time. *The O'Reilly Factor* has been on the air for four years, and they say the ratings are steadily rising while the overall prime-time ratings for cable news networks are sinking. Sister Mary Claudia, can you hear me over the harps?

Doesn't matter. If the good sister's not in touch, there are always people like the Reverend and Mrs. Dennis N. of Georgia:

> Mr. O'Reilly, you have lost us as viewers. We are sure your lies are born of ignorance. Repent while you still can.

Thanks for the concern, but it's too late, Reverend.

☼

If you've tuned in to *The O'Reilly Factor*, you know that I usually have five guests on my hour-long program. You might see me interviewing George W. Bush about the latest wrinkle in his campaign. Or bugging former special prosecutor Kenneth Starr about his refusal to go public with all he suspects about the Clintons and their sleazy shenanigans. Or getting former White House chief of staff Leon Panetta to admit that the Clinton administration doesn't know what happened to some $1 billion it sent to Haiti. Some people think I'm a tough interviewer, but I think I'm fair. And I'm appreciative of my guests. It takes guts for some of these people to come on the *Factor*, because they don't know which way I'm gonna go.

Sometimes I bring on my paid on-air consultants, like Newt Gingrich, Geraldine Ferraro, and Dick Morris. They don't usually agree with each other, as you might expect, and they don't usually agree with me. And I always begin each program with a "Talking Point." You'll see what I mean as you read this book, because I use a few here. And I always give the floor at the end of the program to viewer reactions, which are by far the liveliest in all of broadcasting. Some of those comments are scattered throughout these pages.

If you haven't seen *The O'Reilly Factor*, you might be wondering whether I'm conservative, liberal, libertarian, or exactly what. I hope you're still wondering when you do catch my program and also after you've read this book, my first attempt to put my thoughts in print.

See, I don't want to fit any of those labels, because I believe that the truth doesn't have labels. When I see corruption, I try to expose it. When I see exploitation, I try to fight it. That's my political position.

And in this book, just as on the *Factor*, I will not waste your time. Count on it. I will get to the pith quickly and undiplomatically—even if the pith pithes you off. Sorry, but that's not my problem. I tell it. You hear it. The truth is *often* annoying. It's always easier to look the other way. But it is essential that we all look at American life the way it *really* is today. If we don't do that job, we're gonna lose the battles to the frauds, fools, and thieves—the kind of people you are going to be hearing about in this book.

I love doing the *Factor*. I'm proud of my work. But television can be frustrating because there are so many subjects every day, and so little time every night. So I decided to write a book that would have no commercial interruptions and no director signaling me that a segment's got to end. I took my time writing this book, and I hope you will take your time reading it and thinking about my ideas. What I've tried to do here is give a blunt look at our times, which are very complicated. America in the twenty-first century can be a savage place, full of ridiculous situations and idiotic people. Life in the U.S.A. can also be fun and rewarding. But to make that happen, you have to separate the good from the bad from the ridiculous. I'm trying to help you do that . . . in a none-too-gentle way.

The O'Reilly Factor, the book, is divided into three sections. The first part of the book deals with what you as an individual are up against in your life as an American: That means things like your status in society, money, sex, and the ever-present media. Then we focus on personal relationships—the important ties that bind you to family, friends, and bosses. The final chapters concern America itself and what is happening to the country today.

I won't spoon over any *Chicken Soup* advice here. We're not gonna get "in the zone" or use New Age claptrap or find answers in any Mars-Venus conflict. This is just the straight story as I've lived it and you've lived it. You'll see.

1. THE CLASS factor

NOTE TO REV. JESSE JACKSON: Sorry, Jesse. You're wrong. Racism gets all the ink, but the heart of America's somewhat unfair social setup is class, not race. This fact might cut into your power base, but it's true.

The question for this age in America is: What class are you?

Never thought about it? You should. Each one of us is born into a very specific economic and social class, regardless of color. Most of us remain in that class, for better or worse, until the day we die. The more observant among us can usually sum up a complete stranger's class background within minutes.

Politicians don't usually talk about class. It might open a dangerous door. Advertisers want us to believe we're all one class: the *consuming* class, equal as long as we keep spending. The rich want us to believe that anyone can make the quantum leap from bowling league to country club by just working a little harder. That's supposed to keep us motivated and quiet.

But does class really matter? Would every blue-collar family be happier and more productive if a long-lost relative died and a trust fund flew in the window overnight?

No, but class is not just about money. It is about opportunity for your kids or dashed hopes, about education or minds that close down for good, about enduring values or materialism that comes out as greed or self-indulgence or complete disregard for others. It is the bottom line, in a way, for every problem I talk about in this book. Class attitudes can be involved in unfair tax laws, or government indifference about our terrible drug problem, or what kind of entertainment is available at the local movie house. Class plays a role in gun control laws that restrict personal freedom for the little guy and in casual enforcement of drunk driving laws.

As someone once said, "Class in America is like sex in Victorian times: People believe that if no one talks about it, it will just go away."

♯

Whatever I have done or will do in this life, I'm working-class Irish American Bill O'Reilly. No one ever told me or my sister that we were pretty far down the social totem pole while we were growing up in 1960s America. We took for granted that it was normal to buy cars only when they were secondhand, that every family clipped coupons to save money, and that luncheon meats were the special of the day. The municipal pool in our town on Long Island, New York, was pretty seedy, and we took the Greyhound bus to Miami for our annual vacation, but since air travel and private pools simply did not exist in our world, we never thought we were missing anything.

RIDICULOUS NOTE: Deprivation works both ways, it seems. I'll never forget my astonishment reading that First Lady Jackie Kennedy learned about Green Stamps from a White House employee. This elegant, cultured upper-class young woman was delighted to find that these stamps, which were given out by retailers like supermarkets as a reward for shopping, could be redeemed for "free" electric blankets and the like. For a time, wealthy Mrs. Kennedy collected the stamps like mad.

My parents, who loved us both and wanted the best for us, believed that "the best" was playing it safe in life and not straying too far from the neighborhood. One of my grandfathers walked a police beat in Brooklyn, the other was a train conductor, my mother's mother was a telephone operator, and my uncle was a fireman. My sister became a nurse. I was expected to become a teacher or, if I got very lucky, a lawyer. My mother, not wanting me to become a nonconformist in the 1970s, would not rest until I wore a "leisure suit."

My father, who never made more than $35,000 a year while exhausting himself commuting daily from Levittown to New York City to work as currency accountant for an oil company, took for granted that college for his son meant one thing above all: employment security. He and my mother graduated from college, but they did not remember the experience as a life-altering event. Dad didn't want me rocking the boat or getting big ideas. He looked ready to throw up when I told him I was going to study abroad during my junior year.

"Why do you want to do that?" he snorted. "You could start on the football team!"

He didn't know, as I did by then, that the privileged classes saw the college years as an opportunity for learning a great many things that did not necessarily involve going home on weekends. Sure, some rich students I knew may have grandstanded about hangovers in Spain and sexy nights beside the canals in Venice, but they also learned from experience about different cultures and ways of thinking and saw firsthand some of the great achievements of European art and learning.

Of course, my father had never met such people of privilege, nor did he care to. He was proud of his spartan life with its fast foods, yearly three-week-long vacation, and four Robert Hall suits hanging in a small closet in a three-bedroom, one-bathroom home. All of his friends lived much the same way and were just as proud.

Most of my childhood friends stayed in the neighborhood, married each other, and now live fairly comfortable middle-class lives. Some of them are happy, some aren't. But few of them realize how much their lives have been defined for them, even laid out for them, by a class system that discourages most of us from moving up the social ladder, no matter how hard we work.

Could some of them be happier or more productive if they had had the opportunity to go to graduate school to become architects or physicians or cancer researchers? Yes. It's not that one type of job is more important than another; it's that each of us should have the opportunity to use our own talents and follow our own dreams. A mind *is* a terrible thing to waste if you're held back by race or by gender. It is just as great a waste when you're held back by class. Right, Rev. Jackson?

Ƕ

A great scientist, J. B. S. Haldane, was asked the most important thing he had learned in his years of study. "That God must love beetles," he replied, "because he created so many different kinds of them."

American politicians, businesspeople, and media moguls have to love the middle and working classes because we exist in such huge numbers. If they didn't exactly create us, they do their best to keep us there. We make them prosperous. McDonald's, Burger King, and the like can't survive by supplying takeout only to the rich in Palm Beach, Malibu, and the Hamptons.

Without us, say good-bye to country music and rap, slasher flicks and Home Shopping Network, the Gap and SUVs, Jerry Springer and Oprah, malls and malt liquor, tattoo parlors and trailer parks, Myrtle Beach and Branson, Missouri, professional wrestling and the *National Enquirer*.

TALKING POINT: This country hums along economically because of the toil and the tastes of the working class . . . and the big-profit boys will do almost anything to keep it that way. Factor that into the price of your next Happy Meal.

✻

In Barry Levinson's great movie *Diner*, the working-class heroes drive out into the country and spot a beautiful blonde riding her horse across the fields in the cool of the morning. Poised and confident, she chats briefly with them and rides on. "You ever get the feeling," asks one of the young men, "that there's something going on that we don't know about?"

Like most working-class kids, I first learned about the class system and its rigidity when I left home in Levittown for the wider world. As a freshman at Marist College in Poughkeepsie, New York, a fine and affordable school, I was like most of my class: "ethnic" instead of old-line WASP, smack-dab in the middle of the middle class, and a little rough around the edges in social situations.

Vassar, at that time still a tony women-only college that boasted Jane Fonda as an alumna, was nearby, but Marist guys were not considered prizes at Vassar dances. The Ivy Leaguers up from Princeton or down from Cornell got the dates; we were treated like hired help. Our clever response to such snobbery? We overturned the punch bowl . . . thus proving their point!

Even when our hormones weren't raging out of control, my college pals and I were far from being Ivy League material. None of my friends came from families that could afford the tuition there, nor could they benefit from the old-school-tie tradition of preference for the children of alumni. We certainly couldn't dress as well as a Princeton Tiger or hold up our end of a conversation about regattas.

Following the path that seemed destined for me, I became a high school teacher after graduation. There's no job more important, and few are more difficult. But I was ambitious for the larger stage and left after two years to go to Boston University for a master's degree in journalism. From the campus of this mostly middle-class school my friends and I could look across the Charles River at MIT and Harvard, observing that more than a stretch of dirty water separated us. Our degrees would not open as many doors as degrees earned over there. Our fathers did not have friends waiting to interview us for fast-track jobs as soon as we got our sheepskin. Many of my classmates set their sights lower than they should have, in my view, because they believed they were already behind in the race.

Years later, in an effort to bring all sorts of people together in a creative mix, Harvard's John Kennedy School of Government accepted me for postgraduate study when I was in the middle of my broadcasting career. Suddenly Bill O'Reilly was in a world where no new friend was named Vinny, Stevie, or Serge, and there were no girls called Amber, Tiffany, or Jennifer. Many of my new classmates had three names, and they expected to hear all three of them: Stephen Tristen Copen, Robin Braden Crosfield.

It was the first time I actually knew people who never had to think about money. Their clothing was understated but top-quality, their cars were European and well tuned, and their rooms hinted of exotic vacations and sprawling family properties. Winter skiing in Grindelwald? A must. I learned that a "cottage" could be a twenty-two-room mansion on a northeastern beach or a "camp" a forty-acre property on a lake in the Adirondacks with houses and outbuildings more than a century old.

My classmates were impeccably polite and welcoming, by the way. We might go out together to a restaurant down the way for Thai food. That was fun, even when I was the only one who didn't know how to order my meal in Thai.

CLASS FROM THE PAST: When President Ronald Reagan was nearly killed by a madman's bullet, he put on a brave front to calm the American public. Traveling west to his Santa Barbara ranch to recuperate, he stopped to rest in Chicago and made a brief statement. As he prepared to speak, local officials were horrified by his deep wheezing and weak voice. But when he stepped up to the mike, Reagan spoke strongly, taking a slight breath between every few words to keep his voice steady. It was an actor's trick, but it was also a class act in a time of national concern.

I studied my Harvard classmates more intently than my political courses at the Kennedy school. I had a nice enough tuxedo, I thought, but a friend might have several. Oh, and it's déclassé to say "tuxedo" or "tux," old boy—it's "evening clothes" or "formal wear." Because the point was not really the material things themselves: It was having the right *attitude*, which meant acting a certain way and using the terms and accents of the elite. One rule was not to be "pretentious." A neighbor in Levittown might save up money and take pride in new drapes. No class. The upper classes refer to "curtains," not "drapes," "rugs," not "carpets," and so forth. The expensive cars and clothing were never flashy, never too colorful, never ornamented.

Generally speaking, my Harvard classmates remained outwardly calm in all situations. Everything was under control. No one "acted out." No swearing or arm waving or bear hugs. No panic at exam time. Things were *expected* to go well. They always had. The Harvard campus was like a giant theme park—perhaps Privilege World—where life worked out happily ever after and everyone's clothes fit perfectly.

RIDICULOUS NOTE: Well-fitting clothes, fine cars, and piles of money don't necessarily add up to "class." The host of lavish parties at his estate in the Hamptons, rap star and recording entrepreneur Sean "Puff Daddy" Combs was once a working-class kid from the New York City area. Martha Stewart, the self-made mistress of good taste, is a neighbor and frequent guest, and so are some of the most talked-about celebrities in the Hamptons and Hollywood. But Mr. Combs was recently indicted for three separate gun-related charges, including bribery. Too bad. These things "just aren't done," Mr. Combs. Don't know if we'll be stopping by next summer.

Meanwhile, a part of the Harvard world was studying *me*.

To my surprise, many of the faculty and students had seen me anchoring *Inside Edition*, a nationally broadcast infotainment TV show that might delve into such politically significant subjects as Madonna's decision to have a baby. Harvard people watch this kind of program? Well, they found it *amusing*.

That's fair. The wealthy and privileged deserve some comic relief:

Glimpses of jaded celebrities and stories about bizarre occurrences among the commonfolk can fascinate people who rarely associate with working stiffs.

The Harvardites weren't consciously acting superior; in fact, they were very nice people for the most part, and many were studying politics so that they could help others. But they were generally clueless about the lives, the thoughts, and the dreams of working-class Americans. Such subjects do not come up over the macaroons and out-of-season raspberries at the club.

RIDICULOUS NOTE: Maybe it's not *always* easy for the upper classes. When George Herbert Walker Bush ran for president in 1988, a Texas politician ridiculed him for "being born on third base and thinking he hit a triple." In 2000 a computer whiz named Zack Exley founded a website that wickedly made fun of the presidential campaign website of George W. Bush. He supported this venture, in part, by selling such bumper stickers as "Don't Blame Dubya . . . He's a Victim of Social Promotion." (Politics is serious, but don't take it too seriously. In the interest of bipartisanship, let me say that the bumper sticker of the year reads: "Vote for Nixon in 2000 . . . He's not as stiff as Gore!")

RIDICULOUS NOTE: One thing I didn't have to learn at Harvard is that classy rich people don't cheat the help. "Only vulgar people insult their servants," a Boston grande dame said once. (Are you listening, Leona Helmsley?) I already had seen bad behavior over and again in the world of broadcasting. For example, Kirstie Alley, star of the TV sitcom *Veronica's Closet*, brought new meaning to the word "gratitude." To anyone who would listen she announced that she wanted to share the rewards of a successful season with her hardworking staff. Somehow, money seemed too vulgar to the multimillionaire Kirstie. So she gave each of her lucky minions a live canary. In a way, one could say, she flipped all her coworkers the bird.

Ϫ

VIEWER TIME-OUT: "O'Reilly, I don't know if you're a conservative or a liberal, but you come off as one of the most obnoxious, self-righteous journalists I have ever seen. I am forced to sit there in revulsion and fascination at what you say. I can't take my eyes off someone so completely full of himself." (Scott M., Kerrville, Texas)

Not *really* being too full of myself, I think, I'm going to take a break now from my personal odyssey from Levittown to Harvard and eventually to *The O'Reilly Factor*, a national TV program where I get to spout my opinions every night. That journey has been strange, treacherous, and very enlightening, but I'll return to it later.

I've mentioned my beginnings here to underscore the point of this opening chapter: The way you look, sound, carry yourself, dress, and even smile is very, very important to your life and career in today's America. The system is cleverly designed so that a lucky few will get rich and grab power, and those people are an even smaller group than the ones who inherit money and power generation after generation. Barring an alien invasion from outer space, the president elected in November 2000 will be a "legacy," as the term goes in fraternity life. Both Gore and Bush are privileged heirs of established political families.

If you aren't interested in competing for the richest prizes yourself, why should you care? Because the goals and attitudes of the establishment affect the lives of everyone in the nation. Sure, the rich and powerful will encourage you to "be all that you can be"—but only in the army! With its low pay and lousy housing (thanks to the indifference of the politicians at the top of American government), the Pentagon needs all the working-class soldiers it can get.

BULLETIN: America is not supposed to have a class system, but it does. Even if the rules aren't as rigid or oppressive as in India or Britain or Spain, class issues influence your life every day, and you ought to think about it.

RIDICULOUS NOTE: As we all know, our embarrassing president sold nights in the historic Lincoln Bedroom to anyone who would cough up soft money for his reelection in 1996. Aside from the legalities of this quid pro quo, it was extremely bad taste. I guess living in the elegant White House doesn't necessarily teach you social niceties. Compare the behavior of his good friends the Kennedys of Hyannis, Massachusetts: In April 1999 they offered a weekend in their famous family compound to anyone who contributed $100,000 to the Democratic National Party. But even these wealthy contributors were expected to remember their proper place in society as "not quite our sort." They would not be allowed to stay overnight in the compound, although the Kennedy staff would graciously find them a hotel nearby.

BACKUP STATS: There are about 280 million Americans now, but less than 150,000 of us earned more than a million dollars in 1997 (the most recent statistics available). That's the story from the Center on Budget and Policy Priorities, a nonprofit organization that specializes in tax analysis. Here's another way of looking at it: The 2.7 million richest Americans have as much cash on hand as the 100 million of their fellow citizens at the bottom of the ladder.

A tiny, exclusionary group with loads of money rules America financially. Yes, as the novelist F. Scott Fitzgerald said, the rich are different from you and me. And I say they want it to stay that way. I know it, you know it, and *they* know it!

THIS JUST IN: "Four score and seven years ago our fathers brought forth on this continent, a new nation, conceived in liberty, and dedicated to the proposition that all men are created equal." —President Abraham Lincoln, November 19, 1863

Ḍ

But isn't the business, political, and social establishment what capitalism is all about? Communist leaders Lenin and Stalin didn't like it, and neither did Mao. Castro says he can't stand it, either, but he makes an exception for himself: His estimated worth is more than $300 million.

Winston Churchill said that democracy was the worst possible form of government, except for all the others. Maybe we can say the same about capitalism. For all of its faults, it gives most hardworking people a chance to improve themselves economically, even as the deck is stacked in favor of the privileged few.

RIDICULOUS NOTE: Polo and yacht races may be the most upscale of sports activities, but golf still betrays its origins among the wealthy, leisured classes. According to *Sports Illustrated*, PGA tour player Notah Begay went behind bars in February 2000 after his second drunk driving conviction in a five-year period. Begay, who won two PGA events in 1999 and earned $250,000 in the first two months of the twenty-first century, had a light enough sentence to begin with: a total of seven days in a detention center in New Mexico. But authorities evidently felt that having to sleep there was punishment enough for endangering other people's lives by drinking and driving. He was allowed "off campus" every day to train at his usual gym, have lunch at his house, practice golf all afternoon, eat dinner at the clubhouse, and then have his chauffeur return him to the detention center. That's twelve hours a day on the loose out of the slammer while "serving time."

Here are the choices most of us face in such a system: Get bitter or get *busy*. When you understand the game, you can take charge of how you want to live. You can choose the life that makes the most sense for you—in Levittown or in the rat race or in the spotlight or in a small town in the West—only when you find out what your options really are.

And if you don't believe class is important in your life, you might want to ask yourselves some questions like these:

- Did my spouse or I turn down a chance for another job because of the fear of "not fitting in"?

- Did someone in my family not stand up for himself or a family member after some injustice because he didn't feel he was good enough?

- Do I miss out on some social or sports activity I like because I'm afraid everyone else involved in it dresses better or has more income?

- Have I discouraged my children from chasing an ambitious goal because I'm afraid they won't be happy or comfortable in an upper-class situation?

- Do I refuse to learn something—Alpine skiing, computer skills, wine collecting, field hockey—because I think that other people are already way ahead of me and I would be acting "above my station"?

Get the point? Good.

Now on to how the Class Factor is propped up by the Money Factor.

2. THE MONEY factor

BACKUP STATS: Half of American households have savings of less than $1,200, according to the Census Bureau. Out of a total population of 280 million, some 36 million of us are financially poor. No one is giving these people a sure thing in the commodities markets.

So where is all the money of this hardworking country with its booming economy and skyrocketing stock market? Here's a clue: Only about 4 million of our fellow citizens, or less than 2 percent of us, have assets of at least $1 million apiece (and in many cases much, much more). And that money doesn't just sit in the bank. It steadily grows as the real estate market tightens in the big cities or stocks race up the charts because of "consumer confidence." In other words, the rich get richer because we in the middle class are working harder and spending more than ever.

The story of most of us lies in the middle. According to the National Taxpayers Union, the *median income* for two-earner families in America is $55,000 a year. That means half take in more than that, and half earn less.

The class system as related to race plays a role: Single-income white households have a median income of $39,000, while single-income black households have a median income of $25,000. And the earnings gap between rich and poor is widening . . .

TALKING POINT: These figures are no accident. The powers that be, the establishment, want you to have just enough cash to keep on buying material things and necessities, but not enough money to become independent of the system.

THE PEOPLE'S VOICE: And there's no defined border between business and politics. In 2000 ninety-year-old great-grandmother Doris Haddock, a retired secretary from southern California, made it to the steps of the Capitol in Washington, D.C., after fourteen months walking across the country to bring attention to the need for campaign finance reform. The feisty Granny D., as she became known nationwide, pulled no punches: "Shame on you, [Senator] Mitch McConnell and those who raise untold millions of dollars in exchange for public policy. Shame on you, Senators and Congressmen, who have turned this headquarters of a great and self-governing people into a bawdy house."

I'm reminded of conservative humorist P. J. O'Rourke's definition of the three branches of government: not the legislative, executive, and judicial system we learned about in school, but "money, television, and B.S."

※

For the life of me, I can't figure out why so many smart Americans don't, can't, or won't see that our government has been corrupted by special-interest money. That's why guys like Bill Clinton can get elected president, while people with principles can't even enter the race. Without money they're forced to sit on the sidelines while the games go on. The big-money boys and girls don't want people who are burdened with inconvenient principles; they want deal makers, people they can "work with."

The unions buy candidates . . . the corporations buy candidates . . . the political machines buy politicians. You're right, Granny D. It *is* a bawdy house, but without the fun.

BULLETIN: Am I saying you should devote your life to making big bucks in order to be happy? No way. But here's the problem with having too little money: You are at the mercy of other people, people *who do not care about you!* Without substantial assets, your whole life is in the hands of people whom you cannot control, like bosses and bankers and public officials. These people can terrorize you and make you do things that are not at all to your advantage or in the best interests of your family and community. This is not good!

Worse, in the country designed by very smart men like Thomas Jefferson and James Madison to be "for the people," there are two systems of justice.

RIDICULOUS NOTE: New York mob boss John Gotti has been put away for life in federal prison in Illinois for heinous crimes too numerous to mention, but he feasts on fresh mozzarella flown in to please his palate. The so-called Dapper Don earns his name, even behind bars. But death rows in many states are jam-packed with poverty-stricken losers, often aimless young men, whose court-appointed lawyers couldn't find the men's room. Too many of these men convicted of murder and rape have been found innocent at nearly the last moment because of new techniques of testing DNA. Of course, DNA told the opposite story about O. J. Simpson, loud and clear, but his high-priced "Dream Team" waltzed nimbly around that little nuisance.

Yes, money buys too much in America, like clever attorneys who specialize in confusing, manipulating, and intimidating juries. In the political world it prevents real reform of campaign financing, allows our elected officials to evade their fiscal responsibilities, and corrupts law enforcement of all kinds of crimes at all levels of government.

What kind of democracy is that? And what happened to our famous safeguards?

Well, one of them—and believe me, I practice it every day—is freedom of the press. A watchdog press, like it or not when certain reporters overstep the rules of common decency and fair play, can be the voter's best protection against exploitation by the powerful.

Except the people who own and control much of the press and other media are the very rich themselves. They like to hang out with other big-money types. They like to discuss the things that really matter, at least to the elite: the blight of increased tourism in the south of France and the Tuscan hills of northern Italy, or the high cost of really fine truffles, or the depressing problem of finding servants who speak English well. Newspaper publishers, TV bosses, and "talking heads" of the high-profile political broadcasts are not spending next weekend in Levittown or Youngstown or Middletown. They are crowded together in overpriced houses on Martha's Vineyard or in the Malibu colony, and they are not discussing political reform over their glasses of designer water or Cristal vodka (actually, it will be another vodka label by the time this book reaches you; the defining fads change quickly in these free-spending days!). No, they are not discussing anything that is going to benefit you and me, unless by accident.

RIDICULOUS NOTE: Many of us can be grossly faddish—it's becoming the American way. Down the block from my office in Manhattan you can be a piker and buy a cup of regular coffee, Starbucks blend, for $1.85 plus tax. You should be ashamed of yourself! The Starbucks chain of coffee shops offers a Latte Grande for $3.80 plus tax. Better yet, a Large Mocha Frappe costs $4.30 plus tax. And this is a country where 43 million families make less than $35,000 a year. I'll let you do the math on that one. And don't expect any free refills.

In short, this country has developed a ridiculous blind spot: the power and glorification of money.

This is truly an affliction. It is holding us back as a nation, as a community. The true heroes of America are not the new Internet billionaires or the overpaid sports stars and movie actors or the wise guys who jack up their company's stocks. The true heroes of America are the men, women, and teenagers who go to work for a modest wage, fulfill their responsibilities to their families and friends, and are kind and generous to others— because that's the right way to live.

In other words, I'm talking about the majority of Americans. You know who you are. You rarely appear on a news broadcast or get to see your picture in the paper. But you and your parents and grandparents have defeated evil dictators, freed millions of people enslaved by oppression, and created a country where everyday folks can succeed and lead happy lives. The working people of the United States are the most important ingredient in the enduring American story.

But the rich and powerful have forgotten or never learned that bedrock truth. Or they simply don't care. They concentrate their energies on making themselves richer, more powerful, and better known—as if the rest of us don't count.

⌨

BULLETIN: The American system does not want you to keep the money that you manage to earn or acquire.

It starts in the political sphere from Congress down to your state legislature down to your county government or local city council. Each of these levels of bureaucracy wants your money very, very badly. The most efficient way, as they have discovered, is to tax those things that you *must* have, the necessities of life.

To support yourself and your family, you have to earn a salary. They tax it. Most of us have to drive to work. Gasoline is heavily taxed. We have to live in a house. Property taxes have gone through the roof! Nassau County, New York, where I live, has literally been bankrupted by the Republican-controlled cronyist government, which paid huge salaries to public workers and loaded the payroll with patronage jobs. How did these elected officials deal with the problem they created? You guessed it. Our property taxes were increased by 10 percent overnight. These clowns spent money like crazy, and we citizens had no say in the tax levy. Instituting good programs and properly managing tax revenues is hard; ratcheting up the tax rate is easy.

Do you need a telephone, electricity, water, heating oil, or gas? You sure do, and these utilities are surely taxed.

RIDICULOUS NOTE: I swear this is true. On an episode of *The Phil Donahue Show* some years ago, members of the studio audience were debating the merits of a certain federal program. One man stood up and interrupted angrily, "Why should taxpayers pay for this? Why doesn't the government pay for it?" Have we got a problem in communication here?

✍

And where does your money go? Well, some of it subsidizes tobacco companies so that their addicting drug can continue to be made available to people who will die of tobacco-related problems like cancer and heart disease. John McCain made an issue of these subsidies, and you can bet the establishment hit back at him in the Republican primaries of 2000.

Or your taxes support PBS-TV, whose elitist programming continues to lose viewer support because of commercial operations like the Learning Channel and Discovery Channel that produce similar but more effective programming. And how about the $3.5 billion in Medicare *over*payments that the federal government admitted in March 2000?

Or your taxes pay for—well, you already know that the list is endless. How much of your money has been thrown into the Big Dig, the gaping hole in downtown Boston that may someday be completed as a tunnel and will certainly be history's most expensive highway project at about $12 billion, if not more? I don't want to think about it. Or about subsidies for ethanol, or for farms that will never again pay for themselves.

Sure, there might be something on this list that benefits someone somewhere in the short term, but should the rest of us pay for it? And shouldn't our opinion matter when our money is being spent?

BULLETIN: Throwing our tax dollars away has become the new national pastime, replacing baseball!

RIDICULOUS NOTE: Jesse Jackson, who likes to call himself a "creative capitalist," has four not-for-profit organizations, yet he does not itemize on any of his tax returns. We do get some very interesting hints, however. His Rainbow/Push organization reported $1.3 million in travel and convention expenses in one year alone. Who got that money, which averages an astronomical $3,500 a day? Which corporations support the reverend's activities? How does he live so comfortably and travel in such high style? Why does the IRS look the other way? Why are the laws on disclosure of not-for-profit income and expenses being ignored? No, I don't have the answers . . . yet.

Corporations, whose executives are much shrewder than government bureaucrats, seduce us with the best advertising that money can buy. Who wouldn't want to live in those fantasy worlds of sparkling private pools and deserted tropical beaches and romantic suites in lavishly appointed hotels?

And if we so-called adults can be tricked senseless by the clever shills of Madison Avenue, pity our poor children. The ads are designed to make them think that they are the most deprived creatures alive because they don't own expensive designer clothing or high-tech toys and games.

You know this, of course. You probably deal with it again and again. But we should all stick together on some basic principles here:

- Money doesn't buy love or happiness. We have to help our children understand that the proof of affection is *not* an overpriced gift. Otherwise, we are helping the advertisers set them up for a frustrating life of trying to cope with their problems by racking up credit card bills at the mall.

- The commercials lie. We need to sit down with our children and help them learn how to "read" the sly visual language of advertising. Is the rocket ship toy really flying, as it seems to be, or is it being manipulated? Is fast-cutting from shot to shot making a toy jeep seem to go faster than it really does? Are the happy, attractive children in the spot happy and attractive *because* they are wearing clothing from the Gap? If our children become sophisticated about ad techniques, they may be less likely to be fooled by Madison Avenue—*or Washington, D.C.*—for the rest of their lives.

- We need to set a good example. I don't mean that we hoard every extra penny or talk all the time about interest rates, but we will save our children a lot of grief in their futures if we show them how to save and invest. I remember my first piggy bank. I remember watching the assets grow. Most important, I remember how and why I decided to spend it at last. I bet you do, too. That was a very important lesson in making the right choices.

- And we shouldn't forget that most of us had to be taught to share with others. Some of you go to churches where you "tithe," or give 10 percent of your income to the work of God. Others make a habit of supporting charities that have a special meaning in their lives. If we teach our children the rewards of being generous to others, we will be introducing them to one of life's great pleasures.

TALKING POINT: Money spent wisely can buy you personal freedom. With enough money you can ignore unreasonable demands and avoid humiliating financial situations: *They* won't be able to control your life. Don't waste your money on foolish material cravings, like the silly gas-guzzling SUVs littering your neighborhood. No, money can help you fulfill your potential as a human being: *Earn it, save it, and then shut up about it.*

Is it really that easy? Well, in the twenty-first century in the United States of America, it is. Jobs are plentiful, if you really want to work. Maybe they're too plentiful, when it comes to our kids. Teachers tell us that more and more teenagers are dropping out of school because they can get a job that starts a good income stream right away.

Unfortunately those jobs, for the most part, are not going to offer much upward mobility in the long run. What our parents told us is still true for our children: First of all, college is a must. Then they have to play to their natural talents and develop them for the marketplace. And they have to be prepared, if they really want to bring in the bucks, to work their butts off.

RIDICULOUS NOTE: Of course, there are all kinds of ways to jump the turnstiles in money-mad America, if you have no sense of shame. Anette Sorenson of Denmark was arrested in lower Manhattan for leaving her infant in a baby carriage outside a restaurant while she dined inside. When the authorities accepted her argument that this behavior is the custom in Copenhagen and dropped charges, she followed an American custom and sued the city of New York for $20 million. She had been humiliated! She had suffered! Lower Manhattan is not Copenhagen, Anette. Being arrested may have been the luckiest moment of your life, and your baby's. This is no way to pick up easy money.

Of course, not everyone wants to work long hours just to amass a lot of disposable income. For most people, the old-fashioned virtues of spending wisely and saving can make life comfortable. When my father with his $35,000 top salary left a very nice chunk of change to my mother at his death, I was surprised.

I shouldn't have been. As I've mentioned, he never bought a new car. Instead, he always got a "deal" from his friend Carmine at a local dealership and saved thousands of dollars on automobile expenses over the years. Also, "pre-owned" cars cost much less to insure. He thought it was insane to spend $400, say, on the "luxury" of a moon roof. He could see the moon by walking out onto our front lawn and looking up at the sky.

Since he came from a generation and a class that were very leery of the stock market, my father put his savings into bonds that yielded higher interest than the banks. Eventually he built a solid bond portfolio that was insured and paid healthy interest. Since he always reinvested the yields, the portfolio grew into serious money.

When our family went out to eat, a rare treat, we didn't waste money on appetizers, if only because we didn't go to the kind of restaurants that offered appetizers. Typically the pasta dish was spaghetti, and that was it. No linguine, fettuccine, rigatoni, etceterini, etceterini, to confuse the issue.

Is this the way everyone should live? Well, no. It's not even the way I've lived since I discovered that meat loaf, hot dogs, and tuna are not the only foods available in America. I won't be able to retire as early as my father did because he chose to live in his frugal way, and I respect that choice.

But, thanks to Dad, I am always conscious of what I'm spending, as we all should be, all of the time. I may splurge on an expensive dinner, but you'll never see me walking out of a store with fifteen pairs of dress shoes. I can visit Cape Cod without having to buy a ceramic beer mug to commemorate the occasion. I do not redecorate my house on a regular basis just because the colors of the wallpaper begin to bore me.

We all make our own choices about spending, and that's fine, as long as we really do make our own choices without being tricked by ads, shanghaied by telephone offers, or shamed into keeping up with the neighbors. My fine dinner might be your season ticket to baseball games or the opera. It's just that we have to remember, as the ancients said, "Everything in moderation."

In your home today, if Dad isn't spending thousands of dollars on golf equipment he doesn't really need and Mom isn't throwing good money at the local "boutiques," then your children will have less of a case when they start whining for the twentieth Beanie Baby.

I wasn't any less selfish about toys or more sensible about money than any other kid, but I had the great gift of parents who set an example by thinking carefully about their money. They weren't spending wildly on themselves or the house. Why should I be any different? I took common sense about money for granted.

RIDICULOUS NOTE: "Preferred customer"? Or target of opportunity? Corporate America never rests in trying to get us to fork over our money for sweepstakes scams, useless and overpriced merchandise, or high-rate credit cards. Like many of us, Alessandra Scalise was dazzled when, out of nowhere, Charter One Bank sent her a Platinum credit card with a $5,000 line of credit. Nice-looking piece of plastic, but Alessandra didn't rush out and buy anything. Her mother wouldn't let her: Alessandra had just turned three years old.

A possible wild card on the money question is the spendthrift spouse. Think about this very seriously when wedding bells are on the horizon. Financial compatibility is right up there with sex and religion.

My wife and I spend money readily on vacations, books, movies and plays, sporting events, blue jeans, moderately priced Italian food, charities, Christmas and birthday gifts for our family and friends, cable TV, classic CDs, a nice house, an okay car, and traditional clothing. We don't skimp on our health. I get the best pair of glasses I can find.

What we don't buy is a list that's almost un-American, since we don't fall for the $4 frappacinos or the $400 cashmere scarves: no designer coffee, tobacco products, furs, jewelry, trendy cars, shirts with polo ponies on them, souvenirs of any kind from anywhere, expensive barbecue grill or tools, first-class airline tickets, silk or linen clothing, or any product at all labeled "gourmet" or "fat-free." And you won't catch either of us wearing clothing with a logo; for advertising the manufacturer, we expect the clothing gratis!

That's just us, of course. But it works. Since we've agreed on the guidelines, we don't have to quarrel about spending. Since we both try to make spending *a conscious act* at all times, we don't find ourselves shocked at the end of the month by a mound of bills for things we can't believe we bought.

BACKUP STATS: Don't you "save" money when you buy a "⅓ off" fur coat with plastic? Well, let's say the $900 original price has been dropped a third—to $600. If you pay only the minimum charge due on your card each month, interest charges will triple the price you pay in the long run, and your "bargain" will cost $1,800. And that's not counting any late payment fees in the lean months.

THIS JUST IN: "Happiness lies not in the mere possession of money; it lies in the joy of achievement, in the thrill of creative effort. The joy and moral stimulation of work no longer must be forgotten in the mad chase of evanescent profits." —President Franklin Delano Roosevelt, first inaugural address, 1933

📺

You don't have to be reminded that money, or the lack of it, can be a constant problem in your daily life. But what about these questions about the influences of money outside the household?

- Am I in credit card debt because I buy things I don't need—because TV ads make it look as if *everyone else* has them? Am I spending too much money, in other words, because the advertisers have got their claws in me?

- Are the elected officials in my town looking out for the interests of the middle class, or are they kowtowing to the big-money bankers, insurance companies, lawyers, developers, and so forth when they pass ordinances or make zoning decisions?

- Is my child going to get less of an education because she can't afford to go to the private high school across town or a college away from home?

- Are my taxes a larger share of my average-sized income than the taxes of the rich guy across town who has lower property tax rates "grandfathered in" or special tax breaks available only to the wealthy?

- Who gets the most money in campaign contributions at election time—the official who is already in office (and has been making deals over the years) or the new guy or gal who wants to bring government back home to the people?

Yes, other people's money can shape your life, and so does the government's ability to take your money in the form of taxes and use it in ways you do not approve of.

Now, how do we go from the Money Factor to the Sex Factor? Easy. They are both just about everywhere in American life.

3. THE SEX factor

Has America gone crazy about sex, or what? Sure, sex has been getting us in big trouble since the Garden of Eden. Most of us can't have a happy, successful life without it, but you have to control this powerful force or it will control you, and maybe cause you to lose the things in life that are most important to you.

In today's world, perhaps more than ever before, sex is being used as a kind of currency. Some people barter sexual favors for a push up the ladder to success. That can work in the short term; in the long term, sexual exploitation almost always leads to disaster. Your parents were right about that. And if you're like most of us, you know someone who played the game the wrong way and may be burned for life.

Today's sex madhouse got really started in the 1960s, when the invention of "the pill" helped start "the sexual revolution" and the superheated economy of the Vietnam War era pumped up the level of disposable income.

Suddenly it seemed easy to be casual about sex, youthfulness was the hottest commodity going, and then the 1970s saw the spread of these ideas to every level of society in every part of the country. This was the kind of thinking that led former Miss America Bess Myerson to comment, "We used to dress like Jackie Kennedy; now we're dressing like Caroline."

And what about the days of so-called open marriages, swingers' clubs, kinky newspaper personal ads, and serial one-night stands? Just look at the broken homes, ruined careers, and chronic sexually transmitted diseases. (AIDS is the worst, but having incurable "minor" STD infections is no picnic.)

I'm not calling for abstinence here. That would be intrusive and ridiculous. But sex has got to be a balance between torrid passion and a little voice in the back stairs of the brain that remembers common sense. Even if only 1 percent of your brain cells can think straight during a romantic encounter, listen up! Use protection. Make dead sure that no one else is going to be hurt by this encounter. Respect your partner before and after.

RIDICULOUS NOTE: There's a difference between sexual honesty and smarmy excuse-making, of course. Jane Smiley, writing in the Clinton-friendly magazine the *New Yorker*, offered this odd reasoning for trusting the portly POTUS: "The [Lewinsky] incident showed at least the President's desire to make a connection with another person . . . This desire to connect is something I trust." Restrain yourself, Ms. Smiley. You'd be better off trusting that guy on the corner who's offering to sell you the Rolex watch.

Sex is supposed to be a private activity between consenting adults who are honest with each other, sharing pleasure and affection and then shut up afterward.

Men, if a woman shares her body, take it as a gift of affection, not proof that you're stud of the month.

Ladies, if you said yes without being forced, then don't brag to your coworkers or your homegals.

TALKING POINT: In this very dangerous sexual age, the most vital piece of advice you can get is to keep your sex life private. I mean, tell *no one* what you do! (This *especially* means you, ladies.) Otherwise, you are likely to be scrutinized, and no good can come of that.

I know it, you know it, and the gossips should *never* know it.

RIDICULOUS NOTE: Researchers at Johns Hopkins have found that straining too heavily during sex can induce six to twelve hours of amnesia. This effect is called the Valsalva Maneuver. So Clinton had a good medical excuse for his, uh, foggy grand jury testimony about his relations with Monica Lewinsky? And they weren't trivial, anyway. No. Under oath, there are *no* trivialities. By the way, what was the name of that maneuver again?

❏

Actually we Americans, especially working stiffs, may be fooling ourselves about our sexuality. There's a lot of wishful thinking around.

BACKUP STATS: For example, *American Demographics Magazine* reports that the average American adult—man or woman, heterosexual or homosexual, foot fetishist or "lipstick Lesbian"—reports fifty-eight "sexual episodes" a year. Using my calculator, this came out to slightly more than once a week.

There's even less passion among the best educated, it seems. The magazine reveals that they have the least amount of sex.

I'm not sure what that means, but I do believe that most of us work too hard to have much energy left over at the end of the day for serious romance, and the alarm goes off too early in the morning for a sunrise surprise.

We can't all be Bill Clinton or Madonna. And would we remember Romeo and Juliet as great lovers if they had made it alive into adulthood, much less middle age? They'd be like the rest of us, I imagine: bone-weary after working our tails off and dealing with traffic or commuter trains . . . and after chasing our supercharged kids around the house or trying to communicate with our teenagers in something approaching English . . . and after dealing with irrational people for much of the day, only to have a quiet evening at home interrupted by telemarketing calls.

When you think about it, "fifty-eight sexual episodes" sounds like quite an achievement for the hardworking middle-class couple trying to keep ahead of financial obligations and determined to raise children in the right way.

Talk about headaches. In that scenario, they never end. And here's some advice for upgrading the sex deal: Turn off the TV. (Making an exception for my program, of course.)

⌂

Still, if we aren't having sex on a daily basis, we are *thinking* about it all the time. I mean, *all* the time.

That's especially true of the guys. Since our origins in East Africa maybe 200,000 years ago, the human male has wanted to have sex, sex, and more sex . . . especially with attractive women. Tastes change over the centuries or are developed in different ways in different cultures. The tall, slender bathing beauties on the beach at Rio de Janeiro are a far cry from the desirable pink, plump nudes of western European art in the seventeenth to nineteenth centuries. In parts of Africa today, bared breasts, no matter how smooth and lovely to the American male eye, are scarcely noticed. But when American women wear skirts that reveal their calves in Africa, the local people are outraged: Women's legs arouse lust. Each place and time has its own ideas about sexual attractiveness, but the basic idea is the same: Whatever the local standard of female beauty, men want to possess it.

You can always find grant money, it seems, to study this kind of thing. The most recent research in the United States shows that the physical characteristic that is most important to most men is the woman's *face*. And the faces considered most attractive are likely to be the most symmetrical. Okay, but the rule still holds: If the woman looks good, guys will want to have sex with her. Are you hearing this, ladies?

Now, I know I'm not being politically correct here. Some women, and men, too, will argue that "relationships" are more important than looks. And what about personality or intelligence or a positive self-image in choosing a female companion? Surely today's liberated, gentrified, sensitized male cares first and foremost about those qualities.

Well, I would answer that these women are either more sensitive than most men or are just fooling themselves. As for the men who say such things, they're lying. Dump them right now, ladies. At the first meeting, and for a long time afterward, looks carry the day. The other stuff develops slowly. I'll give the nod to love theorist Zsa Zsa Gabor, who said, "One of my theories is that men love with their eyes; women love with their ears." By the way, Zsa Zsa's hearing was apparently excellent.

RIDICULOUS NOTE: As the world knows, actor Hugh Grant was arrested one warm Los Angeles night in the summer of 1996 as prostitute Divine Brown was performing oral sex on him. Could his "relationship" with the stunningly beautiful Elizabeth Hurley be saved? Gossip columnists speculated, and Ms. Hurley was photographed looking royally teed off. And now these "beautiful people" are evidently on the rocks. Grant has explained, "She has the best pair in London." Romantic? Hugh has it down. Problem is, Liz seems to be fed up.

✄

BULLETIN: There's nothing wrong with men lusting all the time for beautiful women, as long as we are housebroken. Constant desire keeps men mentally occupied and out of trouble. *We must have* our sexual fantasies, ladies. Otherwise, we'll be even more enslaved to sports on the tube than we are now. Trust me on this.

Women are different. I guess you've heard that before. Well, believe it, and no rigid feminist ideology should blind anyone to common sense on this subject.

Yes, most women really do hope to establish some emotional connection with the man they date and go to bed with. That is a noble goal. At the same time, they also expect the man to feel much the same way, even if the relationship is not serious. That is known as lunacy.

THIS JUST IN: "Nobody will ever win the Battle of the Sexes. There's just too much fraternizing with the enemy." —Henry Kissinger, former U.S. secretary of state

No matter what a man says, ladies, he is saying it to get you to have sex with him. Even the dimmest guys know how to read your mannerisms or listen to your conversation and dope out what ideas or entertainment will appeal to your mind-set. It's in the genes. They will deceive you!

And if you fall for it—as you should not—you can be hurt and confused, and things really start to get messy. On the other hand, if you play with the cards we've all been dealt, then you can make good choices, have a lot of fun, and someday, maybe, find that male companionship that the magazines promise, but it takes hard work and a lot of luck in real life.

RIDICULOUS NOTE: When women expect too much, they get hurt, and then they get angry. Perhaps that's why *New York Post* columnist Andrea Peyser took out after Mick Jagger with some contempt when he recently fathered a child out of wedlock: "Mick is, sadly, a grandfather with a pituitary problem, a wealthy midget possessing all the self-control of a Chihuahua revved up on Viagra." Andrea, calm down a little. If Jagger's wife, the always perceptive Jerry Hall, didn't know after all this time that her husband would shag a walrus, then she really is as dumb as she looks.

Are all men pigs? No, we're just what we are. Take us for that, and with luck you'll find a guy you can put up with. Fair?

BULLETIN: We can't trifle with God. After the snake deal went down in Genesis, Jehovah said to Adam, a total wimp who screwed up everything for the rest of us, "I will put enmity between you and the woman." What God meant, I think, is that giving men and women a different outlook on sex would keep things exciting and create a brand-new species: lawyers.

⚔

Men and women do share one reaction to sex, at least in modern America: We're prudes. Much of the rest of the world, with the very notable exception of the Islamic countries, finds our prudishness, or squeamishness, about sex bewildering and even hilarious.

RIDICULOUS NOTE: Get this: Danish high schoolers can take a class at the sex museum in Copenhagen. The "audiovisual aids" include X-rated flicks of the sort Mayor Rudy Giuliani has been chasing out of midtown Manhattan and rubber devices that, well, I'm still not sure what all of them are for. But these young Scandinavians took it all in stride. In fact, the class looked like any group of American teenagers trying to stay awake during last-period plane geometry, slumped down in their seats and glancing at their watches. One kid was so jaded about the whole thing that he was intently reading a soccer magazine.

We can thank our Puritan forebears for the American reserve on sexual issues. But it now turns out that the Puritans weren't quite so sobersided. They actually wore very colorful clothes, saving those black and white costumes for the Sabbath. They become very distressed whenever their supplies of strong drink ran out. But one part of the familiar image is true and, unfortunately, became part of their legal code in the seventeeth century, with some traces left over in the law today in parts of New England: Sex was to be controlled, if not driven underground. (An exception, obviously, is openly gay Congressman Barney Frank's district in Massachusetts.)

But what happens when the prudes take control? Just like the teapot on the boil, sexual desire has to have an outlet, or all hell breaks loose. That is why such a prudish society produces a constant stream of sexy films, ads, Internet offers, books, pop songs, and on and on.

Our entertainment media are fixated on sex because they know we can't resist it, and they think it will help them get deeper into our wallets.

We watch the babes and hunks, and stay on the couch for the commercial "messages." Sex will defeat talent any day in the all-important ratings that determine how much the broadcaster can charge advertisers by the second. Situation comedies, police dramas, daytime soaps, tabloid-TV "news," interview programs—they're loaded with sexual content, from flesh shots to smirking suggestions.

What is the hit comedy *Friends* but a show about sex? The six attractive young leads are either having sex or talking about it whenever you happen to surf in . . . Sex is what they do. Sure, they take a lot of breaks at the local coffee house, but for all that sex activity and imagining, they need to be wired to the max.

But the constant sex of TV and movies doesn't get me all worked up about declining values and ready to mount a moral high horse. As advertisers know, they are giving us what we want. Those who are really upset are definitely in the minority; those who pretend to be upset are down-right phonies. Both groups are perfectly free to change the channel to PBS, C-Span, or whatever—or read a book!

Our children do not need TV to tell them about sex. And once they reach puberty, they are going to find sex stuff somewhere, no matter what parents try. I'd rather know a teenager was watching *Zena, the Warrior Princess* than linking up to an X-rated Internet chat room or logging on to sites put up by the likes of Bob Guccione or Larry Flynt. Thanks to our traditional Puritanism, TV sex is still pretty tame in America. It's more tease than sleaze.

RIDICULOUS NOTE: Sex can't always save a TV show, particularly if it's really a lost cause. When meaty Roseanne saw her talk show ratings going down the toilet, she tried to save the situation by announcing to *George* magazine that she would like to have sex with equally beefy Bill Clinton. She offered to "get a beret and the whole deal." Her show sank out of sight. There are some things no one wants to imagine.

It's time that we all lighten up about sex, accept the reality of the situation, and keep our sexual activities where they belong: in the privacy of the bedroom or hot tub, or in the case of Pamela Anderson, on the Internet.

But Pam is being wrongheaded. Keep sex private. Nothing's more offensive than flaunting sexuality in public, and the most offensive spectacles of all are Gay Pride events. Bearded, paunchy guys prancing around in bras and high heels do not impress the straight majority as an act of political liberation; in fact, they tee off quite a few of us who don't want to see this nonsense in the street.

Dykes on Bikes? Take a hike! Can't you "express yourself" without throwing it in our faces?

When I'm walking down the street with a five-year-old, I don't want to have to try to explain why Jack is dressed up like Jill or Jill is wearing a buzz cut. The kid shouldn't have to be dealing with any sexual ideas at all, much less a couple of thousand folks marching around in drag or half-naked in order to "celebrate their sexuality." Give us all a break. Express your sexuality where the rest of us do, if we have any sense: at home, with the blinds drawn.

On the other hand, religious fanatics who demonize gays and other alternative groups aren't covering themselves with glory, either. Yes, I know about the references to homosexuality as "an abomination" in Leviticus, but I also know what the Old Testament says about slavery. As long as a sexual issue is not intruding on your freedom or endangering your kids, leave it to God to sort it out. The Deity is a lot smarter than we are. That's also in the Bible.

And here on earth our legal system is the place to go to sort out problems such as civil rights being violated because of sexual preference. To someone gay who is the victim of discrimination or abuse, I say exchange the high heels for a sensible business suit, because that's appropriate for the playing field, and hire a lawyer who will put the screws to whatever bastards are interfering with your rights to *private sexual expression.*

¤

Where does Bill O'Reilly get off talking about sex? I was raised a Roman Catholic and had a parochial education . . . Need I say more?

In case you don't know this from your own experience or from the stand-up comics or from the plays and movies, a Catholic school education is heavy on sex. There is almost as much sex as math. I'm not exaggerating. And like math, the figures didn't always add up.

How did the teachers describe most sex outside of marriage? A mortal sin that was a one-way express ticket to the hothouse. Heavy petting? Go right in, son. Lucifer is waiting to see you now. The nuns would actually ask if a French kiss was worth risking eternity in the roaring flames. (A smart aleck, I figured that the answer depended upon the quality of the smoochee and knew that such an impure thought would earn me four Hail Marys after confession.) Well worth it.

The rigid Catholic school approach did not work. It's easy to ridicule it. But to be fair, the nuns, priests, and our parents were doing their best to prepare us for a "tough world out there." No pill and no abortion meant a very good chance of unwanted babies and ruined lives in the 1950s.

But times have changed, and so has the church. That puts all the more responsibility on Catholic parents, like all parents in this wide-open society, to address sexual issues with our children as the citizenry of Tammany Hall days used to vote, "early and often."

How early? Well, if the family is watching Neve Campbell or somebody similar frolicking around, seeming to have the best time ever as a free-spirited sexual sprite but never suffering any consequences from her amazing sexual adventures, it is probably time to talk about the differences between exploitative fantasy and harsh reality.

How often? You'll know by the questions your kid's ask.

BULLETIN: You need to find a strategy for discussing sex with your children. It should probably go like this: "You are special, very special, and you should always behave that way."

I like to call this strategy Operation Elevation. Here's how it works: From the time your children can comprehend complete sentences, make clear that you and your spouse expect behavior that is better than the norm. Because they are special, they will be held to higher standards of conduct. In other words, you are elevating their self-image by persuading them of their self-worth.

And when they see other kids harming their bodies by drinking, smoking, taking drugs, or engaging in irresponsible sex, explain that these losers do *not* value themselves highly. They're doing themselves in because they're unhappy about their lives; they don't feel popular enough or attractive enough, so they fall for the short-term illusion of substance-induced kicks or cheap sexual thrills. Continue to emphasize to your kids that their behavior should reflect the special status they have in your eyes.

THIS JUST IN: "There's nothing wrong with teenagers that reasoning with them won't aggravate." —Anonymous

Are you in danger of losing your kids if you're stubborn about this message? No. The danger comes when you make today's common mistake of wanting to be your child's friend instead of parent. Teenagers have their own friends. They lose them and make new ones. But they have only one set of parents, and that is God's gift to provide mature love, protection, guidance, and an enduring set of values.

It's tempting to get the short-term reward of having children hug you and thank you for loosing the reins, like agreeing to let them stay out too late "this one time" or go to an unsupervised party "because it's just a few friends." You want to aim for something much more rewarding: the grown child who comes back to you at some point and thanks you for creating a sense of honor in your home. Hold to the high standards of behavior out of dignity, of course, and not from a sense of snobbishness. Poor conduct should be unacceptable in your house because you are not the kind of people who cheat, steal, exploit others, or abuse yourselves with drugs or alcohol. Your family is *better* than that.

And if there's a period of rebellion, just grit your teeth and hold on. Under the surface, your message will still be at work: The child who truly values himself will be far less likely than others to be duped into bad, crazy, or dangerous behaviors.

Besides, children are more sensible than they let on. When I was teaching high school in a working-class suburb of Miami some years ago, there was a sudden epidemic of sex-oriented graffiti on the school walls, and some of it was pretty vile. The unpopular principal ranted and made threats, which made the whole activity seem even cooler, to some of the students.

I took a different approach, telling my classes that the graffiti "artists" were obviously sexually immature and had little sense of self-worth. My comments whipped around the campus like a stolen biology test. No one wanted to be thought sexually immature. The smut stopped.

⌖

When your child reaches eighteen, it's all over. You've done your job; the ship is launched. You can hope that you've raised someone who will join the forces of good in America, not a candidate for an entry-level job in the porno industry. It won't be long before your son/daughter and daughter-in-law/son-in-law are having their own children, probably, and looking around at the world of malls, media, and mass-market culture in a new light. Now it's their turn.

With any luck you can relax and have fun again. You've been *chaperoned* for years, if you think about it. Now you don't have to worry about corrupting an impressionable teenager; you can be frivolous about sex again.

For me, that means Tyra Banks in Victoria's Secret catalogs (can you believe you get these free?); Sarah Michelle Gellar in a tight T-shirt chasing a vampire or Jacqueline Bisset in a very wet T-shirt in *The Deep*; Vanessa Williams doing anything anywhere; Melanie Griffith before the lip implants and Sharon Stone reacting with such openness to Michael Douglas; Betty Grable in hot pants and Kim Basinger in no pants; Marilyn Monroe looking exhausted and the Spice Girls looking as if they know what they are singing (with the sound muted). And I'm talking about the full range from Mouseketeer Annette Funicello, when I was ten years old, to Connie Chung reading the news today (call me crazy, but she can tell me about Kosovo anytime).

RIDICULOUS NOTE: Yes, sex is such a personal thing, and so intuitive. How did former Oregon senator Bob Packwood, booted out of office because a number of women accused him of sexual harassment, *know* that Monica Lewinsky never had sex with Bill Clinton? "My bones tell me she did not," he explained. And what bones were *they*, Bob? Hillary Clinton used her own intuition about sex to explain to a White House aide that her husband's goal with Monica was to "offer spiritual advice to a very troubled young woman."

Packwood and Hillary Clinton have one thing in common. They are dupes about sex. Don't you be. Respect it and teach your children about it. Control it; don't let it control you. Have fun and be safe. And never, never take suggestive photos to Kmart for development.

The media would never give this kind of advice about sex. And that's not the only thing the media won't do. Onward now . . .

4. THE MEDIA factor

You've just seen one huge problem with the media. What is said, right or wrong, can never really be taken back. Rebuttals never really offset the first bad impression. Lies take on a life of their own. That's why all political experts, even if they piously claim otherwise on interview shows, believe that so-called negative advertising works in a campaign.

In a famous campaign in the rural Southeast half a century ago, one candidate labeled his opponent, whose daughter had moved to New York City to go to acting school, "father of a thespian." The accuser won, of course. Some of his backwoods voters had no idea that a thespian is just someone who acts on the stage. The word sounded sexual and bad; ill-educated voters acted just on the sound.

TALKING POINT: The media—TV, radio, newspapers, magazines, even billboards—are deeply involved in your personal life for much of your waking hours. The media keep you company, and they can entertain, inform, and inspire you. That's good. They can also shape your opinions, behavior, tastes, and desires. That's not so good. And they can be used by powerful people to seduce and persuade you and often lie to you. That's dishonest, sometimes downright evil, and *always* there in your face.

Here's a plan: You and your family have to learn how to use the media, or they will use you. No, it's worse than that. The media barons will *control* you. And you won't even know it.

This is the ultimate one-way relationship. The movers and shakers of the American media don't care about you. The forces of mass communication are directed *at* you; they are not designed to "open a dialogue." As a friend of Donald Trump's once said about the manipulative tycoon, "He sends, but he does not receive."

To protect yourself and your family from getting hurt by the media, you should learn all you can about this tempting, powerful, and sometimes dangerous combination of forces.

📺

For twenty-five years, or more than half my life, I've made a living in TV, radio, and print. I am about to give you inside stuff that you will get nowhere else.

Because of computers, cable, and satellites, you have more choices than ever before. Traditional TV and radio broadcasters are panicking. The daily news flow is no longer controlled by a few middle-aged white guys in Manhattan. Newspapers are dying off one by one across the country or diversifying into other lines of business.

Because this situation is also opening up all kinds of opportunities for other news and entertainment sources, that's good news for you. The bad news, which is going to become more obvious very soon, is that this huge increase in competing media outlets has already caused standards to collapse. It will only get worse.

Picture what happens when a torrential rainstorm causes the glutted sewers of Chicago to overflow and flood the streets. Got it? Well, you're looking at the current media landscape. There's a lot of untreated waste floating around, some of it toxic.

From now on, you will have to put on your waders and look carefully to separate the truth from the lies and distortions, the skillful reporting from the idiotic.

RIDICULOUS NOTE: Should you ever put all your trust in one news source? Only if you like to put all of your retirement funds in one high-tech stock. Here's what I mean. On February 24, 1999, President Clinton met with the opposition Republican congressional leadership at the White House. How did it go? A very friendly get-together, according to the *Los Angeles Times* headline: "Clinton, GOP Leaders Meet in a Spirit of Cooperation." But the readers of the *New York Times* got quite a different story from the same event: "GOP Chiefs and President Confer, Coolly." What really happened? I don't know. I wasn't there. Neither were you. And that's the problem.

When I left teaching to enter the master's program in broadcast journalism at Boston University, the news business had just been dramatically transformed by someone who may never have existed: the source or combination of sources in the Watergate story known as Deep Throat. Overnight, journalism was not just a job, not even a profession . . . it was a *calling*.

Like most of my journalism classmates, I was a true believer. Remember, this was before the explosion of news programs and the Hollywood-level contracts for TV anchors and star reporters. Bob Woodward and Carl Bernstein, who earned the credit for toppling an administration, still looked like newshounds, not rich celebrities. They were little guys who had taken enormous risks.

At B.U. we wanted to be like them. We wanted to right wrongs, clean up corruption, and safeguard democracy. I mean every word of this. Back in the mid-1970s most journalism students were on a mission.

A quarter of a century later that idealism is in tatters. There are still some great reporters around, and I am trying my best to be one of them, though it's a full-time, never-ending job. The true believers have not all given up yet.

But we aren't blind to the new realities, either. There are also legions of shameless, agenda-driven, power-mad hacks who believe that the news is a vehicle to bring you *them*. Journalism is a business. And the business of business is to make money. The men and women who can do that best—no surprise—are the charlatans, opportunists, and, worst of all, the bean counters.

These are the people who thrive in newsrooms where politics rule and conformity is the order of the day. Such places are treacherous for reporters of talent, courage, and originality. For all I know, conformity is the best way to run Xerox or Microsoft or Qualcomm (although I suspect it explains the "go along to get along" wasteful spending down sinkholes at the Pentagon), but it is death to truth-telling.

📺

Since someone first sharpened a reed and wrote an exposé of a dishonest yak merchant on a wet clay tablet, good reporters have been obnoxious malcontents who despise corrupt authority. Am I looking in the mirror? I'll take the Fifth on that.

But it's not easy, especially for someone just coming into the business today. I get away with my head-on attacks on government corruption and political hypocrisy for very simple reasons: I'm known, I attract an audience, and that brings in the advertising bucks. In other words, as Yogi Berra might put it: "Keep watching, and you'll see me." You know what I mean. This particular "obnoxious malcontent who despises corrupt authority" is on the air only because so many of you click the remote to the Fox News Channel when I come on to make waves.

Without such support I'd be handed a one-way ticket to Sioux Falls, South Dakota. And every young man and woman coming into broadcast or print journalism today senses that. You can see it in their tight smiles as they're working their first gigs. Many of these young people are smart, and some of them have high ideals, but they fear going against the culture of blow-dried, Pan-Cake-made-up, preppie-clad conformity. Are they giving you the news or advertising for Ralph Lauren? You have to look closely to decide, and that's just what the media big folks want. As broadcast veteran and Watergate-era reporter Daniel Schorr said recently, journalism "may have become a tail on a big kite—the media industry."

If viewers get too upset by some truth-telling journalists, they might not sit still for the bottom line: the commercials.

VIEWER TIME-OUT: A lady in Jacksonville, Florida, exercised her free speech rights by writing, "I know I can't make this letter as blistering as I would like so I'll just say shame, shame, shame on you for telling Reverend Reggie Jackson you don't care what homosexuals do in their private lives." Many people share this viewer's opinion, but I hope they don't share her ability to pay attention. On this occasion I had actually interviewed former Green Bay Packers defensive lineman Reggie White, now a full-time preacher who doesn't much like gays and their ways. Hey, pay attention, lady! Unlike some people in broadcasting, I expect a two-way street with my viewers. I'm working hard here. Listen up, okay? Then say whatever you want.

RIDICULOUS NOTE: Bill Clinton began his political career in the post-Watergate era. That's probably why he and most of the Clintonites have always shied away from the press. And that has to be why he looked stunned at some of the questions lobbed his way at his first press conference after a year of dodging the media during the Lewinsky mess. "Why do you think some people have been so mean to you?" asked a young wire service reporter. Another marshmallow came from an on-air TV personality: "Mr. President, do you think your wife would make a good senator?" Clinton responded deftly, of course, but he had to wonder about this new *post*-post-Watergate generation. Simple, Mr. President. Too many of the watchdogs have become lapdogs.

✍

Okay, things are going well for me right now. There are a heck of a lot of people out there who want to hear the truth, as I tell it. But don't get the idea that even the most experienced, tested media rainmakers can always avoid evil intrigue and backstage schemes. Yes, evil. I've seen evil many times in the media world.

In the late 1980s I was based in New York covering breaking news for ABC News. The toughest battle was not in getting assigned good stories but in getting them on the air. There were one hundred network correspondents and only enough airtime for less than half of us on the three major ABC news programs: *World News Tonight* with Peter Jennings, *Nightline* with Ted Koppel, and *Good Morning, America*. The competition for airtime ranged from ferocious to vicious. This was Ego City big-time.

If you've read my novel *Those Who Trespass*, you might think I exaggerated some of the cutthroat competition over airtime to write a more exciting thriller. No way. If anything, I had to choose just a few examples out of hundreds in order to keep the story on track. The truth is much, much worse. In the novel a few of the most ambitious showboaters meet untimely ends. That was fun to write. In real life they keep rising to the top. (Not that anyone in my novel *really* resembles anyone I've ever met!)

For some unknown reason Peter Jennings liked me and my work, so I appeared on *World News Tonight* quite often. But Jennings's appreciation was equaled by the loathing of the senior *Nightline* producer, who banned me from ever appearing on that fine program. What had I done to this man? Not a thing. Was there something about my style of reporting that he disliked? No. It was an illogical personal hatred—not a rare thing in the world of network news—and there was nothing I could do about it.

What difference did it make? Let me tell you a story, and you be the judge . . .

Late one chilly November afternoon I got a panicked call from the New York assignment desk. A building had collapsed in Bridgeport, Connecticut, trapping dozens of workers in the debris as night was falling. Our ABC affiliate in New Haven was preparing video coverage for the Jennings program, and I'd been tapped to do the voice-over for this breaking story. The problem was that the raw video footage would not reach New York until about half an hour before national airtime. Could I write and edit the story and tape the voice-over in time to lead off *World News Tonight*?

Of course! No problem. (In case you haven't noticed, I'm a cocky bastard.)

Now, I don't know how this whole thing sounds to anyone outside broadcasting, but I can tell you, the adrenaline was pumping. The story had to be written while new information kept coming in. I had to choose the shots, put them in a dramatic order, and make my words fit the footage. I had to explain a terrible disaster very clearly to viewers across the country—and also show respect for the victims and their families as the rescue efforts continued.

In other words, I really could have blown it . . . but thank God I didn't. My story topped the program. Peter was happy with my piece but mostly with the fact that I'd made it possible for us to beat both CBS and NBC. Neither one managed to air the story until much later in their newscasts.

Then, incredibly, someone at *Nightline* assigned me to go to the scene for a live report. I hopped in my car and raced like Evel Knievel up to Bridgeport. I was on a roll. Here was my chance to change that producer's mind. I was on top of the story already, I had time to shape the *Nightline* segment in my head, and I was psyched about answering Ted Koppel's questions live on national television. As athletes say, I was in the zone.

There was chaos at the disaster site, but with the help of two excellent ABC producers I immediately began shooting interviews and getting the most up-to-date information on tape. We were pelted by a freezing rain, but that didn't matter. *Nightline* mattered.

After about an hour of this feverish activity, one of the producers ran up to say that New York wanted me to call the office immediately. This was before cell phones, so I used the phone in the satellite truck.

It takes a lot to leave me dumbstruck, but this phone call did it. My blood rises when I think about it today. I was told I was being dumped from the story I had developed in favor of a reporter from WABC-TV, the local ABC station in New York City. This *never* happens. When a network news correspondent is on the scene, that correspondent is *always* used by a network news program. And since everyone in the business knows this, I could see that the decision had been made for one reason, and one reason only: to humiliate Bill O'Reilly.

There was nothing I could do about the situation. The faces on the screen are not the power behind the cameras. I was one of the grunts, I guess, from their point of view.

When word about this backstabbing got out, the producers of *Good Morning, America*, who were decent human beings, got in touch with me and assigned six live shots for the next morning. Exhaustion took over, so I checked into the Bridgeport Hilton to catch some sleep before my 4:00 A.M. wake-up call.

But the bedside phone startled me awake at 1:00 A.M. Shouting on the other end of the line was my powerful *Nightline* enemy himself: "O'Reilly, get your ass back out to the building site! We might have to update the situation for the West Coast feed!" Because of the three-hour time difference, of course, *Nightline* can be changed when necessary for the folks on the West Coast.

I was only half-awake but not brain-dead, so I had the sense to ask if Koppel was still in the studio. The producer exploded in obscenities. I had just called his bluff. If Ted had already gone home, there was no way to update the program. Ted was long gone, it turned out. More games were being played at my expense. No West Coast update was actually planned.

This was getting dirty as well as irrational. Pulling a Linda Tripp long before that lovely hit the spotlight, I flicked on my cassette recorder to tape what had become an incredible tirade. The *Nightline* producer was giving new meaning to the word "ballistic."

Finally he hung up, probably smashing the receiver to bits. But I went peacefully back to sleep. I had caught him acting way out of line, and he should have known it.

RIDICULOUS NOTE: Don't confuse the fine journalist Ted Koppel with this ridiculous producer. In a live interview during the NATO action in the Balkans, Ted was interviewing a Serbian official who denied any wrongdoing by his countrymen in Kosovo, despite a long list of evidence to the contrary. Finally Ted snapped and said, "This is bullshit!" Some one hundred complaints were logged by ABC News, but Ted was right. Sorry about the language, but innocent people were being tortured, raped, and killed. Did these one hundred viewers want a soothing bedtime story or the harsh truth? I vote for truth.

There were no problems in Bridgeport the next day. I did the live shots from the site in the morning, filed a fresh report for Jennings, and then drove home to New York. The story was over. At least, as the old saying goes, yesterday's newspaper can be used to wrap fish. Yesterday's TV story just vanishes into space.

As it turned out, the news story was over, but not the media story. The following morning an ABC vice-president called me into his office to accuse me of "refusing an assignment." Let me explain that this was no trivial matter. Such a "refusal" is a firing offense in our business. (Ever wonder what happened to NBC's famous Scud Stud of the Persian Gulf War? He refused an assignment. So long, Arthur Kent.)

According to this network "suit," the *Nightline* producer filed a complaint that said I had directly refused to do a report for his program; in addition, he accused me of laziness (and probably bestiality), but I'd stopped listening. Rising to my full height of six feet four and looming over the veep's desk, I pulled out my recorder and hit the Play button.

The man's mouth dropped open as he listened. I stopped the tape and explained that the whole thing was a setup. Koppel had gone home.

"You secretly taped an employee of ABC News?" the vice-president gasped.

Yeah, I sure did. And it saved my ass. The incident was dropped.

⎙

Why should you care about my run-in with a martinet? Because it's typical, and that has an effect on the news you get in your home.

Everyone in network news can tell you stories of betrayal and deception. For many good journalists the atmosphere becomes so poisonous that they pack up and leave. Not too many capable reporters relish playing office politics. So you, as a viewer expecting to get an accurate news broadcast, are not being informed by the best and brightest. In many cases they've gone off and left the newsroom to the least and the most ruthless.

There are many exceptions to the rule. Some on-air reporters manage to keep themselves away from the politicking. Too often, though, one charlatan left unchecked can influence news coverage, slant opinion, and ruin anyone who objects to the corruption of journalistic ideals.

THIS JUST IN: "The power of instantaneous sight and sound is without precedent in mankind's history. This is an awesome power. It has limitless capabilities for good—and for evil. And it carries with it awesome responsibilities . . ." —Federal Communications Commission Chairman Newton Minow, speaking to the National Association of Broadcasters, May 9, 1961

But the media universe has expanded—and that is breaking up the news monopolies. Ten years ago you had to swallow whatever a few national outlets stuffed down your throat. "National news" meant "network news." For years it was "Uncle" Walter Cronkite, Harry Reasoner, and the tag team of Huntley-Brinkley. These were all fine journalists, but they were cut from the same cloth, and so were their bosses.

Today their successors have lost millions in audience share to cable and the Internet. Now the old guard has to *compete* . . . and they don't like it. They claim that the flood of start-up news outlets is lowering reportorial standards. Well, that's part of the changing picture, but the best will soon rise to the top. Meanwhile, your news is no longer censored by a few powerful, self-absorbed, sometimes corrupt broadcast executives.

Okay, "censor" is a hot-button word, but consider this . . .

In 1962 FBI chief J. Edgar Hoover discovered from wiretaps that President John Kennedy occasionally "entertained" Judith Campbell (later known as Judith Campbell Exner) in private lunches at the White House. Miss Campbell, whom JFK met through his friend Frank Sinatra, was allowed the special privilege of entering the presidential mansion through a back entrance. Since his inauguration, the attractive brunet had telephoned the commander in chief about seventy times on his private phone.

This was not just slam-bam thank-you-ma'am hanky-panky. Campbell was also sleeping with Sam "Momo" Giancana, unchallenged boss of the Chicago Mafia, who claimed that he had helped Kennedy win the election by stuffing ballet boxes in Illinois and pouring money into the West Virginia primary. Giancana was also involved with the CIA in a plot to murder Fidel Castro. Campbell called her White House boyfriend at least once from the mobster's home.

Kennedy wisely cut his ties with Campbell after Hoover revealed what he knew, but the national security implications of this whole sordid affair are enormous. And parts of the story soon leaked to members of the press. But did any of our TV "uncles" tell us about it at the time? No way. Did any editorialists write about the situation? No. Did a young reporter convince his managing editor to run the story? No.

Why? Because the fix was in. Many people in Washington knew about Kennedy's reckless womanizing, but the editors who controlled the news outlets of the day were charmed by this brash young president. Nobody dared print the first word of scandal. There'd be no more dinner parties at the White House or at Hyannis.

The mob, fixed elections, secret money, CIA misconduct, a harlot in Camelot—you think this story would be hushed up today? Heck, no. Judy and Momo would be household names! Cable would go nuts. Giancana's house would be staked out with scores of satellite trucks. Geraldo would be outraged that the story was being discussed even as he discussed it. Tim Russert would be blowing steam on NBC News while Alan Dershowitz would tell anyone who would listen that Momo was the victim of discrimination and innuendo. And there probably aren't yet enough news outlets for all of the Republicans who would be lining up to go on the attack.

Would all of this brouhaha be a good thing? Yes.

And I'm not saying that as an anti-Kennedy remark. There should have been just as much outrage when the tragedy of his assassination in 1963 was hardly investigated at all by the mainstream press. Once again, they circled the wagons. The Warren Commission Report, which was overseen by establishment figures who wanted to calm the waters, was accepted at face value. But it was as fantastic as anything Rod Serling was writing for *The Twilight Zone* in those days. Only years later did a cottage industry of Kennedy conspiracy books emerge, but it was a case of too little, too late. The trail of evidence was cold, and many key witnesses were dead.

⌕

Not long afterward, no one on nightly news or in the print press challenged Lyndon Johnson's version of the Gulf of Tonkin incident that became his excuse for our massive involvement in Vietnam.

Remember? Allegedly a tiny North Vietnamese gunboat menaced a giant U.S. warship. So because of this mouse, the elephant would eventually put millions of young men in harm's way on the other side of the world for reasons no one ever really explained. Tell me I'm arrogant, but I *know* that this cock-and-bull story would not get by me on today's *The O'Reilly Factor*—or on other cable shows and Internet magazines. There are too many of us today who are not paid lackeys of the establishment. And more than one of us would be on the ground within hours, getting the real story from the guys on both ships.

BULLETIN: No one should long for "the good old days" of news controlled by the powers of Washington, New York, and Hollywood. Thanks to increased competition, there will be no more sweetheart deals between political power brokers and media titans. You are now much more likely to hear all sides of a story. Sometimes that's more information and more scandal that you might want to hear, but it's your right and your job as a citizen to face up to it. The news choices of today are an important change in your life. They help you decide what kind of country you want.

RIDICULOUS NOTE: The first rule of TV viewing is, use common sense. A friend who dates a soap opera actress swears that well-dressed, sane-looking middle-aged women approach his date on the street and say something like, "You shouldn't be out with this guy. You should marry Tony." Tony is the character on the show who is in love with the character she plays. My friend asked his girlfriend why she doesn't explain the difference. "It doesn't do any good," she says. On the other hand, viewers can be too distrustful of their own eyes and ears. Pollsters have found that as many as one American in twenty-five believes that landings on the moon and Mars have been staged in the Arizona desert.

⌗

If I'm upbeat about news competition, I'm bored stiff by the entertainment competition. What gives here? You know what I mean. We surf through seventy channels, and there's nothing interesting to watch! How can this happen? Seventy different channels, for cryin' out loud!

For example, my cable system gives me the traditional stuff: CBS, NBC, Fox, and ABC with their tired laugh-track sitcoms and predictable pulp dramas about cops, lawyers, and doctors.

Next come the never-ending newsmagazines—for which I have to take the blame, I admit. Here's the story:

The newsmagazine explosion started with a whimper in 1989 with *Inside Edition*, a hybrid of news and entertainment reports anchored by Sir David Frost. Aimed at a blue-collar audience, it emphasized emotional stories and sexy babes. After three weeks, Sir David was sacked and given a ticket on the Concorde back to London. The show was tanking. It wasn't exactly his fault: What nut thought that this dapper, manicured Brit would appeal to the working-class target audience?

Enter your humble correspondent. *Inside Edition* producers Bob Young and John Tomlin hired me away from ABC News and I wound up replacing Frost. The three of us revised the format to include aggressive investigative reporting—my strong suit—and also to sharpen up the entertainment stuff with a punchy point of view. The result: Our show became a monster success in syndication.

Well, you know what happened next. Following the television rule that a successful program inspires ten clones, the networks jumped in with *Dateline*, *48 Hours*, and so forth, all of them combining emotional stories and consumer investigations to the saturation point. These are often fine programs, but too many clones of *Inside Edition* send you looking for something else on the box.

⋈

So here we are, surfing again. Ever notice the star power of monkeys and snakes on cable? Someone drops a tiny camera into a reptile's underground home and we can watch the family writhe around in its typical leisure-time activities down there.

Nope. Boring. *Click . . .*

Howler monkeys are jumping from tree to tree in Costa Rica, howling away. I can take about twenty seconds of that. *Click . . .*

I have a choice of four sports channels that specialize in bad puns. Some young man in a plaid jacket with a clashing tie winks at me and smirks, "Yeah . . . he . . . could . . . go . . . all . . . the . . . way." *Click, click . . .*

I gather that Rhoda and Mary are mad at Lou because . . . *Click . . .*

VH1 wants me to understand why onetime teen idol Leif Garrett is depressed these days. He must be watching cable. *Click . . .*

Lifetime has brought together a gaggle of women who all hate the fact that men always . . . *Click . . .*

MSNBC, Fox News Channel, and CNN are all covering the same tornado in Texas. On all three channels the same fire chief is looking very grim. I sympathize but . . . *Click . . .*

Bill Kurtis is investigating some prisons where the prisoners are not very happy. How does Bill find these stories? Have I lost my competitive edge? *Click . . .*

Richie and the Fonz are mad at Chachi because . . . *Click . . .*

Elvis is singing "The Clam" in the movie *Clambake*. The words go, "Do the clam, do the clam, grab your bashful baby by the hand." *Click* extra fast . . .

Sipowicz and Simone are roughing up some skell. Seen it. *Click . . .*

HBO has some rough-looking chick riding in the back of a New York taxi, legs splayed apart, telling the driver about her S&M fantasies. He looks confused. He is from Armenia. *Click . . .*

Bravo features a very grainy movie from Spain. A young shepherd is talking sincerely to his goats. *Click . . .*

The History Channel, known in the trade as the Hitler Channel, is offering more of its never-ending Nazi footage. This time, the Stuka bombers are strafing . . . Crete? *Click* . . .

MTV offers a program about dating for dumb people. The word "awesome" is used eight times in thirty seconds. *Click* . . .

Garth Brooks . . . *Click* . . .

Racing cars . . . *Click* . . .

Fake wrestling . . . *Click* . . .

Connie Stevens . . . *Help!*

Why is this happening? Has my TV set turned on me? Is it me? Am I jaded?

I don't know, but in a panic I run out of the house and down to the local movie theater. There's got to be something there that's original. I choose *Eyes Wide Shut*, the famous final movie of the great director Stanley Kubrick, starring Tom Cruise and Nicole Kidman. It is bad beyond belief. I know it, you know it (if you saw it), and the reviewers and producers know it. *I am in pain here.*

I know the same thing has happened to you. Boredom! Our buddy television is letting us down big-time when it comes to entertainment. And things are probably going to get worse, moving from the unspeakably bad into a new realm that would frighten Stephen King.

BULLETIN: Why can't the entertainment guys hire me to help out? Here's an example. The fine but depressing cop show *NYPD Blue* should go to Disney World one week. Both Russell and Kirkendall could wear shorts and skimpy tops, a great way to spike ratings. Rick Schroder could pick up some nice waitress at Adventureland. Sipowicz could pummel a pickpocket working the Magic Kingdom. The show always has peppy dialogue. Sipowicz: "You take my meaning here, Goofy?" Is that my phone ringing?

Radio isn't doing much better than TV. Listen to talk radio. Why are the most successful talk show hosts conservative? Well, it's probably because liberals, whatever you think of their views, are usually nonjudgmental. They make exceptions for Ken Starr, Linda Tripp, and Newt Gingrich, but Chinagate? Naw. Buddhist fund-raisers? Nope. High taxes?

Yawn. Welfare reform? Zzzzz. Liberals are just not easily annoyed—unless they happen to find themselves within earshot of Rush Limbaugh. He can get them ranting and raving.

And conservatives? Well, in this country they get teed off regularly. Liberals can look the other way when Clinton fools around in the Oval Office, but conservatives are *outraged*. Find me a conservative who doesn't want to sound off about "the collapse of the American way of life" or the idea of global warming. Hell, some right-wingers would have to see desert sand dunes in their backyard before they'd cop to that.

So if a radio producer can find someone who eggs on conservative listeners to spout off and prods liberals into shouting back, he's got a hit show. The best host is the guy or gal who can get the most listeners extremely *annoyed*—over and over and over again.

After a while, though, the intense verbal action on the right gets predictable and stale. It's not easy for the talk show hosts to get livid every day, even though they think that Bill and Hillary Clinton are not *acceptable*. They've got to hope that Al Gore and his Buddhist nuns, his zinc royalties, and his creative memories will take up the slack.

◻

If TV is boring and talk radio just recycles the same old ideas, where *do* we turn? You can learn from magazines and newspapers, but they become predictable, too. When's the last time Americans rushed out to the local newsstand to get a story hot off the presses? I believe I know. It was the night of Nixon's "Saturday Night Massacre" almost three decades ago.

RIDICULOUS NOTE: Not every magazine is afraid of innovation. Here's how *Sports Illustrated* explained its swimsuit issue of winter 2000: "To us, swimsuit models are strangers on a plane: the two-dimensional world they inhabit. To them, we are just plain strange: readers saddled with a one-dimensional obsession. If only there were a way to bridge the divide . . ." The bridge? 3-D photographs, with specs provided so that the dimensions of Daniela, Heidi, Estella, Audrey, Lujan, and their friends meet journalistic standards. The last time I used 3-D glasses to, uh, read a magazine it was a Mighty Mouse comic book. Do I want to think about what this means? No, I don't. Do I want to use dopey paper glasses to see babes in bikinis? No, I don't.

I believe we're going to turn away from TV, radio, and print journalism in the twenty-first century. Our new best friend? The computer. And if you're one of those people who shrink back from the computer, take a deep breath. You *have* to learn, and it isn't hard. If a six-year-old can learn how to go on the Internet and download video games and a nine-year-old can produce Power Point presentations (don't ask), you can learn how to connect up with the entire world for more information, entertainment, instruction, and conversation with people who share your interests. There is a danger of getting addicted to the machine and turning into one yourself.

For now, it's important to know that global media change is in the air. These are the last desperate days for some electronic information outlets. They aren't reacting very well. It's like the lava heading downhill toward Pompeii. Watch closely; there are exciting times ahead.

5. THE DRUG AND ALCOHOL factor

NOTE TO SUE BERMAN, MEMBER OF THE SAN FRANCISCO BOARD OF SUPERVISORS: Have to hand it to you, Sue . . . You've come up with a very original excuse for allowing public drunkenness and drug use to muck up your city's streets and ruin things for law-abiding citizens. You argue that the streets are the "home" of the homeless addicts and alcoholics. We can have cocktails in our homes, you say, so they should be allowed to drink or drug themselves into a stupor in their "home." What about the other things human beings do in the privacy of their homes, Sue? You want those out in the open, too?

TALKING POINT QUESTION: Why is there so much drug and alcohol abuse in America today?

Simple: Alcohol and drugs make huge profits for legal and illegal organizations.

Simple again: The media thrive on the income from beer and liquor ads, and haul in dough from you with CDs, movies, books, and TV programs that glamorize the lives of "social drinkers," dopeheads, and pushers.

Simpler still: Much of the population is bullish on intoxication. And set in their ways. Dedicated pot smokers believe they are "mellow" and look down on crackheads nodding out in alleyways or deserted basements. Young professionals sniffing coke know that they're on top of the world, masters of the universe: The drug tells them so. The country club set, knocking back martinis and Manhattans and Cosmopolitans, looks down on the rednecks at the noisy beer joint across the county line, and the writers and intellectuals at the local college sneer at both groups for being "alkies" but believe that a trip on the latest psychedelic drug is an intellectual adventure. But everyone has one belief in common: I can handle my "drug of choice."

No wonder Nancy Reagan's message—"Just say no!"—never really went anywhere. It got lost in the "feel good" world kept spinning by the powerful forces of corporate advertising, entertainment companies, alcohol manufacturers, and all of us who indulge stupidly. There is big money to be made in the intoxication business. They know how to get into our pockets.

TALKING POINT: If you are after success in America, substance abuse can be your downfall.

Just think of how many mistakes you can make when you're cold sober. When you're inebriated or stoned, your mistake quotient flies to the moon. The more mistakes you make, the tougher your life will be. And your so-called friends have a long memory—just ask George W. Bush and Al Gore, Jr. It's darned hard to get people to listen to your tax-cut proposals or your environmental policies when half the country's giggling at the jokes on *Saturday Night Live*, Jay Leno's *Tonight Show*, *Late Night with Conan O'Brien*, and *The David Letterman Show*. Bet you're not feeling groovy now, George and Al. The country's laughing at the next commander in chief and leader of the free world, and that's ridiculous. Of course, it was already too late for you to learn from that popular anti-Clinton campaign button of 1992: "Inhale to the Chief."

VIEWER TIME-OUT: "Mr. O'Reilly, how dare you dictate to me what I can ingest—whether it be alcohol or drugs? I am a consenting adult. I own myself and consider it an assault on my freedom when you and other absolutist moralists impose your antediluvian values on me. I know you are an old fogy, but even old fogies indulge themselves on occasion." (Jim F., Tobyhanna, Pennsylvania)

You're right about that, Jim. Old fogies *do* indulge themselves on occasion. But this old fogy tries to do so in moderation, and with legal substances, and in situations that are not going to involve driving or rifle practice, or a sleep-over with a girl named Trixie.

Here's the basic problem with consuming intoxicants: the Child Factor. When funny frogs are pushing beer on TV and high-profile actors like Christian Slater and Robert Downey, Jr., go into drug rehab, kids learn that something pretty interesting is going on, and they want to try it, too. No law is going to stop them from "experimenting," as Al Gore puts it. When Woody Harrelson shows up at a movie premiere shoeless but wearing a suit made entirely of hemp, you have to laugh. And I'm sure there's no truth to the rumor that at the cast party later he smoked his suit. But this kind of stunt *sanitizes* the drug issue for kids. And a substantial portion of each generation will lose control and devote their lives to the pursuit of intoxication.

Therein lies the problem. And a solution is nowhere in sight. Not from medical experts, not from government bureaucrats, not from psychological studies, and not, sad to say, from teachers or religious leaders. The drug and alcohol abusers will tune all of these people out.

BACKUP STATS: Somewhere between 4 and 6 million Americans are addicted to hard drugs, according to recent government estimates. Another 14 million of us have a constant problem with alcohol abuse. Both drugs and alcohol fuel crime and social problems. No study has ever shown otherwise.

MORE BACKUP STATS: In large cities, according to the Office of Drug Control Policy, between 50 and 75 percent of males arrested test positive for drugs. The percentage is even higher for women. Meanwhile, the staggering total of tax money spent by local, state, and federal agencies to combat drugs is about $30 billion. (That's "billion with a *b*," as Ronald Reagan used to say.) And yet, virtually anyone who wants to buy illegal drugs can find them, as the authorities freely admit.

Public policy will *never* put an end to drug addiction. That's why most of the chattering on TV and elsewhere about treatment and legalization and crackdowns is bogus. Intoxication is an extremely personal matter. It can only be dealt with effectively on the individual level. Here's why . . .

It's natural for people to want a quick relief from pain, physical or emotional. We want the hurt to stop. Right now.

Drugs and alcohol, unlike some products, do exactly what they are advertised to do: They make you feel good without any effort on your part. Getting drunk or high is easy. It's the lazy, self-indulgent way to escape from the challenges of real life. When you are feeling some kind of emotional discomfort, absorbing a chemical that brings relief becomes very attractive, *especially* when others around you, or in the media, are taking the same shortcut to oblivion.

THIS JUST IN: *"intoxication* [See also TOXICATION.] 1. The action of poisoning; (an instance of) the state of being poisoned . . . The corruption of the moral or mental faculties; a cause or occasion of this. 2. The action of inebriating or making someone stupid, insensible, or disordered in intellect, with a drug or alcoholic liquor; the condition of being so stupefied or disordered . . ." —*The New Shorter Oxford English Dictionary*, 1993

♉

Despite all of the jokes about drink and Irish Americans, I was sixteen before I was exposed to full-blown intoxication. When a friend's parents left town, he didn't go quite as far as the Tom Cruise character in *Risky Business*, but he did throw a giant party complete with cases of hard liquor and beer. This was pretty wild stuff in our neighborhood in our day. By the end of the evening, there was serious damage to the house and also to many of the teenage partygoers, who either had passed out or were painfully regurgitating. Some of them could have used medical attention, though everyone survived.

I still don't understand why, but I did not join the drinking. Dr Pepper in hand, I was the sober observer. To this day I can see the images of my out-of-control friends. Some of them got goofy, others became hostile, and quite a few acted in ways that none of us ever mentioned afterward. I was amazed by what alcohol could do. It forever changed my opinion about certain people there that night.

Before then, I had regarded alcohol as an adult habit, like smoking cigars or going to Vegas. My parents were light drinkers. They didn't drink enough to have mood changes or stumble around the living room. My folks never felt the need to discuss drinking or drugs with me. They didn't have to. My father did not tolerate other kinds of nonsense; I knew that coming home drunk or even tipsy would be extremely risky. Did I know that my grandfather was an alcoholic who died from liver disease? Not really. The subject wasn't talked about. It was just something that happened to an old man.

As for me, drink never had an appeal. But some of my friends took to drugs and alcohol, and the results weren't pretty. In our quiet working-class suburb alone, three friends were killed by drug abuse: an overdose, a drowning while stoned, and AIDS transmitted by a needle. Three other guys in town became addicted to heroin and wound up in jail. And *this* was Levittown, not Haight-Ashbury or Amsterdam!

Was alcohol a less dangerous way to ruin your life? Only in a manner of speaking. More than a few kids in our neighborhood washed out on booze. Their vital signs may indicate that they're still alive, but they've chosen a slow form of suicide.

VIEWER TIME-OUT: "O'Reilly, what are you—the morality police? Haven't you ever made a mistake? Your position on marijuana is a crock. The best thing you could do would be to lay back and stoke one up." (Laurie B., Seattle, Washington)

Oh, I've made quite a few mistakes, Laurie. No question about that. And if you want to carry your argument about morality police a little further, some people might say that we all have the right to destroy our lives and our careers with drug and alcohol abuse. Why is it any of my business?

Well, one good reason is that the abuser is almost certainly going to hurt other people.

◻

Something like 75 percent of all physical abuse against helpless little kids is committed by inebriated adults. That's what the child abuse agencies tell me. Some of these abusers probably thought they would just "lay back and stoke one up."

But that's only part of the "collateral damage" of self-indulgent drug and alcohol abuse. Unwanted pregnancies are often the result of drugged or drunken couplings, especially among teenagers. Sexually transmitted diseases, including AIDS, are often passed around when people are too intoxicated to use protection. Alcohol alone is involved in fully half of all murders, accidental deaths, and suicides in the United States, and in almost half of all fatal car accidents, according to the National Institutes of Health.

Add drugs to the mix, and you can trace most of the social problems we face in America to chemical abuse of some kind (or kinds). The majority of the pathetic homeless people living miserably on streets across the country cannot keep themselves sober. High school dropouts have a high rate of substance abuse. The list goes on.

RIDICULOUS NOTE: Even kids have a low tolerance for druggies when the shoe's on the other foot. When actor/comedian Norm MacDonald gave a paid talk to students at Connecticut's Quinnipiac College, his speech was so slurred that some young people in the audience started booing and making rude comments. Norm cut short his remarks, whatever they were. A college spokesperson said he would not be paid because he was "clearly on something." Norm snapped back that the students were all drunk. Stay tuned. Well, no, don't stay tuned. This is too ridiculous. Hey, Norm, we'll leave the light on for you.

So why are the few Americans who speak out against drugs labeled morality police, bluenoses, or religious zealots? Got me. Since, as I've just demonstrated, substance abuse usually does not take place in a vacuum and since millions of innocent bystanders get hurt or killed, society has to wake up and deal effectively with the problem. It's time for a national outcry.

If you don't know it, you should now. I know it, and the victims of drug abuse know it.

But the federal government? Not a clue.

BACKUP STATS: To stop drugs from getting to your hometown, the feds alone spend $15 billion *every year.* It hasn't worked, and it will never work. No matter where you live, I'm willing to bet some zonked-out kid could find a drug source within a few miles of your home. And I never bet to lose. How much of the illegal drugs coming to the U.S.A. did the DEA,

FBI, U.S. Customs, and the Coast Guard *combined* seize last year? Here's what they themselves estimate: about 10 percent. The home team is losing big, folks.

We also send American tax dollars to places like Mexico, Thailand, Colombia, and Turkey so that local authorities will stop the drugs at the source. Does anyone on this earth besides our chuckleheaded politicians actually believe that throwing millions at corrupt officials in underdeveloped countries is an effective program for ending drug trafficking?

RIDICULOUS NOTE: Not long ago, the Clinton administration's comically weak "Drug Czar" General Barry McCaffrey publicly expressed his admiration for Mexico's top general because the man had taken such a tough stand on drugs. About a month later this admirable Mexican role model was arrested. He had been caught supervising the transshipment of drugs to the U.S.A. Good call, Barry! How about the guys in Colombia? Got any drug war heroes down there?

📺

If payments to local authorities and interdiction at the borders don't work, how about the other ideas we hear tossed around all the time?

Legalization? Not on your life. When Switzerland legalized drug use in Zurich in the early 1990s, I hopped on a plane to check out the program. What I saw was a real-life spectacle of horror that turned my stomach. Hundreds of addicts roamed through the bustling center of town, shooting up in plain view of pedestrians, including children. Many of the addicts were filthy and panhandled aggressively.

Because of this noble experiment, a famously beautiful city park was transformed into a dreadful slum. There were piles of used, dirty needles and bloodstained cotton balls stacked under the linden trees. Fortunately the proud citizens of Zurich did not take this outrage lying down. They forced the Swiss government to reverse its wrongheaded policy.

In this country legalization would be even worse for at least two reasons: the sheer numbers of potential users in our growing population and the simple fact that users do not like to do drugs alone. Users want company so badly that they will share their drugs, illegal or legal, expensive or free. If you think it's easy for your kids to get their hands on cigarettes and booze now—and it is!—just you wait until the day some town or state makes the mistake of legalizing heroin, coke, and pot. It would be a nightmare.

Could you keep your kids "clean" in that situation? Wouldn't be easy, because they don't have to be "bad" kids or hoodlums or even losers when drug use is okay with the law. If society allows it, then it must be all right. And if drugs are legal, think of how many places your kids could go to get high, doze it off, and come home without a trace.

And if legalization passes, can Madison Avenue be far behind? Or Wall Street? Will some legal drug producer get enough cash to buy the rights to change John Lennon's famous anthem to "Give Coke a Chance" and play it in the background of a TV spot? And air it during the Super Bowl? And who will be the highly paid spokespersons for this thriving new industry? Richard Dreyfuss? Whitney Houston? Stacy Keach? How about the losing candidate for U.S. president in November 2000? That would make Bob Dole's Viagra ad look like an act of statesmanship.

THIS JUST IN: "Even useful medicines like heroin and morphine are hurtful when taken habitually for nontherapeutic purposes, while poisons like cannabis, caffeine, coca products, tobacco, and beverage alcohol . . . should not be promoted in our society—and, above all, not under any circumstances permitted to be exploited for commercial profit." —Rufus King, author of *The Drug Hang-Up*, 1972

📺

Well, there's another approach that gets a lot of attention, but not enough thought: Would spending federal dollars to open thousands of drug rehab centers cure the problem?

No.

Hold that thought.

No.

BACKUP STATS: When the think-tank Rand Corporation organized a massive study of drug rehab, the results were dismal. Only 13 percent of hard-core cocaine abusers stayed clean after they were released from rehab. Experts estimate that anywhere from 60 to 80 percent of drug addicts want nothing to do with rehab programs. (Hint: That's what "addict" means.)

The problem with well-meaning do-gooders who push for expensive rehab programs is that they aren't looking closely at the reality of drug use. Only a tiny minority are motivated to enter rehab, and motivation is the key. Without it, no therapy will work. Every drug counselor will tell you that.

The true addict has turned away from all personal and social responsibility. Is the baby crying? Get high, and you won't hear it. Have you lost your job for being out of it most of the time? Now you can stay out of it all the time. That's the addict's way of thinking: Life is lived for the purpose of getting high.

Do you find this attitude hard to understand? So do I. We're lucky. And we're not *better* than people who become addicts, but *smarter.* Because, and make no mistake about it, at a certain point the addict made a stupid choice. Society has to do something to make that choice more difficult.

¤

The truth is obvious: The only solution to the drug problem in America is to deal directly with users as the law requires.

The U.S. Constitution does not guarantee any American the right to walk around intoxicated. Therefore, laws have been put in place, and those laws should be vigorously enforced in a humane way.

As you probably know, the courts have ruled that the authorities have the right to drug-test everyone who is arrested, no matter what the reason. Why? Because the state has a right and probably an obligation to know the physical condition of people taken into custody. Using new high-tech mobile machines like SYVAETS, large-scale drug testing is possible now for about a dollar a test.

You probably don't hear many good things about the state of Alabama in today's media, but a new drug program there points the way to a saner future.

All prisoners are now tested as soon as they're booked. The majority— no surprise—have drugs or alcohol in their blood. The test results are passed along to the courts. All convicted suspects are given a choice:

forced drug rehab in a prison drug facility or a longer sentence with the general prison population. More than 90 percent opt for rehab.

Hundreds of pages of statistics on this new program already prove its unusual effectiveness: Of the five thousand participants so far, twice as many criminals stay off drugs upon release than those without rehab. For years after release the ex-cons must submit to regular drug testing.

Wait a minute . . . How does this rehab program differ from the rehab centers that our tax dollars could set up by the thousands? Remember the word "motivation"?

The Alabama program works so well because of three factors. First, the hard-core drug customer is forcibly taken off the street and kept away from the drug-using environment. That cuts down the temptation.

Second, the close monitoring after release provides a strong incentive to keep clean: If you test positive for drugs, you're hauled back to prison rehab. No exceptions. Unlike the state of Florida, Alabama wouldn't be cutting any slack to New York Yankees slugger Daryl Strawberry.

Third, this program takes customers by the bushel away from the local pusher man. It attacks profit in the drug marketplace.

What's the lesson here? It's that the feds should shift the billions in the "drug war" budget to *coerced* drug treatment in all fifty states. The addict population has remained stable for the past ten years, according to the experts. That means there's a finite number of adult Americans who ruin their lives ingesting narcotics. Keeping these hard-core addicts off the streets for a year or more, depending on their crimes, would mean far fewer customers for the dealers. That would immediately damage their financial bottom line.

BACKUP STATS: Some 7 million Americans buy a total of 331 tons of cocaine each year, according to the Rand Corporation. Take half of these users off the streets and place them in forced rehab, and the U.S. coke market would collapse. You can count on it.

BULLETIN: To support this new approach, prosecutors and judges should ensure that pushers get slammed with big-time mandatory prison sentences. That would put the risk-reward ratio of dealing squarely against these merchants of death.

How does forced rehab work? Well, it should be humane, as I've said. The point is to give the drug-addicted criminal a fighting chance to succeed in society upon release. This means psychiatric drug counseling, educational classes, job training, and job placement. That's a sensible and fair formula for giving drug-addicted criminals a leg up on leading a productive life. Sound rehab cleans up the users, tries to get to the source of their emotional problems, and provides them with the tools to succeed.

This is good, smart policy.

But it won't work if it isn't tough, too.

If the released addict commits another crime and is returned to the system, the second time around should be much stricter. Such criminals should be given rehab again, but in a more intense setting. They should have to work long hours in addition to their treatment. Their sentences should be doubled. After all, society has already invested a lot of time and money in their recovery, and they blew it off. The taxpayers who foot the bills are owed a no-nonsense carrot-and-stick approach to repeat offenders.

◻

Am I wrong? Well, some people think so.

They complain that forced drug rehab is inherently racist because it would affect more blacks than whites. This is absolute nonsense. It is also self-defeating prattle from "advocates" who really ought to know better. (And probably do . . .)

What's racist about investing billions of federal dollars in helping drug-addicted criminals—many of them poor and badly educated—get a second chance to succeed in our competitive society? If more members of minority groups are addicted, then more members of minority groups are going to benefit. Forced drug rehab is an opportunity, not a punishment. Racism, if we think clearly for a minute, is allowing the drug problem to fester and grow in minority communities that are falling further away every day from the American Dream. Racism is expecting less responsibility from minorities than from the rest of society.

Then there's the disease excuse.

It goes like this: Drug addiction is a disease, so society has no right to punish addicts for their illness. Well, this kind of ridiculous argument makes *me* ill. We need to stop feeling sorry for people who career out of control, and begin to impose sanctions on them. What do the experts say? They disagree. You'll find just as many researchers arguing that drug addiction and alcoholism are *not* diseases as the reverse.

I don't know who's right, but I do know this: Millions of former addicts and alcoholics have proved that substance abuse can be conquered by the abuser—by doing just that themselves! And then they are able to keep themselves clean. You can't argue against that kind of track record. People *can* stop drinking and drugging. They cannot stop prostate cancer or a brain tumor by just saying no. Those are diseases.

Oh, and one other thing. As long as addictions are considered to be diseases, then physicians, counselors, and administrators of rehab centers are going to be able to claim reimbursement from insurance companies. And government grants will fund existing and new programs. But if addiction is considered to be just a psychological weakness, not a disease, then the flow of corporate and government checks dries up.

Okay. If *I* can figure out that no attack upon our national drug problem is going to work as well as the Alabama solution of forced rehab for addicted criminals in prison, why can't the federal government get the picture?

Because of the realities of power and class I talked about back in Chapter 1. Washington's rich and powerful don't *care* about the drug problem in American life because it doesn't impact their privileged lives on a day-to-day basis. What nationally known politician lives down the street from an openly functioning drug bazaar, like "the little people" in parts of Harlem or South-Central Los Angeles or Chicago's South Side? I don't know any. Which media mogul or millionaire lobbyist has a five-year-old kid who can explain crack slang to him, because it's used all the time in the neighborhood? Not one. Our lawmakers typically live in secure neighborhoods where you're more likely to run into E.T. than a crack whore.

Well, you can bet I've tried to knock some sense into the powers that be. On *The O'Reilly Factor* I've debated the use of coerced prison rehab with some of the biggest political names in the country. I don't mean to be rude to these people, or to anyone, but we have staked out a no-spin rule on my program. I expect facts and reasonable arguments.

So far, no one has poked a hole in the idea of forced rehab yet, because they can't. They know the truth: Nothing else is working. They know that the "drug war" is a hollow charade that is bilking taxpayers and neglecting addicts. Drug Czar McCaffrey himself admitted on the air to me that his current programs are at least a decade away from making a dent in the drug industry.

And the losing battle provides a darned good career for many of our fellow citizens. The DEA doesn't want to give up a penny of its budget. The czar himself has a nice job that confers status and has such perks as frequent travel. Why rock the boat? We aren't putting pressure on them to change, so they aren't going to change.

BULLETIN: The government could bring the drug problem under control within the next two years by providing block grant monies to states for coerced drug rehab. That's an amazing statement, but it's true! Yet it is not going to happen, because the D.C./Beltway establishment could not care less about this issue.

Consider how important it would be to get even half the nation's drug addicts into forced prison rehab: Crime would fall dramatically, perhaps by as much as 50 percent. The AIDS infection rate would drop. Fewer children would suffer abuse. All of us would see our insurance rates go down. As the drug dealers are driven out of business, inner-city neighborhoods would become more livable overnight. Children going to school would no longer have to walk around junkies nodding out on the sidewalk.

I can cite twenty more examples, but you get the picture. Somehow we've got to make this happen. I believe it, I hope you believe it, and maybe if we keep at it, we can make the big boys in D.C. believe it.

Drugs have created a giant spiderweb of catastrophe that cheapens life in America. Our freedom is threatened when addicts and dealers are given license. Drug dealing, a crime against humanity and a violation of human rights, should be punished harshly. Do you disagree with anything in this paragraph, Drug Czar?

ﾛ

Treating alcoholism is a different problem.

I don't know any effective solution. You can't resort to coerced treatment, because booze is legal. That means that alcoholics can emotionally damage their families and drink themselves to death, but society can do nothing but watch, unless there's physical abuse or drunk driving.

BACKUP STATS: Lest we get jaded . . . The death toll from drunk driving accidents in 1998 was 16,189 children, women, and men. Each one of them was a uniquely individual human being. Every year, according to government estimates, drunk driving crashes cost more than $45 billion—not counting lost wages, physical therapy, and rehabilitation.

Meanwhile, the alcoholic can choose from two kinds of messages. On TV and in print there are campaigns to warn about the dangers of abusing alcohol. Some of them are stark, provocative, and frightening. But the same media outlets also provide glamorous or clever ads. Will the alcoholic put down the glass because of a MADD spot or refill it because of the images of beautiful people in beautiful places having an adman's fantasy of the good life? You know the answer. Booze ads are just peer pressure in a modern form. Alcoholics have heard the message they want to hear since Noah invented viniculture and made a fool of himself by getting drunk and passing out in front of his family.

Still, the drug addict takes drugs for only one reason: to get high. The vast majority of Americans who drink are able to do so responsibly without crossing the line to intoxication. That's a significant difference. It also shows that society is not entirely hypocritical by legalizing booze but not narcotics.

But no one can argue that you *need* alcohol any more than you *need* drugs. You'll have a better life if you avoid both entirely. The whole intoxication thing is a minus for all of us. From broken health to broken friendships, alcohol and drugs are not worth the hassle. Even a so-called minor drug like marijuana has a negative impact. It erodes discipline and is toxic to the body. More kids are in pot rehab than in alcohol rehab.

If I sound like I'm from the Land of Oz, so be it. The *Factor* is here to tell you the straight story: Walk away from the seductive rites of inebriation, and your odds of succeeding in America will soar.

6. THE
JOB factor

NOTE TO BILL RICHARDSON, SECRETARY OF THE DEPARTMENT OF
ENERGY: You found out, what?, fifteen minutes ago that the
Chinese have been looting some of America's most prized nuclear secrets for more than a decade. But I gotta admit, you
took quick action: Your new DOE job guidelines instruct all
employees to report any romantic involvement with a person
from a country that's developing nuclear weaponry. So, to
keep their private lives private, your employees better date
someone from Cameroon or Italy rather than Pakistan or Is-
rael. This is ridiculous, Bill. Your DOE guidelines are DOA. By
the way, instead of scrutinizing the love lives of those in your
charge, you might call up former secretary of energy Hazel
O'Leary and ask her why she gutted security at all of our nuclear facilities. Then call up Attorney General Janet Reno and
ask why she denied a wiretap on Wen Ho Lee's hot computer.
The Chinese certainly got in there, but the FBI couldn't. Do
these two things, Bill, and you'd be doing your job.

Like Bill Richardson, most of us have to work for a living. Most of us
hate something about our jobs, beginning with our bosses. It's no accident
that Johnny Paycheck's country music hit "Take This Job and Shove It"
still gets a lot of play at TGIF parties. Most of us don't think our work
is appreciated or fairly compensated. That's what we tell the pollsters,
anyway. And yet quite a few of us are not planning to retire. Ever.

I guess that means that having a job and doing it well, even when you get teed off or feel exploited, is an important part of life. We all want to make things, or make things happen. You don't have to work in the Department of Energy to deal with baloney, bull, and bilge. There are going to be hassles wherever you get a job—even if you work at home (as one in six of us does these days).

But since work is a fact of life and can also be rewarding, we're better off when we find the job that's best for us. It's too big a chunk of your lifetime to let it go to waste. And our workday directly colors our social life. If we're unfulfilled at work, it's harder to be a happy, generous person.

VIEWER TIME-OUTS: Hey, you probably deal with only one supervisor and some coworkers, right? Not me. I've got hundreds of thousands of supervisors: the viewing public. Last August, on an evening picked at random, here are job evaluations phoned in by some of my supervisors:

8:10 P.M. "This is about O'Reilly. I'm upset because he doesn't know how the intelligence community works. I think he should be jailed for treason."

8:24 P.M. "I normally watch Fox News but not when O'Reilly's on. He is obnoxious and disrespectful to our great president. Please take him off immediately."

8:40 P.M. "I can't take this O'Reilly. I think he's a Nazi."

8:52 P.M. "Doesn't Fox have anyone else who can do this O'Reilly show? He is the most obnoxious man I've ever seen on TV. I'm switching to CNN."

9:00 P.M. "I just finished watching an hour of O'Reilly. I demand to talk with his superior right now."

And you thought you had a bad day at the office?

◻

How do I deal with these reactions? Like Harry Truman. I chose to be in this particular kitchen, I *like* being in this particular kitchen, and I've learned throughout my career how to take the heat.

I had to because I lead the league in dumb on-the-job strategies and unbelievably foolish maneuvers. I recount them here as a warning: Learn from my mistakes. Do NOT try this at work!

◘

I began working at age eleven. Not because I was born with a "work ethic." Not because I was ambitious. I had a strict six-foot-three, two-hundred-pound father who kept a tight grip on his wallet. He had earned every dollar in his pocket, and he intended to hold on to every one of them, as the old Bessie Smith song goes, "until the eagle grins."

So my work life began, as most do, because I wanted money. I started out cutting lawns, baby-sitting, and hunting down lost golf balls to resell them. My first real job was behind the counter at a Carvel ice cream store one summer, and it was great: a buck an hour plus all the ice cream I could swallow (which was quite a bit).

But this was the 1960s, when a dollar an hour was not going to get me to Woodstock. The next summer I struck out on my own and began a house-painting business with some of my thug friends. That gave me my first useful job lesson: Working for yourself is a big advantage *if* you are willing to work hard. And I was. You get to make the choices, but you also have to take responsibility. There's no cushion. You can make good money, but you pay for your mistakes.

My friends and I made a great team. Some weeks we cleared as much as $200 each. My father was delirious with joy. I was *never* going to meet him at the front door asking for cash. I'm not sure he could believe his good luck.

RIDICULOUS NOTE: We teenage capitalists never turned down any good honest work. I guess that's why I'm surprised that Monica Lewinsky turned down a $480,000 job offer from Italian designer Gattinoni. All she had to do was walk back and forth on a fashion show runway in Milan modeling a few of his two-piece "outsized" bathing suits. Ms. Lewinsky found the gig "inappropriate." How nice that propriety has become an option for her.

◘

As I've mentioned, I taught high school after graduating from Marist College. The pay was $5,000 a year at a Catholic school whose philosophy was, "Poverty is good because Jesus was poor." Unfortunately poverty was one of the few things Jesus and I had in common.

I liked being a teacher. I felt I helped some students and kept the rest awake. I always prepared for class because I didn't want to waste their time or mine. But the school's corrupt dictator of a principal took a different approach. He was perfect for the totalitarian system that is American education, laying down foolish rules and ignoring important problems. I mocked him at faculty meetings, but that kind of behavior is a dead end. Nothing was going to change. He had no respect for students or teachers. He just wanted to keep a lid on things.

So I bailed out and went to Boston University for my master's in broadcast journalism. Good training, but no guaranteed meal ticket. My first TV job was at tiny station WNEP-TV in Scranton, Pennsylvania, and I was glad to get it. After driving down from Boston for the interview, I appeared in the station manager's office wearing a powder-blue sports jacket and double-knit slacks. Add the mid-1970s hairstyle, and all six feet four of me looked like a barker at a strip club.

But I was a shoo-in because I agreed to work for $150 a week. This was not smart. After taxes, my take-home pay was about $475 a month. Because there was a rental housing shortage in Scranton, my rent was $250 a month. And I needed to get a new wardrobe pronto to go before the camera and deliver the news with any hope of being taken seriously. Things were *very* tight.

So I did a fairly stupid thing. After less than two weeks on the job, I complained. I should have waited at least a month. But it was okay. This was a family-owned station that patiently heard complaints and tried to be fair. The general manager, who was kind, came up with a plan. For an extra twenty dollars a week, I would write gag lines for the station's Saturday evening monster movie program, *Uncle Ted's Ghoul School*. I signed on.

It was not long before Uncle Ted and I had some pretty fierce "creative differences." An old Scrantonite who had hosted a variety of local programs over decades, the sixty-year-old Ted loved the sauce, and I'm not talking Chef Boyardee here. Ted was usually half in the bag during the telecasts, which were live, and mangled some of my best one-liners. Who cares? Well, let me tell you, you can get caught up in these things. Who was watching moronic monster movies in Scranton late on a Saturday night? Voters for the Emmy awards? Was this any way to meet the local chicks? ("Hey, baby, I'm the guy who writes the gags on . . .") Didn't matter. This was "pride of authorship." Not kindly, I suggested to Uncle Ted that he lighten up on the Scotch and soda before airtime. He came back with a creative suggestion of his own involving my committing an unnatural act with myself.

Like Dean Martin and Jerry Lewis before their famous split, our relationship soon sank to the level of outright hostility. I got pretty steamed. And I took action that might have been a tad inappropriate.

When a movie called *Dracula's Daughter* was scheduled, I arranged with a local mortuary to send over a coffin in exchange for an on-air plug. Then I suggested to the director that Uncle Ted, who looked like a vampire without using makeup, do what vampires do: that is, emerge from a coffin to open his segment.

He adamantly refused. I insisted, even though a technician told me Ted was claustrophobic. I called the general manager, who ordered him to go along with the skit. Cursing a blue streak, our host climbed into the coffin—and I locked it from the outside. When his live insert was cued during the commercial, he pushed with all his might. The lid stayed shut tight. The coffin rocked back and forth on live TV! The mike picked up Ted's muffled scream from inside.

Laughing, I signaled the director to cut back to the movie. Everyone thought the whole thing was hilarious, except Uncle Ted. When the coffin lid was unlocked, he stormed off the set, vowing to kill me when I least expected it. I replaced him as emcee, explaining to the amazed audience that he had accidentally been exposed to some garlic but would return next week.

He did, but I didn't.

No, I wasn't axed as a news reporter, but my gag-writing career was history.

Okay, the whole stunt was immature, but it was *funny*. Did I let it teach me anything about how to play well with others? Naw. I shed no tears for Uncle Ted. After nine months at WNEP, an offer came from a big station in Dallas. I left Scranton for the sprawling, brawling great American Southwest.

RIDICULOUS NOTE: The Clintons, who've been creative about their activities past and present, came up with a new way of giving job evaluations to their employees. According to the *Washington Post*, it depends upon your farewell party. If Bill and Hillary thought you did *great*, lobster is served. A merely good job earns lamb chops. Meatballs mean "just fair." But if you walk in the room and see a spread of cheese and crackers, you know they hate you. What happened when Monica got "transferred"? (Supply your own wisecrack here.)

ᵈ

Back to my career. I hadn't seen anything yet. After the plain dealing of the folks at WNEP-TV, I was twenty-six going on ten in the worldliness department. Suddenly I was swimming among the sharks at WFAA-TV, a powerhouse station. It swarmed with ambitious, aggressive journalists battling each other under the strong thumb of an unsympathetic management.

But I was not going to be knocked aside. I jumped right in—and made every possible political mistake. Openly challenge the arrogant but successful news director? That was me. Blurt out stupid comments in the newsroom? Me, again and again. Mouth off to the producers? On a daily basis. Dumb doesn't even begin to cover it.

VIEWER TIME-OUT: Some things don't change, I guess; here's a *recent* note from a viewer of *The O'Reilly Factor*. "Mr. O'Reilly, once again I heard you describe yourself as a journalist, and that makes this old newsman sick. You'll *never* be a journalist." (Keith H., Honolulu, Hawaii)

So what saved me from being thrown out into the street? Once again, my pay was low, less than $300 a week, so even pain-in-the-ass O'Reilly was a bargain. (No 1970s Lava Lites and shag carpeting on that budget.)

And my work was good. It had to be. The honchos got back at me by torturing me with lousy assignments and mocking the hell out of me. But they had to put me on the air because I came through every time. Boston University had provided the broadcast schooling; WFAA-TV was broadcast boot camp.

Did I mention twenty-six going on ten? Well, that's the only explanation for what brought things to a head. In a staff meeting I stood up and criticized a decision to hire a new anchorwoman. "It's outrageous," I fumed. The room froze. See, I thought it was not sound news practice to bring aboard an untested anchor just because she was supposedly sleeping with one of the station honchos. Wrong, O'Reilly. I found out that it happens *all* the time in the TV news industry. They didn't give that insight at B.U.

So I was suspended for two weeks for "insubordination." I was shocked all over again. What insubordination? I had offered an honest and honorable opinion, and I had offered it in the interest of giving the public a good newscast. Without freedom of speech the managers and owners of a TV station would not be making money. That's the foundation of broadcast journalism. So where does a TV station get off suspending me, or anyone else, for "speaking freely"?

Then a strange thing happened. Jim Simon, at the time the news director for the radio side of WFAA, hired me to work for him during my suspension at *double* my salary. I loved the guy. He was one of journalism's true believers. He knew I'd been sandbagged, and he didn't like it.

So things turned out well for me, despite my big ego and big mouth. The TV management was humiliated. And from all this I learned . . . nothing. After two years I left Dallas, still naive enough to believe that right can always overcome wrong.

📺

Next stop, KMGH-TV in Denver. Paul Thompson, my new boss, hired me on the recommendation of the McHugh-Hoffman consulting firm. He liked my brash style, paid me well, and allowed me free rein to roam all over Colorado in search of stories. Thanks to his faith in me, I broke some big ones. Working this gig was the most fun I've ever had in my life.

But after a year Thompson left for a better job. His replacement, Lucifer the Prince of Darkness, did everything you'd expect from the King of Hell. I fought back and was in constant trouble. Are there nine circles of Hell? I was sent down to level 8 at least. Then, I swear, the Lord intervened, trumping Satan again. I won an Emmy for the best breaking-news coverage in the Rocky Mountain region. It was awarded for a story on an airline skyjacking in Denver.

It takes a lot for a functionary to argue with an on-air Emmy. The award becomes part of the station's advertising, part of the corporate image. Gnashing his teeth in private, the fiend news director got out of my face. But the backbiting continued out of sight in the offices of upper management. I had still not learned that you cannot challenge authority in the workplace without lining up some major forces to support you.

Within a couple of months I left for the East Coast. An Emmy on the cheap coffee table is a fine thing, but it doesn't beat getting respect from the people you break your back for. After I briefly anchored the news in Hartford, Connecticut, CBS offered me a job in New York City—a huge step up the career ladder.

VIEWER TIME-OUT: *Why* did people keep hiring me? Maybe this viewer has the answer. "Mr. O., I find you smug and annoying. I believe you have a personal bias regarding a wide variety of issues. However, for reasons I cannot readily explain, these traits seem to increase my enjoyment of your program." (Zeke U., Leavenworth, Kansas)

At this point I had worked at four different TV stations in five years. So, of course, I was experienced enough now to operate wisely within a large bureaucracy? Yeah, and Al Sharpton cares for all Americans.

I was about as perceptive as a telephone pole. Besides, I had no stomach for playing the corporate game. I enjoyed being a maverick. I relished my defiance of corrupt authority and my doomed crusades for justice in the newsroom. I insisted on being treated with fairness.

So I marched down the halls of CBS like Clint Eastwood. This was the same Dirty Harry attitude that had already got me in so much trouble in three different time zones. I was completely out of my mind. I became notorious.

CELEBRITY SIGHTING: The analogy to Eastwood is deliberate. I admire the man and the actor. He's the same height as I am, came from a working-class background, and made it on his own, rising from his movie debut in *Revenge of the Creature* to become the most successful movie star in the world. He came to Denver to make one of those dopey monkey flicks with his girlfriend at the time, Sondra Locke. Naturally he was surrounded by a phalanx of bodyguards, but your young intrepid reporter O'Reilly was determined to get an interview. I found out where he was staying, bribed the doorman ten dollars for Clint's room number, and knocked on his door without warning at 9:30 one morning, while my cameraman stood back cautiously. A bleary-eyed Clint opened his door, wearing a bathrobe, and pinned me with that patented squinty-eyed look. The camera was rolling, and I cheerfully welcomed him to Denver. In his famous raspy voice he said, "Why don't you guys take a hike?" The cameraman looked closely to see if the star was armed. Shameless, I explained how an interview with me would be great for *his* career. Clint apparently found that amusing and said, "Okay, kid, gimme fifteen minutes and I'll talk to you." Back at the station, my colleagues were stunned by this coup. Clint won greatest-guy status in my eyes. It was three years later that I imitated his walk into CBS.

BULLETIN: Repeat . . . Do *not* do what I did in the workplace. It's not worth it. I've survived and even prospered in the world of TV news, but that's a miracle, believe me. I made my life a thousand times harder than it had to be.

Am I finally wiser? Well, maybe just a better strategist. Now I go into corporate combat *only* when there's no other option. I don't make the mistake of expecting fairness to be in play. I don't waste my own time and blood pressure in back-and-forth with pinheads. That's what my agents and lawyers are for, and they're brilliant at it. It's still true that a man who represents himself has a fool for a lawyer (or agent). I've learned that much.

Enough of my résumé. If you want more of the story of network newsroom intrigue in these turbulent times, it's in the novel I mentioned, *Those Who Trespass.* Let's get off my Job Factor and back to yours . . .

📺

Here's the most important thing you need to know for success: Identify your true talents. We're all born with a grab bag of gifts and gaps. Think deeply about yours; identify them clearly; *then* find out how to use them to make money!

Go back and read that paragraph again. I don't care how old you are. It is never too late to use the gifts God gave you. Not many things are sadder—or more darned annoying—than someone who says, "I wish I had started my own woodworking business" (written a book, moved to a farm, gone back to nursing school, etc., etc.). Get off your duff and do it now!

What keeps people from identifying their talents and using them?

Laziness, insecurity, and lack of discipline. The cure for laziness is work. The cure for insecurity is light-years more complicated, but it should not hold you back. The cure for lack of discipline is to learn to make yourself do what you *do not* want to do, and do it *on time*.

This is not always easy. But it's worth doing, if you want to live comfortably and feel proud of yourself.

And you have to develop strong habits: Get punctual, bring energy and creativity to your work, and stay with a project until it's completed (and then double-check the results). These habits will make you *indispensable*.

Why will discipline make you stand out from everyone else on the job? Because the sad truth is that we live in an undisciplined age. The art of the excuse has been raised to Olympic caliber. In fact, there ought to be a new event in the Sydney Olympics called excuse-making, right after synchronized swimming and those ridiculous ribbon twirlers. The Irish would win the gold medal, a perfect 10, but the U.S.A. team would have a lock on the silver.

Back in real life, though, excuses don't cut it. Your boss wants results, as do his and hers and his, all the way up to the chairman and the stockholders. Excuses are not results. Excuses are not money, and money counts. Sometimes excellence counts, and when it does, no excuse will paper over a half-assed job. Something else: There is never any excuse for not being kind.

THIS JUST IN: "The more that a man exercises himself and asserts his own influence over his work, the less the part that luck plays. It is true in baseball that the greatest single menace that a man has is a willingness to alibi his own failures; the greatest menace to a man's success in business, I think, sometimes is a perfect willingness to excuse himself for his own mistakes." —Baseball General Manager Branch Rickey, 1926

I know "discipline" is not a user-friendly word, but you owe it to yourself to force yourself to do your job well. If the work is beyond your capabilities, face up to the fact and move on. If you have to work extra hours every night, just to keep up, something is probably wrong. It's not how long you work but how much you produce.

If you don't or can't produce, the responsibility for that is yours alone. You don't want to descend into the world of weaseling and blaming others. And you must never take credit for work that is not yours, even if you're a movie producer.

Does playing dirty ever work? The worst human being I've ever worked with prospers in network news, even as I write. A true weaselette—vicious, sneaky, and bloodthirsty—she has never covered a news story, never been in the field, never faced a deadline, and never got behind the desk and appeared before the camera. Doesn't matter. Her skills don't need to be learned; they are ancient. She has accumulated vast power over scores of working reporters by kissing ass and spying on her coworkers. She can damage a career with a well-placed hiss—uh, comment. There is likely to be a clone of this truly dangerous individual lurking in your own workplace. These people are legion.

This particular creature instinctively hated my guts. Naturally, like most other people around the newsroom, I should have smiled and stayed out of her way. Naturally I played right into her hands by openly despising her right back. In fact, I had to make a point of showing my disdain for her. Am I an idiot? The final answer, Regis, is yes.

Unless you go the monk route, you will always run into toxic people like the weaselette. (Heck, what do I know? Even the monasteries might be hotbeds of hypocrisy and scheming. Never been close to finding out, myself.) The disciplined person will take some time to figure out how to deal with such people. It's not that hard, really. Even the worst slime will respond to a little kindness, though you may have to grit your teeth to pass it along.

Jesus and Gandhi would have been kind to the weaselette. O'Reilly wasn't. I think we all know whom to emulate here.

BULLETIN: Why do corporations allow the slime to do so much damage? After years of going *head-to-head* with them, I've finally reached enlightenment. Most of the suits want their employees frightened and on the defensive. The weasels help immensely with that. They provide info, much of it false, to the suits who are isolated in their upstairs offices. These weasels prosper because they are indispensable to many insecure corporate managers, unscrupulous political types on the make, and power-hungry entrepreneurs.

This will never change. Don't waste as much time as I have thinking about these people. Accept them—and dodge 'em.

CELEBRITY SIGHTING: The weasels were waiting for Burt Reynolds, whom I covered during my Dallas gig in 1977. He was shooting *Semi-Tough*. This was just after his famous seminude pictorial in *Cosmopolitan* magazine, when he was a regular on Johnny Carson's *Tonight Show* and was earning over $1 million a year—an incredible sum at the time. Burt took full advantage of Dallas with hot and cold running babes in his hotel suite and fleets of limos. Crowds of fans appeared wherever he went. With that kind of treatment he could have been obnoxious to this young reporter dogging his heels, but he was actually very gracious and I kind of liked him. Once, he took the time to compliment me on a story I'd done about his costar, Robert Preston. But even I had enough smarts to see that he was headed for a fall. He was too cocky to the wrong people and had too many guys named Vinnie and Marty whispering in his ear. Six years later his career blew up after a series of unbelievably foolish racing car movies. Then he lost a dramatic amount of weight, which sparked wildfire rumors in Hollywood that he had AIDS. Actually the problem was linked to a jaw disorder, but the rumors crushed his leading-man status. He's never fully recovered. Quite simply, the press built him up, and the press tore him down.

❏

Nothing succeeds like success, according to the old saying. Here's another one: Nothing makes enemies like success. I know it, you know it, and so does anyone who notices how much the American public loves to see some rich, famous, powerful person get caught in an embarrassing situation.

But you don't have to be famous to have people gunning for you. Once you learn to work hard, honestly, and consistently, you are going to begin to succeed. That will make some people hate you. It's not your fault, and there's nothing you can do about it.

Once again, don't copy my behavior. As I became more successful, a lot of less disciplined people in the business began to resent me. I had no patience for this. I told them to go scratch themselves. Or something like that.

So I made droves of enemies. Which was not smart. Which was a total waste of time. This is what I should have done, and what you should do: Smile and wave good-bye as you rise above them in your career. Let them enjoy the view as you do so. *Never* engage them in a personal way. There's nothing to be gained.

BULLETIN: If I can make it in America, you can, too. It's as simple as that. Starting out, I had *zero* advantages. I'm no genius. You already know that quite a few people think my personality is questionable, at best. But I've always worked my butt off, haven't missed a day of work in ten years, and am never satisfied until my work is better than what other people were putting out. I *paid attention*, tried not to make excuses when I flopped, and realized that the guaranteed route to moving up was making money for my bosses. That's the big picture. Well, most of it. If I had been as disciplined in dealing with toxic coworkers and supervisors as I was in my work, God only knows what would have happened. And God is not talking at this point, because his publicist doesn't think it's time.

A final note about success on the job: It's not worth it if you have to achieve it dishonestly, and that includes screwing (literally and figuratively) coworkers. The vast majority of the many brutal people I've known in TV news got fired or demoted after a period of time.

Call it a karma thing. After getting theirs, they didn't come back into the business. I've tracked them, and I know. Hitler had a run of about fifteen years; the junior Hitlers of the world usually get much less. Even though the occasional animal does sustain material success, ruthless is not the way to go.

I'm no Bible-thumper, but I do believe, as Jesus said, that gaining the whole world is not worth the loss of your soul. Or, if you don't believe in the soul, it's not worth the loss of your peace of mind or your self-respect—unless you have no conscience. And if you have no conscience, you're one of the unluckiest people alive. I mean it. A conscience gets in the way when we want to violate our personal moral code, but a conscience makes sure that in the workplace we work hard, keep it honest, and don't kiss up. There is dignity in honesty.

In the long run your dignity is much more important than your salary, bonuses, and stock options. What you do for others on the job is just as important as what you do for yourself. Are you bringing in big bucks?

Good for you. That's all the more reason to wave at a schoolteacher, or a cop on the beat, or an elder-care nurse when you see one. Their banker probably doesn't give them much respect. We should.

THIS JUST IN: "I believe in the dignity of labor, whether with head or hand; that the world owes no man a living but that it owes every man an opportunity to make a living." —John D. Rockefeller, Jr., 1941

Ḍ

Yes, we're back to money. You have to be realistic on that subject. As I said back in Chapter 2, most American *families* earn less than $50,000 a year. Before deductions, the feds and the state will take about $22,500 in taxes. Then there are sales taxes, property taxes, gasoline taxes, user fees, license fees, and on and on.

In our "tax culture" the wage earner shoulders an enormous burden. As I said in Chapter 1, the American system wants you to have enough money to spend regularly, but not ever, ever enough to become financially independent and call your own shots. Employers and government bureaucrats can hold on to their power only as long as most Americans live from paycheck to paycheck.

Workers must conform to the system in order to support their families. By regularly scaring voters with talk of Social Security and medical aid shortfalls, Washington politicians are able to raise taxes again and again.

BULLETIN: In the twenty-first century we pay more in taxes than any other American citizens since World War II. That is, workers do. If you've inherited wealth, your advisers have figured out how to slash your tax burden with tax-free bonds, trusts, corporations, and other tax-advantaged vehicles. No, it's the wage earners who foot the tax bill. The highest wage earners pay 75 percent of all U.S. income tax, and many in government would like to raise that rate and amass even more power. I thought the American way was to encourage hard-earned success, not penalize it. Wrong again, O'Reilly, you dope!

So you have to prop your eyes wide open on the money issue when you're starting your career. If you opt for security—say, by joining a union or working in a small business or taking a job in the public sector—odds are that you will reach your salary cap early on. You teachers are not going to be taking summer vacations on the Concorde or driving a BMW to PTA meetings. The same goes for you cops, postal workers, truck drivers, and many of the rest of you who keep this country running smoothly. Even out in the business world, unless you are uniquely talented or a hell of a salesperson, it is nearly impossible to get rich working for someone else.

Even doctors and lawyers, who could count on bringing in the dough when I was growing up, are no longer guaranteed an upper-middle-class life. The government has cut back payments for medical services, and the competition is fierce. Specialists make the big money now, but who knows what the future holds for them, as insurers, federal bureaucrats, and HMOs try to cut costs?

BACKUP STATS: Here are some randomly selected annual income estimates from the Bureau of Labor. They can be a kind of guide to what to expect from your future career.

LOS ANGELES—attorney, $83,500; waiter, $12,500 (on the books)

NEW YORK CITY—physical therapist, $67,000; doorman, $14,000 (on the books)

CHICAGO—dentist, $85,000; cook, $13,000

PHILADELPHIA—engineer, $70,000; bartender, $13,000 (on the books)

WASHINGTON, D.C.—airline pilot, $96,000; home-care aide, $14,000

DETROIT—physician, $100,000; crossing guard, $14,500

HOUSTON—gas-drilling manager, $91,000; restaurant host or hostess, $11,600 (on the books)

BOSTON—college professor, $85,000; funeral attendant, $14,500

DALLAS—real estate broker, $80,000; cafeteria worker, $12,500

Across the country, registered nurses generally make around $45,000; store salespersons, around $20,000; mid-level company executives, around $60,000; janitors, around $20,000; bookkeepers, around $25,000; and secretaries, around $25,000.

BULLETIN: *Time* magazine predicts that database administrators, computer-support specialists, and computer scientists will be the hot jobs of the twenty-first century.

These figures underscore the obvious: If you learn a specific skill, you will make more money. And if that skill is needed, you really do well. Capitalism runs on supply and demand.

CELEBRITY SIGHTING: You can go overboard with this capitalism business. Take Elton John. He had to sell off the rights to most of his music when he got into debt up to his toupee. At the point where he had made more than $100 million, he was spending $400,000 a week, according to his accountant. Think of how many candles in the wind that would buy. We once shared a car in L.A. He was doing a private concert for King World, the company that owns *Inside Edition*, *Wheel of Fortune*, and *Jeopardy!* I was invited to the event because of my *Inside Edition* job. The car ride was truly bizarre. Trying to make conversation with John was like trying to teach calculus to a goldfish. Not going to happen. "Where are you living now?" I tried. My traveling companion ruminated for a few moments and finally decided he knew the answer: "Atlanta." This was news. "When did you move from England?" He became confused and said nothing. My final attempt was no more successful: "Which songs mean the most to you after all these years?" He looked as if he would throw up on my shoes. Out came very strange sounds, like the chorus to "Crocodile Rock." He buried his head in his hands. I spent the rest of the ride trying not to disturb an obviously distraught Elton. I learned one thing: Money can't buy good conversation.

📺

Chart your own course, and make your own decisions about the kind of life you want. But if money is important to you, you have to learn a skill that will increase a company's profits or provide a needed service to the community. If you don't, the harsh reality of American life means that you are probably doomed to economic dependence and constant worry.

⌘

I may surprise you here: I truly believe that money is not what we Americans should be focusing on.

Of course, we need it, but *enjoying* a job is worth plenty, too. If you look forward to going to work when you wake up in the morning, you are a success, no matter what your job description. Do you envy the guys and gals with the huge houses out in the suburbs and exurbs? How about their two- or three-hour commutes in the mornings *and* the evenings? And how about the "big nuts" of taxes, mortgages, private school fees, and all the rest that require them to keep their heads down and play the corporate games, losing their dignity so they won't lose their mock-Tudor homes? Sometimes, having money costs too much.

Who knew that writing dopey jokes for *Uncle Ted's Ghoul School* would lead anywhere? I didn't, but I did know that I was never going to give up. I survived, and I've *enjoyed* it, weaselettes and all.

Your life, too, will unfold in ways that you can never imagine if you keep hammering away at your dream with discipline, talent, and goodwill.

Dance around the bastards, never forget your allies, and trust yourself above all.

7. THE
PARENTS factor

Here my book makes a major shift in focus. We go from the world outside back to your home and private life. We're going to think about a frightening, ongoing part of daily living—personal *relationships*. If we don't handle them effectively, we can't have a successful life in modern-day America. I'm going to be brief on this subject, because you're the only one who can figure out how to make your own personal relationships work.

The word "relationship" is an annoying cliché, but it will have to do. It's used by people who want to "share" when I want them to get out of my face, or who "have issues" with me, which is fine—but have them somewhere else.

"Relationship" is also a key word for charlatans and hucksters of every stripe in personal counseling, talk radio, self-help books, self-awareness movements, "inspirational" tapes: That's a growing *industry* of shallow, useless "advice." This hokum is harmless, I guess, if you use it to stay awake on a late-night drive. Otherwise, you'd be better off making personal choices based upon a horoscope column, and that would be ridiculous.

BACKUP STATS: This is the Age of Aquarius, so I looked up the skinny for Aquarians on March 27. "A cycle of good luck is beginning in your place of work. Ask for added duties or a promotion." That was the word from the horoscope column in the *Daily News* of New York. The *New York Post* had a different take: "What you are faced with today is beyond your powers to alter or modify. You will just have to live with it as best you can." I hope I don't have to tell you that believing any of this rubbish is ridiculous.

So I'll leave the analyzing to shrinks. What comes next are just some O'Reilly observations. Take them for what they're worth to you. If you don't like 'em, dump 'em.

◻

Let's begin with parents, and let's begin with some common sense: *Forget all the bad stuff they did to you when you were a kid.*

Wipe it out. Zero. Nada.

"But," you say, "they blah, blah, blah." So what? In the first place, maybe they weren't as bad as you think, but so what? Maybe they had reasons for their bad behavior, but so what? Maybe they were just downright cruel, selfish, unreasonable schmucks, but the question remains, so what?

None of this ancient history should matter to you today. The shrinks disagree at $200 an hour, or whatever they can pry out of you. But if you start probing into the past, whining about all your grievances and bad memories, there's no end to it. Will you be healed? Never. You will just wallow in victimization. You won't overcome your emotional problems, you'll be excusing them. You know what you're doing? You're paying an analyst to be your ally against your absent parents.

And you're wasting your life and money. Here's what you have to do, beginning right now: Face your problems on your own. Deal with the cards you're dealt. It's too late for retooling. You're a completed work. What happened, happened. Get it?

Should you forgive your parents? You'd be better off if you could. If you can't forgive them, then drop the grudges. Otherwise, you're just looking for revenge, and that keeps you from enjoying life in the present.

BULLETIN: If you're hung up on your parents' mistakes, you're allowing them to keep doing to you over and over whatever they did in the first

NOVELL

EL PASO

SCHERING – PLOUGH

TRAVELERS – ST PAUL INS.

EXXON – MOBIL

place. It's you, not Mom and Dad, who's keeping the cycle of pain going. Shut it off.

If you can begin to live in the present, and take responsibility for your emotional state, you will be ahead of 90 percent of the population. Stick to basics. Are you sad today because your father spanked you too hard for no reason thirty years ago? You *could* make an appointment with the shrink. Or you could get off the couch and exercise in the fresh air, or eat a healthful fresh meal instead of junk food, or stop feeling sorry for yourself and call a friend who may be having problems much worse than yours and needs to talk. These things work. That's what the British mean by "stiff upper lip." It got them through World War II.

Yes, I know there's such a thing as clinical depression that requires treatment. I'm not talking about that. You know what I'm talking about.

Remember, your parents had to compete with changes in the media and other parts of society that have only become harder to fight. The rise of TV started the decline of parental status in America.

Once the tube began lighting up the nation's living rooms in the early 1950s, parents made a bargain with the devil. Here was a cheap, easy way to keep kids quiet. The working dad didn't come home to a lot of chatter at the dinner table. The kids were eating off the TV trays—American ingenuity at its best, or what?—in the den or living room. And they didn't require a hot meal made from scratch, thanks to the invention of the Swanson TV Dinner. A perfect fit on the wobbly trays. If you were better off than we were, which would be no stretch, you could get yourself a portable refrigerette and roll it into the living room on casters and put it right beside the glowing TV.

And there was no more reading stories at bedtime. The kids dozed off, glassy-eyed, and could be carried to bed. That is, *if* that's the choice parents made. The TV dominated the household—not by putting a gun to their heads, but by giving the relief of escapism and keeping the urchins quiet.

The family storytelling now came from demented strangers: people with names like Howdy Doody, Spanky and Buckwheat, Pinky Lee, and some chubby woman on *Romper Room*. They weren't always so hot, but the tube was cool. Kids couldn't get enough of it.

And as parents stayed in the next room for quality time with each other, or whatever, the kids soon found much better parents on TV. There was Ozzie Nelson, who kicked my dad's butt all over the yard. He was funny and always understanding—and seemed to have enough in his wallet, when it mattered. (If you're too young to recall the Nelson family, then think of Bill Cosby's Dr. Huxtable.) Back in my teen years Shirley, matriarch of the Partridge Family, was pretty, perky, extra nice, well dressed, and freshly made-up—*and* she played in a rock band! Sorry, Mom.

THIS JUST IN: "Parents can no longer control the atmosphere of the home and have lost even the will to do so. With great subtlety and energy, television enters not only the room, but also the tastes of old and young alike, appealing to the immediately pleasant and subverting whatever does not conform to it." —Allan Bloom, *The Closing of the American Mind*, 1987

This stuff has been going on for nearly five decades. The father on TV "knew best," not the one in the house. The father on TV would give us what we want. When little Ricky Nelson got a new guitar on *The Adventures of Ozzie and Harriet*, I asked my father why he couldn't be more like Mr. Nelson and buy *me* a guitar. I was too young to understand the word he called Ozzie.

But kids were watching because their parents had given in to the media. That abdication of responsibility started a chain reaction of events that put pressure on parents to live up to a scriptwriter's ideal.

RIDICULOUS NOTE: Speaking of responsibility, Dr. Bernard Lewinsky reacted to his daughter's Oval Office activities by blaming Bill Clinton, calling the most powerful man in the world "totally irresponsible." Monica's stepmom, Barbara, added that Bill was "a butthead." But is a totally irresponsible butthead the only adult in the picture here?

Here's how it worked: The parents gave up part of their job to TV, TV brought in pretty pictures of perfect family life, and the kids glued to this mental bubble gum began having *unreasonable* expectations of their own human, unscripted parents. Most parents want to do what's best for their kids, though it's not always easy to know what that is. With TV images and ad temptations millions of American parents came under siege. TV, according to one writer, "fed a sense of generational superiority" in the kids who watched it. I know exactly what he means, and so do you.

I expected only one thing from my dad: Leave me alive to celebrate my next birthday. Today's kids expect much, much more. Demand it, even. Like, parents must have perfect attendance at games, dance recitals, you name it. They have to understand their kids' pain in wanting what "the other kids" have, and that means making enough money to keep their own kids happy. They are supposed to be kind and patient in the face of a kid's barbaric fits and "acting out."

Satisfying the desires of children can be an overwhelming task. Worse, it can distract parents from paying attention to the really important parental duties: teaching discipline, morality, and the truth about how the world works. Then, almost as important, there's encouraging your kids' imagination and explaining to them the art of conversation and the joy of *thinking*.

SPOT TEST: Are you training your child to compete and succeed in a ruthless and competitive world? Or are you just trying to make him or her *like* you? If the honest answer is the second choice, big trouble is brewing in your house.

⌗

I well remember all of the parents in my neighborhood when I was growing up. Except for a couple of actual maniacs, they were all pretty much the same, similar to my own working-class parents. The exceptions, who were boozehounds or had violent tempers, were an embarrassment to everyone else. I stayed away from them, and so did their own children, if they could. This was a painful situation. I felt sorry for those kids and went out of my way to include them in our street games.

I've already explained my parents' blue-collar backgrounds and their college educations. When it came to raising my sister and me, background won out over newfangled education every time. Just like their parents, they believed in "Spare the rod, spoil the child" and "Children should be seen, not heard." And we heard almost every night about the children starving in Korea. Boy, did they starve. There seemed to be an endless supply of them. Today, I guess, it's Kosovo or Chechnya, but the lesson's the same, and it's a good one: You are one lucky kid, so shut up and eat!

My father, particularly, would have won praise from Mussolini for his, uh, child-rearing practices. "One more time and you'll be sorry" was not an empty threat. In our house there were never any "time-outs" but plenty of "knockouts." Sorry, I guess I'm getting carried away with nostalgia. To be fair, they were really more like TKOs.

My parents and their friends were not wicked, cruel, abusive, or un-feeling. Just the opposite on all counts. The thing is, they were *afraid*. I didn't know that then, and I probably wouldn't have cared or understood, but it's clear to me now.

Growing up in the dark depths of a worldwide depression drilled fear into them. They'd seen banks fail, families get evicted, factories close down, soup kitchens open. When they heard the song "Brother, Can You Spare a Dime?," it wasn't just vaudeville.

Then came the most terrifying war in history. My dad was a naval offi-cer who was given major responsibility in the American occupation of Japan, a huge task. Yet when he came back home, he took a low-level ac-countant's job at a major oil company and never moved up or left for an-other challenge, even though he hated every minute of it. He did not "express himself" through his work; he was simply unhappy. He was stuck, and so were most of the other parents in our neighborhood.

You're right: This is a puzzle. How come big macho O'Reilly, leader of men on foreign soil, let his working life go flat on home turf? It's hard for later generations to understand, but this was not a rare thing for people his age. He was afraid, that's all. He was afraid to take a chance. When an opportunity came up, he saw the risk right away, but not the reward. Tal-ented, educated, he could have done big things with his life, except for that one dominant fear: that he would make a mistake and fall forever into unemployment. So he stayed where he was and took the crap that was regularly dished out there. His fear also shaped the way he ran his family.

As you already know, I rebelled against the claustrophobic existence of Levittown. I knew I had to make it on my own. No one could ever call me, as Marilyn Quayle called George W. Bush in 1999, "a guy that never ac-complished anything . . . Everything he got Daddy took care of."

I knew how to fight. I went out of my way to give grief to my bosses when I thought they were wrong, unfair, stupid, or corrupt. As I said in a recent interview in New York's *Daily News*, "I don't want people to like me. I want them to respect me and watch the program." Maybe my rough edges are a reaction to the way my father's generation had to live. I'm not paying any shrink to find out.

What did my father feel about my choices and my behavior, especially as I began to be successful? I'm not sure. Was he proud? Was he jealous? Did he think I was a fool because someday I'd be pushed aside and would be grateful to get a bean-counting job at a low level, just for the security? I don't know. I never discussed it with him before he died. We each did what was right for us, because of the time and place we were born. I guess that's the answer. But I regret that he couldn't take more chances. He would have been a happier man. He would have had the dignity he deserved.

◻

When we become parents, the first thing most of us say is that we won't "make the same mistakes" our own folks made. That's why today's kids have more "lip" than the kids I grew up with. I cannot imagine defying my father in his presence (think: Jackie Gleason without a gut). When I see so many kids disobeying their parents in public places today, or even hitting them, I laugh out loud. If I had acted anything like that, I would have ended up in traction. Would the neighbors complain? Would the cops be called? Right. The neighbors would tell their kids to take a lesson from my condition, and the cops would have treated Dad to a beer.

RIDICULOUS NOTE: Chief White House "enabler" Hillary Rodham Clinton wrote that "it takes a village" to raise children. My parents and their friends thought that it takes parents. They were sorry that some of my friends had maniacs for parents, but they didn't interfere. And they didn't want anyone poking their nose in our house, either.

THIS JUST IN: "Discipline is a symbol of caring to a child. He needs guidance. If there is love, there is no such thing as being too tough with a child. A parent must also not be afraid to hang himself. If you have never been hated by your children, you have never been a parent." —Bette Davis, *The Lonely Life*, 1962

Did I take my father's discipline with a cheerful heart? Are you nuts? There were times when my heart was black with the urge for revenge. I thought I *hated* him, although it was not really hatred but frustration. It didn't seem fair to get felony punishments for such misdemeanors as knocking over the neighbors' garbage cans, hurling snowballs at passing cars, yawning while serving mass as an altar boy, punching Tommy Massey for sucking up to our teacher, tossing a cherry bomb under the bedroom window of a neighbor who annoyed me, shooting Justin MacDevitt in the back with BBs, or just provoking Dad with my brooding facial expressions. These were *trivial* offenses! But no matter how angry I got, I never tried to get back at my father. I'm proud of that.

My parents deserved respect. Most parents do. That doesn't mean that any kid should take abuse. Once you finish high school, you should leave such toxic parents as alcoholics, drug abusers, sex abusers, and so on. Just hit the road. Don't even think of trying to even the score. It is courageous and dignified to walk away without trying to strike back. If a parent abandons you, shows jealousy toward you, or has no real interest in your welfare, disengage. Don't descend to his or her level. You'll be a better person.

My parents certainly did not fit these descriptions, though neither of them had sophisticated "parenting skills." They didn't have books by the likes of Bill Cosby and Paul Reiser, and they knew enough to know that, as far as they were concerned, Dr. Spock was full of it. They didn't know terms like "self-esteem," "play dates," and "acting out." They wanted us to become good citizens who could support ourselves someday.

But Mom and Dad didn't approach this goal in the same way. While he dominated the big picture, she was responsible for the micro work of child rearing. Both would say, "You will do what I say when I say it," but she was much slower on the trigger. Sometimes she even felt sorry enough for our mistakes or offenses to hide them from my father. This wasn't license; it was a reprieve. It was something like the poet Robert Frost said once: "The father is always a Republican toward his son, and his mother's always a Democrat."

Many of you, I bet, had parents similar to mine. They made a gazillion mistakes—no question about it—but they *tried* to do the right things. If they didn't teach me certain life skills, that's because no one had ever passed along these skills to them. My friends and I were beasts. That was considered the normal childhood state in my neighborhood. You got our attention with displays of superior force.

No one taught us how to think, how to deal effectively with adversity, or even the basics of behaving well in polite society.

But, as you can guess from the beginning of this chapter, I long ago forgave my parents for not being as sophisticated and understanding as the Nelsons, the Andersons of *Father Knows Best*, the Cleavers of *Leave It to Beaver*, and Cosby's Huxtable family.

✿

I see that I've talked so much about parental discipline that I've skewed the picture. I wasn't a fiend all of the time, and so I wasn't punished all of the time, either. My father was a lively man with a sense of humor. He wasn't heartless, and he wasn't stupid about the human heart. That's what this next little story shows, I think.

Dad was a neighborhood legend for being able to co-opt kids into doing chores for him for free. The other adults were mystified. They never figured out how "Mr. O" managed this trick, but the secret was simple, if you understood my dad: He gave out great advice to kids and always paid attention to what they had to say. They were happy to do small jobs with him because they liked to hang out with him.

Since my father commuted with his car pool to the city around 6:30 in the morning and didn't get home until about 7:00 at night, he missed most of my ball games in the Central Nassau Little League. That was fine with me. The guys in my neighborhood despised the "Little League dads" who showed up at every game and whined because their sons weren't getting enough playing time. They were ridiculous, and sometimes the apple didn't fall far from the tree. Their spoiled kids could be a real pain.

The most obnoxious of these kids was Eggy, whose real name was Eddie. Because his father never missed a game and always interfered with play, Eddie was on the field much more than his skills would have deserved. My thuggish friends and I resented this, of course. In revenge we tagged him "Eggy." Yes, it was stupid, but then so were we.

Since I was leader of the pack, Eddie's father threatened me with bodily harm if I didn't lay off. A big mistake. That made the problem even worse and stoked our creative juices. Eddie became "Ham and Eggy" or "Scrambled Eggy." By the time we reached "Eggy Benedict," the kid snapped.

One steamy August night my gang was playing stickball in the street near Eddie's split-level house. When he came out to join us, he hit a barrage of Eggy jokes. He ran back inside. Moments later his father, red-faced and making guttural noises, raced out of the house and made a run right at me. I quickly gathered from the visible evidence that he was not interested in a calm conversation about issues. So I bolted. I was quick, but for an old geezer (probably all of forty, now that I look back!) this guy could really haul. I fled toward my street, expecting him to slow down and give up at any second. But he kept right on rolling.

He knew where I lived, and he was close behind. I desperately considered my options. They were all rotten. I could see that I couldn't run fast enough to lose him. If I ran inside my house for safety, my father would become involved—and that was suicide. If I kept on running around the block, there was a good chance that Eddie's father might catch me. The curses streaming out of his mouth suggested that this would not be pleasant.

Sweating and panting, I finally thought, screw it. I ran into my house. Eddie's father came right behind me and through the front door—without stopping to knock. I ran upstairs into my room. Eddie's father stopped in the living room, startling the hell out of Dad, who was drinking a cold one and reading the paper.

Quaking in my room, I heard loud voices erupt downstairs. The few words I could make out were not complimentary to me. Suddenly the conversation stopped completely. There was a moment of awful silence. Then I heard the front door close. My mother's voice was saying something about calming down.

The words "calm down" were never good news.

Next, I heard my father's footsteps on the stairs. Decades later I can *still* hear my father's footsteps on the stairs. Remember those stories at night around the campfire? This was much, much worse.

My father, who had a no-knock policy in our house, barged into the room. I was sitting on my bed, intently staring at my dirty sneakers. My six-foot-three father loomed over me. I hunched in my shoulders, prepared for loud yelling and perhaps a couple of hard punches on the arm.

Then my father shocked me nearly senseless.

"Lookit," he said, in a fairly reasonable tone.

What was this? With my full and amazed attention, he went on. "Eggy's father is a nut. So stop calling Eggy, Eggy. The kid's got enough problems, and I don't want this guy comin' to the house again. Got it?"

Yes. I got it, okay, and I never forgot it.

My father simply turned and left the room. As usual, the footsteps going down the stairs were much better than the other kind.

The truth is, I had a behavioral problem that would have turned Cosby's Dr. Huxtable into a foaming-at-the-mouth lunatic. That night, though, Dad attacked the problem in a way that got through my thick head. I didn't reform overnight, but I got to thinking. Eggy *did* have enough problems. We were picking on him because we thought he was getting something we deserved on the ball field, but we had the whole thing upside down. He was the victim of a very strange father. I didn't want to be a bully. And I guess my father knew that. Eggy became Eddie again.

♉

Most of the time, I'm sorry to say, I didn't figure out where my father was coming from. I was just afraid of him. Thank God, long before he died, I began to understand how much he cared for his family.

I also understood that surviving his rigid, sometimes brutal regime gave me discipline and motivation, the values that have been essential to my success. Put another way: After living with my father for seventeen years (only three years less than the Nelsons' show lasted on TV), I was never frightened by anything ever again. He had immunized me against fear.

Your parents may have done the same. But whatever they did, as I've already said but want to say again, we'd be smart to take the good from our parents, as is, and turn the bad to our advantage.

As we grow older, we watch our parents decline, passing the torch to us. No longer do they appear to be, as we thought as kids, always in command and all-knowing. They can become dependent, demanding, and confused. It is our job then to take over as *their* parents, in a way. We have to help them out, and we should do so gladly, no matter what the frustration or the expense. Even if your parents still get under your skin, it is your job to help them. And don't expect any pats on the back. This is a nonnegotiable obligation.

Finally you must ensure that your parents live out their lives with dignity. Do so, and good things will happen in your life. Besides, your kids will be watching . . . and taking notes.

VIEWER TIME-OUT: Am I sounding preachy? Don't mean to. But some in the audience aren't convinced. "O'Reilly, I know you're proud of your pomposity, but couldn't you just say 'I think' once in a while? You can be just as pompous by saying 'I think.' " (Marvin B., West Valley City, Utah)

Okay, Marvin, "I think" what I've said about the Parent Factor is worth saying. If you want to, get back to me on that. I'm always ready for feedback.

THIS JUST IN: "Where does the family start? It starts with a young man falling in love with a girl—no superior alternative has yet been found." —Winston Churchill, 1950

Right. So that's why we're going to move from the Parent Factor to the Dating Factor.

8. THE
DATING factor

The year was 1990. I found myself standing on a stage in a Mafia-run catering hall in Bayside, Queens. The occasion was a Bachelor Auction to benefit the American Cancer Society. Your humble correspondent was the object of a bidding war between two very nice young women: One was a pretty Irish nurse, the other a dark-haired Jewish stockbroker. The bidding, incredibly, was up to more than $3,000 for a date with me! Was this nuts or what?

As I stood there, I couldn't believe that two young women were willing to pay this kind of money to go out with a guy who was the world's worst date until his mid-twenties. But I have plenty of excuses to explain why it took me so long to get it right.

When I was growing up, dating was restricted—or so I thought—to healthy young teenagers from California with names like Annette and Gidget. Those were serious babes who had guys panting over them as they sat on the beach at Malibu, batting their false eyelashes. In other words, to this working-class teenager, dating was a fantasy, something far away and a bit frightening.

That attitude toward dating was common in the 1950s and 1960s, because American society was much more innocent. But look at how society has changed. Dating now begins in grammar school and extends to the AARP. Ex-spouses back on the market, aging singles, exes back on the market again, widows, widowers, exes yet again back on the market—they're all dating till they drop. Go to your local senior citizens center if you really want to see love in bloom.

At all ages and from all backgrounds, the Dating Factor works best when you start with low expectations. Don't greet your partner with an unspoken agenda a mile long. Don't expect her or him to fulfill all your fantasies (hey, when did that last happen in real life?). Just try to have a good time. Relax. Maybe, if you stay cool, Mr. or Mrs. Right (Right Now?) will show up.

You can trust me on this. I was a serial dater through three decades. And I usually had a great time on all of my dates. Why? Because I never had any expectations. It was enough for me that the lady actually showed up. That was a plus, to begin with. If the evening got interesting or led to something else, I was thrilled.

◻

VIEWER TIME-OUT: "Mr. O'Reilly, I cannot for the life of me understand those silly women who think you have sex appeal." (Helen S., Mediapolis, Iowa)

According to the calendar, I came of dating age in the mid-1960s. But there was an obstacle, thanks to my upbringing. Since I was enrolled in an all-boys Catholic high school, I was clueless for much too long about how to approach the opposite sex. And, as I've mentioned, the nuns and the brothers weren't exactly helpful on this issue.

I know you can guess that the subject didn't come up by itself in my household. And I was *not* going to bring it up. Some well-intentioned somebody—not my parents, of course—gave me a copy of Ann Landers's *Do's and Don'ts of Teenage Dating*. Man, Old Ann was tough! She made dating sound like marine boot camp.

Her training manual was thorough, and there were more don'ts than do's. She described in detail just how close together a boy and girl should dance—*no* cheek-to-cheek! When would it be right to hold a girl's hand? Not until the *third* date. And what about French kissing, the bane of the nuns? Yes, but only after the boy and girl are officially engaged to be married.

You'll not be surprised to learn that Old Ann was dead set against teenage sex. If we ignored her advice and did have sex, we would become outcasts in the community. Our lives would be ruined. But that was only part of it. Possibly we'd wind up in a hospital someplace with a disease that she couldn't even name because it was so gross.

But Ann did not have to worry about me. I was as far away from the action as Lawrence Welk, because I had no one to *don't* with, even if I wanted to *do*. I had my wandering eyes on Sharon, a girl in our neighborhood, but I was hopelessly shy. Also, I was not top-notch in the grooming department. It would be years before I'd learn to slap on a little Brut aftershave and get that double-knit shirt collar to fit just right.

Of course, there are two sides to every question. Ann Landers had made her point, but on the other side was Hugh Hefner, who seemed to be having one *hell* of a time with no hospital in sight. *Playboy* magazine answered the rules and regulations of the Landers training manual with four-color photos of what was *under* those bulky sweaters the neighborhood girls were wearing then. It was all over for me. Game, set, match, tournament to Hugh!

The question: How could I join Hugh's club?

Unfortunately the answer was clear: I couldn't. In the first place, as we know, I was Catholic . . . and would be blasted down to Hell. How was Hugh getting away with it? I actually wrote this question to the "Playboy Advisor" several times. Somehow the "Advisor" never found time to respond. He probably thought I was being some kind of smart aleck. But I was dead serious. I wanted to know. In the photos Hugh often looked dazed and exhausted, but, I surmised, not from saying a lot of Hail Marys for penance.

There was another obstacle to joining his club. There were no naked babes slinking around my neighborhood or, as far as I knew, anywhere else on Long Island. Obviously the first thing naked babes did was migrate to Chicago, where Hugh welcomed them warmly at his Playboy mansion. I looked in the library to see if there was a good college in the Windy City.

But there was an even bigger hurdle: Young O'Reilly had no moves. Count them: none. So far as boy-girl interaction was concerned, I was pathetic. So were all of my friends, for all of the same reasons. So we played a lot of football and got very good at it. We imagined a lot. And we kept reading those *Playboy*s. Every issue was like butter.

Ϫ

THIS JUST IN: "I'm not denyin' that the women are foolish: God Almighty made 'em to match the men." —George Eliot

Meanwhile, other kids in the neighborhood leapt ahead of me. Those of us on the sidelines liked to say, when a couple we knew got hot and heavy, "They are young and in love, and nobody understands." We were joking, but we were jealous. And we were quoting Paul Anka's song "Puppy Love," because we wanted to get some of that action, too.

Finally I got lucky. The girl was only a year older in age, but decades ahead of me in experience. We'd met when I taught swimming one summer at the pool in Babylon, Long Island. The year was 1968, when young women were burning bras in public places and hordes of kids were staging love-ins. Those things seemed very far away and hard to imagine. I was operating at a much different level. I asked her to a movie. My thought was, That will reduce the time for awkward conversation.

"Sure," she said. "Why don't we go to the drive-in?"

The drive-in. The *drive-in?* You mean the outdoor theater where you sit in a dark car for four hours watching double features starring Annette and Frankie? *That* drive-in?

"Yes."

Yes! Marv Albert couldn't have said it any better.

Hugh's face immediately popped into my head, grinning that wicked grin. I wondered if I should get a pipe or show up in my pajamas.

So we went to the drive-in in my maroon Mercury Comet, and this girl reduced me to rubble. Toward the end of Annette and Frankie's second adventure, I had reached second base and had a good lead toward third. But it's all in the timing, of course, and her parents had a non-negotiable curfew. When I left her at her door, I gently kissed her good night. She said she had had a good time. I couldn't reply very clearly. My tongue had lost all feeling.

When I glanced in the living room mirror as I walked in the door at home, I realized I was covered with red welts. Not good. My mother was waiting up holding the fort, and red welts probably meant interrogation. I mumbled something about poison oak. Mom seemed to buy that excuse and said good night. Now that I think about it, she probably wanted me out of the room and upstairs in my bedroom before she broke out laughing. Did I mention that dating has something to do with parenting?

It was that first, lucky drive-in experience that turned me into a dating lunatic. Refined, cultured girls didn't particularly take to me, but working-class girls seemed to like me just fine. I had a car, a sense of humor, and plenty of packs of chewing gum.

BULLETIN: I never bragged about my dating exploits, and that includes this book. It's cheap for a guy to have sex with a girl, then broadcast it. This was a stupid double standard, and it's still out there today. If I was fooling around with someone, why would I look down on *her* for having sex with *me?* That makes me the jerk. When a girl showed me some affection, I was grateful. God knows it didn't happen *that* often.

If I was a good date, and I think I was, it's because I followed this rule: I didn't go out with anyone I didn't like, just to get some action, and I kept my mouth shut tight afterward.

And why spoil a good time by arguing over something? When you're having a date, you're not trying to make a point on *The Factor*. I always tried to be accommodating. I wasn't auditioning anybody for a life partnership right away. I usually found fun, because that's what I was looking for. Girls understood this. Most wanted the same thing.

📺

The 1970s and early 1980s were the best dating years of all time, with the possible exception of ancient Rome. The books tell you that the Roaring Twenties were pretty wild, but I put my money on the disco years. The energy rocking through those dance clubs was geologic. Talk about low expectations. Everyone was there for one reason: to meet new people. That was enough. As far as I know, no one felt uneasy or suspicious. We were all out for fun.

Drugs were around, but they weren't in your face, if you didn't want them. I never did drugs and avoided the women who took them. My thing was the music: I was a dancing *machine*. Sock it to me, Donna Summer! Let's shake this place, Gloria Gaynor! Get down!

Now, this was the lad of a quarter century ago, okay? But I make no apologies. I loved the all-out dancing, and quite a few girls loved to dance with me. The dancing got me dates. The dancing said (since you couldn't hear any words in those places under the rotating mirror balls), Hey, let's have some fun and see what happens next. Even Catholic girls had their inhibitions lowered by the howls of the Bee Gees or Sylvester. A few hours at clubs like Septembers or Shenanigans and most of my dates wanted to extend the evening at their place or mine.

By 1975 I was regularly on TV, and that was the greatest dating advantage a man could wish for. I was recognized instantly: Fame leads to dates, at least with some women. Is Puff Daddy one heck of a handsome devil, or is Jennifer Lopez all over him because of his clout?

During my TV gigs in Dallas, Denver, Boston, and Portland, Oregon, I was shameless:

"Hi, my name's O'Reilly. Perhaps you've seen me making a fool of myself (heh, heh) on Channel 9. Oh, you have? Can I buy you a drink or take you to Vegas?"

Yeah, this was pretty shallow, but if you're listening to lyrics like "We're doin' it, doin' it, doin' it" four nights a week, you might be pretty shallow, too.

Since I've dated hundreds of women in my life, I think I've learned a thing or two about the opposite sex. How could I not? The biggest thing I've learned, as I mentioned in "The Sex Factor," is that men and women have different agendas in the romance department. This bears repeating. Women usually want to find the one Mr. Right of their dreams, and men want to find all the dream girls they can get their hands on.

◻

If you are young and single today, the disco years must sound as far back as the Dark Ages. AIDS and other STDs have changed dating forever. Fear is now part of the equation. Having multiple partners became dangerous, and going out with a stranger after a night of hot dancing can earn you a death sentence—and there's no appeal to the U.S. Supreme Court.

From the late 1980s to the present, dating has been more of a serious mission than harmless recreation. There is a goal. Find someone—that is, *one* someone—and the quicker the better.

But I was young and single at a great time to be young and single. I admit it: I miss those carefree dating days. I liked meeting almost all of those women, and most of them had a good time with me. That's not bragging, that's communication!

Looking back even further, I'm glad my dating started late in my teens. The "Puppy Love" crowd that started dating a lot earlier usually wound up getting married early. Not many of those marriages lasted. Looks like our folks were right about that one, too.

It's a radically different dating world for teenagers in the twenty-first century, and it will change even more dramatically, I believe. It seems as if most young kids today know everything they need to know about dating by the time they're fourteen. If they don't, they're sure putting on a good front.

Teenage sexual innocence has been drowned in *Dawson's Creek*, mocked in *The Party of Five*, and had a stake driven through its heart by *Buffy, the Vampire Slayer*. There are no drive-ins anymore, but teenagers hardly need them, as I did, to discover sex. Stories about oral sex at teen parties or in community parks are no longer rare on the news cycle. (Is this the "presidential legacy" Clinton leaves to the nation?)

BACKUP STATS: According to one study reported in 1997 in the *Journal of the American Medical Association*, about 17 percent of twelve- and thirteen-year-old American teenagers admitted having sexual intercourse. Others that age report engaging in oral sex because they believe, wrongly, that there's no chance of contracting an STD.

Now there is cybersex or technosex on the Internet. Use e-mail, and you will be scammed by unsolicited messages from "little Debbie" or whomever, who has just turned eighteen and wants to show you nude pix of her friends at the birthday party.

RIDICULOUS NOTE: One of my researchers went to his local small-town library one afternoon to look up info about the alleged Watergate source, Deep Throat. Suddenly nude photos of luscious young women popped onto the screen, as young mothers walked by with their children looking for picture books. "Goodness," said the amazed librarian. "I didn't know there were cookies like that in our search engine!" It's funny. But it's pathetic, too.

But the old, familiar technologies are not getting left behind. For three bucks a minute and up, phone sex is available. You don't even have to know Monica's home number, as Bill did, but you do have to be at least eighteen . . . or *sound* eighteen . . . or be able to *count* to eighteen.

Can this be good? I don't think so. Dating was exciting to me because it was a slow buildup to something special—I'm talking about the best kind of dating. Now immediate gratification is the order of the day. The thrill of the chase has been replaced by the predictability of the computer or the convenience of the videocassette.

Why risk rejection with a live human being when you can make all of your fantasies come true with the push of a button? And you can always charge it!

I forecast a dating recession in America soon.

THIS JUST IN: Someone asked Mark Twain this question: "In a world without women what would men become?" He didn't miss a beat: "Scarce, sir. Mighty scarce."

☐

If you're one of those who still believe that dating is a great social teacher, forget what's going on. Just get out there and do it! You'll learn about different types of people. That way, when you decide it's time to settle down, you're more likely to pick the right person for your personality and temperament, and vice versa.

BULLETIN: Because of the way our American society is structured, dating is about the only way to choose a good spouse, and that decision is probably the most important you will ever make. A mistake can become a disaster that will ruin your life—and someone else's—forever. So get good at dating, and hang it up when the right person comes along.

Evaluate others the way you evaluate a car or a house or a new suit. Is this one really right for you? At the same time, don't make snap judgments. Give the other person a chance; sometimes she's nervous or having a bad night. Remember? It's happened to you, too, if you're human.

And if you pay attention, you will learn a lot about a person fast. When I was in college and could barely afford shoes (which isn't that unusual in your college years), I asked out a young woman who knew my financial situation. When we went to some modest restaurant off campus, she ordered lobster, by far the most expensive dish on the menu. That's all I needed to know. This was one hell of a selfish woman, with no consideration for me and my wallet.

Another woman asked me point-blank—on our second date—what my "intentions" were. I was just as frank: "I intend to take you to a medium-priced restaurant, then go to a dance club, and then try to convince you to give me a back rub." She was not amused. She did not find this admirable sincerity charming! In fact, she brooded for most of the evening. The back rub idea apparently rubbed her the wrong way (please forgive me).

But, hey, don't worry about rejection. It will happen. It happens to everyone. In my business you meet some of the most physically attractive women on the planet. You'd be amazed by how many of them are insecure because they've been rejected along the way. It can be a lonely planet, unless we keep trying to get to know each other better.

If you're nice to your dates, things will someday fall your way. But be smart, too. Don't get desperate, because then you might make the fatal mistake of letting someone exploit you. You don't have to be "in a relationship" all the time. There's nothing wrong with who you are when you happen to be single. Sometimes it will work out much better if you just take your time, let the pressure ease off, and become close to someone slowly.

But if you do find someone with whom you have that unmistakable chemistry, and by some miracle there's an old drive-in movie nearby, well . . . take advantage of it.

I wish I could say that I took advantage of the Bachelor Auction that started this chapter. But things did not work out. After spending $3,500 to go out with me, the dark-haired woman understandably got very intense. I took her out to a nice restaurant and tried to keep the conversation light— my usual first-date strategy. She was having none of that. Since she was wearing a low-cut blouse that would make the Victoria's Secret catalog blink, it was all I could do to make eye contact, and she enjoyed my dilemma. By the time dessert arrived, she was asking me where our "relationship" was heading. Now, keep in mind that this lady had plunked down 3,500 bucks for a few hours with your humble correspondent. I kind of felt guilty because I knew the "relationship" was fast heading south. Finally I looked her in the eye, perhaps for the third time all evening, and said what all guys say: "It's not you. It's me." Remember, this was way before Seinfeld ever got on the air.

⌘

A final word. Like Ann Landers, I've come up with a little manual for dealing with the opposite sex, but my point of view is not the same. Bring on the cheek-to-cheek, the heavy petting, and the home runs, but not *ever* with any of the following prohibited, *ridiculous* lines:

He says,

"I've never met anyone quite like you." Please.

"You remind me of my mom." Run, lady.

"Sex isn't really that important." Run very fast.

"Look, I just want to talk to you. Nothing will happen if I come in." Lock the door.

"I haven't felt this way about a woman in years." If said on the first date, call the cops.

"Just one more drink won't hurt." Take his keys and drive home without him.

"Want to see my tattoo?" Begin coughing, and do not stop. Tell him you picked up something in the Amazon rain forest.

But it's not just the guys who come out with the ridiculous lines. Your reporter has tirelessly collected a few gems from the other side:

She says,

"Let's be friends." Fine. Date her best friend.

"My sister's got two beautiful kids." Whatever you do, do not have sex with this woman.

"I'm not that kind of girl." Get the telephone number of her best friend right now.

"Where do you buy your clothes?" Get to a mirror fast.

"I'm *so* tired of the dating scene." Fella, she has *designs* on you.

"My ex-boyfriend . . ." She's still in love.

"When I graduated from Vassar . . ." Run.

"My mother says . . ." Run faster.

"Once I make up my mind about a guy . . ." Lock the door.

"I feel we have a soul connection." Dial 911.

"Christmas with my folks would be nice." That's it. Your dating days are done.

With this little manual, you can survive the Dating Factor. But there isn't a manual in the world to help you survive the Spouse Factor. That's coming up next.

9. THE
SPOUSE factor

Since I am beyond dumb in this area and haven't a clue why some marriages succeed and others fail, what can I tell you about the subject? (Of course, *marriages* don't fail. People who are married fail.)

Marriage is a very intense microscope that reveals and illuminates the character faults—and also all of the good qualities—that a man and woman bring to their partnership. Sometimes there are serious, even dangerous, disagreements that cannot ever be mended. Sometimes it's just the old question of how to pronounce "tomato." And we've all seen marriages that are just doomed from the beginning. Everyone knows it but the bride and groom, and maybe their friends can't even explain what's going to go wrong, but instinct says, This is one heck of a mistake.

But marriage is vitally important to having a successful life. Even if I'm a dunderhead on the subject, my observations come from experience. I'm sharing them because, well, I'm a sharing kind of guy.

Besides, even I might *know* as much as the experts, who are all over the lot.

RIDICULOUS NOTE: "Relationship expert" Barbara DeAngelis has made a ton of money giving advice about love in her eight best-selling books and a TV infomercial, *Making Love Work*. A busy gal, but busier than you might think: She is now working on her *fifth* marriage. I guess the American public isn't demanding rock-solid qualifications in this area. So I'll press on.

Staying married is a bear. The marriage experts admit that; many of them have divorces as final if not as frequent as Miss DeAngelis. Right now, about 56 percent of American adults are legally married for the first, second, or nth time. About one in ten American adults is divorced and hasn't remarried.

Divorce has been legal in America since colonial times. Back in England it had required an act of Parliament, which cost a lot of shillings. Divorce would not become legal there until 1857, but the first American divorce was recognized more than two centuries before, in 1639, by a Puritan court. The couple didn't have to make much of a case—something about growing apart over witchcraft, I'd guess—because settlers in the New World wanted little to do with the restrictive codes of the Old.

They were a practical lot, too. Why make two adults suffer a living Hell when both wanted out? Let St. Peter figure it out later at the entry to the real Hell. Or, as the writer Heywood Hale Broun put it once, "The desire for divorce is the only important factor. The reasons do not matter."

Divorce became so common later in the days of our Founding Fathers that Thomas Jefferson would handle a number of cases as a lawyer. He once declared that it was cruel "to chain a man to misery until death." Okay, Tom, but what about the ladies? Some of your compatriots—those Adams boys leap to mind—were not exactly a bundle of laughs around the house.

As America expanded westward, thousands of men left their wives in the East and were never heard from again. Divorce became even more common then. Wives sitting lonely by the fireside knew that homesteading could be fatal, especially if you ran into a teed-off Apache like Cochise or somebody. If the years passed without a word, many American women simply bailed out of their marriages.

Another factor in these decisions was life expectancy. At the end of the nineteenth century it was less than fifty years for the average white man.

That pretty much prevented the problem of having a midlife crisis; you were likely to be underground before it happened. Those were pretty rough times for trophy wives and Corvette dealers. If your man was in Tombstone at age fifty, he was probably under a tombstone. So you rigged up the buggy and rode down to the lawyer's office.

Most of us forget about the freedom of these earlier days because of— here it comes up again—the Great Depression. When that sucker hit, nobody had much money, there wasn't much leisure time for fooling around, and folks became pretty conservative. The divorce rate dropped sharply and stayed down during the anxious years of World War II and the boring years of the 1950s. Elizabeth Taylor did her best to shake things up, with some help from the likes of Eddie Fisher, but the average couple didn't even consider the idea of divorce.

Instead, until the 1960s sexual revolution changed everything, most married couples in America fully expected to stay married for life. At least, my folks and their neighbors did. There were no divorces in my entire family from the time the O'Reillys and the Kennedys, my mom's ancestors, got off the boat from Ireland in the 1850s (and, of course, divorce had never been possible in the Emerald Isle before that). More than a century in America without a single divorce! That streak remained unbroken until my aunt got unhitched in the 1970s.

ロ

For some reason, I was inspired to ask my father about marriage a few days after he and my mother celebrated their thirty-fifth wedding anniversary.

"So, uh, Dad. What's marriage *really* like?"

"You have no idea."

Pause.

"Uh, I know. That's why I'm asking."

"You'll see."

Pause. These answers did not, as you see, carry the conversation forward, but I was persistent.

"But . . . I'd like to *prepare* a little."

"Can't prepare."

"Why not?"

He looked at me without any expression.

"You have no idea."

Sitcom stuff? Yes, but it's the truth. Word for word, that was what my father had to say about marriage. He died without being moved to expand upon the subject.

But don't get the idea he was trapped or henpecked or bitter about his marriage. My father loved my mother, and vice versa. There was absolutely no reason, despite the family legacy, for them to stay together otherwise.

And this was a marriage without perks. I've mentioned our brief, cheap vacations. Once, we all rode on a Greyhound bus from Long Island to Fort Lauderdale in the middle of summer. There are no words to describe this excursion. Look at a map, and weep for me.

At home my parents were unashamedly themselves. My father had a temper. My mother was a bit ditzy. He saw to the used cars, and she prepared the Yankee Stadium–style food. He earned little money, and she was no Betty Crocker—don't even *think* Martha Stewart.

But the marriage worked. I'm particularly happy about that, purely for selfish reasons. I would have dreaded having some guy named Larry date my mother after she tossed out my father.

◻

Good as my parents' marriage was, it wasn't tested the way marriages are today. Since the 1960s a couple walking down the aisle or taking their turn at city hall are going to have *huge* expectations.

You know what they are: a big house, late-model cars, and expensive "with-it" clothes, great sex between hard bodies, varied and healthful foods, separate space but mutual interests, stimulating conversation that helps each partner "grow," fun parties and swell vacations, exceptional children who can be bragged about on social occasions and at the office, constant hugging and supportive endearments, old-fashioned considerate behavior and also trendy progressive thinking—and don't forget the intelligent, cheerful, gifted pets.

If that's your agenda, there's a quick route to reality. Run that list by your parents.

Where do we get these expectations? Once again, the Media Factor is partly to blame.

The worst culprits, hands down, are the magazines designed to appeal to women. "Yes, You Can Have It All!" the headline screams. (Take a look at some of these career women who produce this tripe, and you'll see some ladies who are seriously deluding themselves.) Inside the mag, an article might inform female readers that their husbands should be performing deft sexual acts at least three times a week, and then spend the rest of their time at home remodeling the place into *House Beautiful* condition. Mr. Right should also be working long hours on the job so that the kids can dress in Calvin Klein and summer in Nova Scotia, just like the Kennedys or whoever happens to be profiled as the media's ideal family of the month.

No wonder so many American husbands have this frozen grin on their faces *all the time*.

A friend of mine is the perfect example. He has a pretty wife and three kids—and he is their prisoner in his own home. That's how he himself describes it. Lately some of us guys planned a sensational three-day-long adventure in the wild, the kind of break guys have been taking to get sane long before anyone ever heard of Robert Bly and his drums around the campfire. But we had to count our friend out. "If I go on that trip," he told me, "I won't get sex for two months. I don't think I can last two months."

BULLETIN: I argued in the last chapter that *effective* dating can screen out irrational, controlling potential marriage partners. That's why the dating deal is so important. But here's a news flash: Some American men actually *want* to be controlled by women, and, of course, vice versa.

Why would my friend want to be in such a marriage? I don't get it. Can't see it. Whenever I see one partner giving up all power and decision making to a spouse, I'm flabbergasted. To me, this is truly tragic. I can't understand why anyone would want to give up his or her individuality to become a hostage to the wants and needs of a spouse.

Is it a way of avoiding responsibility? Is it an emotional return to childhood? I have no beepin' idea. Dr. Laura probably knows, but I'm afraid to call her: I don't want to get yelled at.

I do know this: The best thing about marriage is the opportunity to make another person's life richer on a daily basis. And I also know that it's not easy. I agree with Robert Louis Stevenson: "A certain sort of talent is indispensable for people who would spend years together and not bore themselves to death." That's why you have to marry someone who complements you, not dominates you; someone who compliments you, not depends too heavily on you, dragging you down. The best partners are the ones who can live life on their own. Does that sound like a contradiction? It isn't.

The second best thing about marriage, as I try to explain in the next chapter, is the chance to raise children who will do positive things in this world. But if you let them see you acting like a doormat or a martyr, you are giving them the wrong message about adult life and companionship.

Dicey as marriage is, it's worth it when two people respect each other's needs and learn to work together—yes, I said *work*—on the day-to-day responsibilities. No, you can't "have it all," because there's too much you have to get done. You can't "have it all," because no one's that lucky. You're lucky if you and your spouse really understand each other even half the time. That's a windfall, I think. Two different people, no matter how much they love each other, are . . . well, always going to be different. That's part of the fun. When it isn't part of the problem!

And the children will challenge and change your relationship with your spouse in hundreds of ways. Yes, the children. "Hey, stop makin' noise and go to sleep. *You do NOT want to make me come up there.*" (Do you ever hear yourself saying these things without even thinking about it? Automatic pilot. Blame it on your parents.)

Because that's what your kids will do. They'll blame everything on you. We'll explain in the next chapter. But first one final word on marriage. Don't do it if you are "just trying things out." Live with the person, date him or her all the time but don't get married unless you can put your spouse's needs above your own. Constantly.

10. THE CHILD factor

In *Bye, Bye, Birdie* Paul Lynde, playing a suburban American parent, unforgettably performed the song "Kids" with its catchy refrain:

> *Kids, what's the matter with kids today?* . . .
> *Why can't they be like I am, perfect in every way?*

Why, indeed? (Well, we'll have to set aside right now some of the childhood stories I've told about myself earlier in this book.)

This is the Golden Age of the Child in America. No question about it, especially in the middle class. Our kids are production numbers. We seem to believe—and they certainly agree!—that they *must* have everything we did *not* have. The perks of today's childhood include play dates, private lessons, organized sports, tutors, electronic gadgets, frequent vacations, camps, theme parks, trendy clothes for play and school. If you've got a kid and a checkbook, you know what I mean.

And *you're* expected to participate. *You* are on call to see it all. If you're a no-show, your child's self-esteem will be in jeopardy. And that's what many believe. In fact, you'll be scorned by the other parents because they *do* realize the true value of self-esteem.

Besides, if you attend the games and recitals and recreational experiences, you will be able to brag much more vividly about your child's accomplishments. And everyone at work wants to hear that, right?

RIDICULOUS NOTE: Pattie Pollard Ash of Greensboro, North Carolina, really wanted her son to do well in soccer. Watching him play a game one day, she took offense at the referee's "unfair" calls. She also took action: Running out onto the field, she punched the official in the mouth. Did I mention the ref was fifteen years old? We're talking high school here, Pattie. Socking that kid didn't play well with the judge, who convicted this overeager soccer mom of assault. She was fined and banned from all soccer games for three years—a catastrophic punishment for a mother of this sort.

So what's *really* going on here?

As you expect by now, I have a theory. In the 1960s, when the establishment couldn't handle the Vietnam War protests and then the sex, drugs, and rock culture that swept the nation, we baby boomers got a tremendous taste of power. This was not my father's Depression-era generation, okay? Just the opposite. Boomers had *power* and also—or so it seemed to many of us at the time—unlimited possibilities.

Whether you were liberal or conservative or, as John McCain likes to say, a vegetarian, you felt that you were going to change the world. Boomers expected to call their own shots in society—forever! Life would be one long journey of accomplishment and self-gratification.

But it didn't happen that way. A lot of us got burned. Reality swept in like a tsunami when we got down to the business of making a living instead of making love not war. The long hair was chopped off, our lifestyles changed overnight, and quite a few of us were brutally disenchanted. One minute some boomers were shouting, "Hey, hey, LBJ. How many kids did you kill today?" The next, or so it seemed, many were fully assimilated into the same over-thirty establishment they had so loudly disdained.

Who could have predicted it? Not the boomers, and certainly not their long-suffering parents. The ego-boosting of rebellion was replaced by the conformity of the workaday world. The dreams that materialized in a marijuana haze went (sorry) up in smoke. When the air cleared, you were sitting behind the same kind of desk your father sat behind until he got the nice gold pocket watch. You were getting his same gut and, God help you, his same personality.

For some disappointed baby boomers, I think, children conveniently stepped in to fill the void. Couples usually waited later than their own parents to have children, so they were more firmly established financially. Their children would become little trophies of the well-lived life. The kids' accomplishments would boost parental ego. Again, the possibilities of the future looked unlimited, if on a much smaller and less idealistic stage than Woodstock One.

Now, this is not the first generation of parents to earn some criticism. Early in the twentieth century George Bernard Shaw wrote, "There may be some doubt as to who are the best people to have charge of children, but there can be no doubt that parents are the worst." Well, he was a smart aleck, but you know what he means. It's tough being a parent. You're right on the firing line much of the time. Sometimes you blow it.

But there *is* a new problem with many of today's parents: They don't view their offspring as little people who have to be molded and disciplined. Something else is going on here. When the children are being used to define a positive self-image for a boomer parent, their whims and feelings will be taken *very* seriously. The kids begin *to rule*.

This is not good.

RIDICULOUS NOTE: A recent study showed that 20 percent of students in the Boston public schools flat out refused to do *any* homework. The superintendent quickly issued a statement that showed remarkable perspicacity. He suggested that the kids' parents were at least partly to blame. What's the man thinking? Is he ignoring the students' need for self-esteem at home?

As you've seen by now, I cannot even imagine telling my dad that his impatience with me and my behavior might cause my self-esteem to suffer.

"I have your self-esteem right here," he'd probably say, and his only son would bolt up the stairs. Did my sister and I refuse to do our homework?

Sure. And we used to have filet mignon every night for supper, too. My father had a big chip on his shoulder about people like Dr. Spock who were, in today's parlance, attempting to "empower" children. Dr. Spock was lucky he never met William O'Reilly, Sr. There would have been violence.

⌗

Now, my father didn't get it totally right, either. But somewhere between his bullheaded autocracy and the permissive idiocy of many boomer parents there's got to be a middle ground. Otherwise, it's not going to be possible to raise children so that they turn out to be happy, productive adults, rather than sad, confused misfits who turn over a large piece of their take-home pay to a shrink with an eye tic. Finding the middle ground is not easy, but parents should try.

And even if you do find that optimum way of raising your children, you get no guarantees that they will turn out okay—much less great.

As I wrote in "Their Labor of Love," an article in *Parade* magazine, the fine actor George Kennedy and his wife, Joan, have adopted their granddaughter. Why take such a drastic step in your golden years? Because three of their four children have become productive, responsible adults, but one is a thirty-five-year-old drug addict who can't kick the habit and take care of her own child. Talking about raising his kids, Kennedy said, "To this day, I don't know what I could have done differently . . . But the truth is that both my wife and I tried as hard as we could."

I believe they did, and their granddaughter is thriving in their home. You can't beat yourself up when a child takes the wrong path after you really have done your best. That's all you can do.

BACKUP STATS: According to the U.S. Census Bureau, about 3.9 million American children are now living with their grandparents, a figure that's risen 75 percent in the last thirty years. Often, the grandchild's mother and father are out of the picture, unable or unwilling to take responsibility.

⌗

To repeat, you will deeply regret it if you don't put in the effort that child raising requires. If you screw up big-time, there is a *huge* chance the kid will mess up his or her life, and the boomerang effect can settle a heavy layer of dust over your golden years.

Of course, it's always easier to explain what *not* to do. Here's an example:

Because of my long legs, I always take an aisle seat in today's crowded airplane cabins. On a recent flight to Los Angeles, a kid behind me, who looked to be about six years old, sharply kicked the back of my seat every fifteen seconds or so, regular as clockwork. I was not soothed by this recreational activity. His mother, sitting next to him, could clearly see what he was doing.

Turning around slowly, I silently gave her my best Clint Eastwood squint-eyed look. This caused her some alarm.

"Ethan," she mumbled. "Don't kick the man's chair. That's not nice."

About thirty seconds later, another kick. I swear he put more sauce into it this time.

"Ethan, didn't Mommy ask you not to do that? You are disturbing the man, Ethan. Please stop it."

The kicking continued.

"Mommy is going to punish you, Ethan, if you don't stop doing that. There'll be no ice cream when we land, and no TV . . ." She was beginning to sound desperate, and I knew this was going nowhere.

Swift as a cheetah, I bounded to my full height and loomed large over Ethan. I stared down at him. I'm certain I made an impression, but he refused to look up, realizing that danger lurked close by. I shifted my glare to his mother and said, "When I comeback from the bathroom, the kicking will cease."

A few minutes later I returned. Ethan was in the middle seat, his mother on the aisle behind me. She had had to switch seats because she couldn't control him.

This was pathetic. It also proved what I already suspected from what I had overheard. Ethan was acting like a brat because he did not *fear* his mother. As her conversation showed, she was a *talker.* I mean, she said entirely too much to her precious son. Sure, reasoning with certain children can work, but Ethan was long past that particular form of rehabilitation.

When your kid is doing something that is obviously wrong, you should only have to say three words: *"Knock it off!"* If the child doesn't stop immediately, you've got a problem. But your child should suddenly have an even *bigger* problem, right then and there.

Is spanking the answer in such a situation? Many Americans think so, but there is a big debate in our country about corporal punishment. I land somewhere in the middle, myself. I wouldn't completely rule out spanking, but laying rough hands on your child should be the very last resort.

I *do* believe in immediate, attention-getting, uncomfortable punishment. I *do* believe in getting right up in your kid's face and explaining in no uncertain terms exactly what is going to happen next. The answer to little Ethan's defiance? Make his life very unpleasant for a while.

You will never teach your kid anything more important than discipline. It's the key to making everything work in the home, at the office, and in social situations.

The high school where I taught those two years in Florida had the reputation of having very tough students. But I never had to use force. Instead, I devised punishments that specifically suited the lawbreakers and their offenses, and I administered these punishments swiftly. I didn't consider any kid's sense of self-esteem. If he or she got out of line, the hammer came down. They knew that they could count on it every time.

You've got to be just as consistent with your kids—you owe it to them! Sure, many a child can be a major pain in the posterior. I believe that they are put on this earth to test us. So, pass the test.

Little Ashley, Ambrose, and Shelley actually want parameters. That makes them feel secure. Inconsistency from a parent is very confusing, even frightening. You are the force that defines their world and the behavior that will get them through it. Have enough guts to teach your children the guidelines that you will enforce. That's a way of giving them stability. Think out punishment strategies, then have enough fortitude to follow through.

That's the stick, but there's also the carrot. When your child does obey and does do the right thing, a reward should follow just as swiftly as punishment would—even if it's only an especially kind word or praise. You should think out your reward strategies as carefully as you've considered punishment strategies.

THIS JUST IN: "Everything must be made as simple as possible, but not one bit simpler." —Albert Einstein

Have I been oversimplifying the "child-raising experience"? Yeah. I mean, I'm a simple kind of guy. Simple is good. When your kid knows that bad behavior is always followed swiftly by predictable punishment, you will be winning the battle. Repeat after me: "Simple is good."

Your children aren't evil. (Probably.) They just need to be *taught*. The great comedian Will Rogers had a different way of saying it: "If any of us had a child that we thought was as bad as we know we are, we would have cause to worry."

◻

Your biggest tests as parents often come in the car, especially when two or more kids are along for the ride. Here's another eyewitness report from the field:

Two brothers, aged nine and eleven, are riding in the backseat of a brand-new Lincoln Town Car. Between them in the strapped-in baby seat is their one-year-old baby sister, fast asleep. Their mom is driving. Riding shotgun is the U.N. observer, me.

It starts about ten minutes into the ride.

"Mommmm, Jeffrey's leaning on me. Stop leaning on everyone, Jeff!" As you probably guessed, Jeffrey is the younger brother.

"I'm not doing anything, Mom. He's lying."

"Keep quiet back there," their mother replies, using a fairly reasonable tone.

"Mommmmm! He's doing it again! He's *leaning!*"

"Liam, stop it," she hisses. "You're going to wake up Rebecca."

Jeff can't resist: "She's already awake, Mom. She's drooling."

"Just *calm down* back there." Her tone was becoming a bit more strident.

"Jeffrey is lying, Mom. He's not telling the truth."

"Am not . . ."

You get the picture. In fact, I'd bet many of you have had starring roles in this picture, or one very similar. Kids get bored faster than Pamela Anderson in a library, and when kids get bored, sound the air-raid sirens.

Of course, nature can be nurtured, as I've been arguing throughout this chapter. It was natural for young boys to get bored in that situation, confined by their seat belts when they'd much rather be racing around outside. But we have a question of competing needs here. If Liam and

Jeffrey had feared their mother, the understandable episode would not have been prolonged into the ordeal it became for everyone involved. (Your observer places himself squarely and prominently on that list.)

But these boys knew from experience—still the best of all teachers—that their mother had no heart for punishment, or even very strong words. They knew that they were relatively free to create holy havoc while she was behind the wheel. Almost every child has the survival instincts of the Viet Cong. Listen up, parents of America: Your children must fear you, and only you can make that happen.

RIDICULOUS NOTE: Recognizing that political hay could be made from the much-publicized school shootings in the American heartland, your House of Representatives debated legislation requiring local school districts to set aside tax dollars to teach "character education" in the classroom. Excuse me? Why is cash required to subsidize character education? Why not just teach it? I suspect the bill is meant to be politically correct. And I know it's completely ridiculous.

I repeat: You are not a good parent unless and until you become the strong authority in your house. That does *not* include physical abuse or psychological brutality. You just need to establish yourself clearly as the person who can make your child's life pleasant or unpleasant, in direct response to the type of behavior that goes on.

And don't make the mistake of trying bribery. Once you start down that slippery slope, you begin accelerating toward warp speed. There won't be enough cookies, cakes, and video games in the world to keep up with the increasing demands. If you bribe to encourage good behavior on one occasion, your kids will be demanding baksheesh on *every* occasion. Depend upon it. They'd be crazy not to!

No, you have to be downright mean—the Wicked Stepmother!—when kids do the wrong things but sweet as Harriet Nelson when they behave correctly. Even the dimmest kid will catch on to that cause-and-effect program. The experts call this behavior modification, but your kid doesn't need to know what it's called to learn how it works.

But childhood turns out to be the easy part. When your kids reach their teen years, then it becomes *Children of the Damned* time for almost every parent in America.

You have to envy teenagers. We adults are usually just muddling through, trying to do our jobs and pay our taxes and figure out what's right, but they know *everything!*

And they're usually willing to share that knowledge with us, unasked. (Just like me, come to think of it.)

Dealing with teenagers might be easier if you were a Rockefeller. At the family mansion north of New York City in Westchester County, just recently opened up to the public, you see a huge estate house on the right as the tour bus takes you up the winding drive. The passengers always exclaim at its great size, and the tour guide explains, "That's the children's house." The mansion is farther on. Giving teenagers their own house is a very good idea—but not very practical for most of us.

We have to live *with* our teenage children. We will earn an advantage if we've established discipline, a moral philosophy, and a consistent tone early on. If we wait until the hormones are in play, it will probably be too late. Disciplined, responsive teenagers do not spring out of the air: They are developed from disciplined tots. Even then, they will be loony, and they will probably emit strange odors. But you'll get through it if you've been working on them in their earlier years.

And your teenagers, even if they don't know it, will be luckier than most. Since they've had the advantage of your discipline for years, they are way ahead of children whose parents are unable or unwilling to give them the right kind of attention and maintain a rational environment.

BACKUP STATS: There are approximately 60 million children under age fourteen in America today. About 18 million of them, or 30 percent, live in single-parent homes, and some 97 percent of those live with a mother, grandmother, or other female relative. There's more: 72 percent of all teenage murderers grow up in homes without a father. Many single moms are doing the best they can. Many of them work hard to support themselves and their children. But the kids are often left alone too much of the time or in the hands of others; they are at a tremendous disadvantage because a parent's time and discipline are in such short supply. This is a dangerous situation, but society can do little about it.

Of course, the swirl of everyday life often leaves little time for important life lessons even in homes where both parents are managing the household together. They have to set aside that time, or it won't happen.

In the teenage years, you will face new challenges. Two are more important than the others: You have to teach your teenagers to become aware of others and also how to *think*.

Let's take awareness first. By nature, kids are egocentric, kind of like Hollywood celebrities. For example, children don't leap out of the womb knowing how to share. They have to be *taught* generosity, just as they have to be taught tolerance and patience.

But they have no chance of succeeding in America today if they do not develop an awareness of the world outside themselves, especially when so many different cultures are coming to this country and joining the famous melting pot. The twenty-first-century world is big, it has many different kinds of people, and your children need to be exposed to that world.

Reading is one effective tool for developing awareness. I know some people who can't resist checking out the medicine cabinet when they are a guest in someone's house. I couldn't care less. Not my business. But I discreetly check out the family bookcase. You'd be surprised how many people have only a few books. Makes me cringe, especially if they have kids. I don't understand it.

Children should learn about reading long before they themselves can read, by adults reading *to* them. They should know as toddlers that there is something magic about printed words.

From the time they learn to read on their own, you should make sure that books are available to them. And you don't have to spend a lot of money. You can get fine secondhand books from garage sales and church benefits, or whatever. And does the word "library" ring a bell?

BACKUP STATS: If you have to have an economic reason, think about this: Reading is the most cost-effective form of entertainment there is. Compare the cost of reading a book borrowed free from the library—say, for a reading time of three to ten hours—with the cost per hour of going to a movie, spending the day at Disney World or some other pricey amusement park, going to a baseball game (and eating there), or even renting a videocassette.

If your children don't take to reading right away, take your time and use your head. It doesn't matter *what* they read. It could be a kids' magazine about some hobby or sport they like. It could be the Sunday funnies or *Mad* magazine. Of course, they are more likely to believe that reading is fun if you are reading books and magazines yourself.

Unless your child has some physical problem or attention disorder, why wouldn't he or she want to enter those exciting worlds that writers create for young imaginations? For me, there was nothing better than the adventures of the Hardy Boys and Chip Hilton, sports superstar. Your child may prefer dog or horse stories, fairy tales, science fiction, nurses, cowboys. Once they get started, they will never stop.

Just make sure that they know that such books exist—and that you will help them find them. You might have to give your child a small reward for reading books, at first. Gold stars worked in my elementary school. You might even have to *make* your child read. But someday there will be a little click—the lightbulb goes on—and reading will become what it should be: a lifelong habit that enriches experience and brings home the wider world outside.

After teaching awareness, you have to teach the use of brainpower.

Your teenagers can never succeed in this world, and they will miss most of what's going on in a changing society, if they can't formulate logical and cogent thoughts. You should start teaching them how to think when they're small, maybe as young as age seven.

Of course, the sad thing is that many adults don't themselves know how to think. You may have to give yourself a short course in rational thought processes. Don't be ashamed. You are only being a true-blue American, for in this country thinking is not widely encouraged. Logical thought is far too difficult and sometimes too painful for most of us. Instead, the national psyche prefers to react emotionally to events. If we *feel* it, it must be true.

Besides, the establishment, including, above all, the media, does not want us to think for ourselves. Better that we laugh, cheer, weep, or just feel good. The establishment knows very well that people who begin thinking for themselves will begin seeing things for what they really are. The powers-that-be much prefer Americans who are easily led, easily distracted, and easily satisfied with lies and spin.

In the interests of full disclosure, let me explain that my folks never taught *me* how to think. They were too busy reacting emotionally to all the stuff happening in their lives. So when I was a kid, I naturally imitated them. I didn't analyze situations; I just reacted. The result: Any conflict or threatening situation or misunderstanding just got much, much worse. All heat, no light.

Everybody in my neighborhood acted the same way. We did what everybody else did. We all yelled and screamed and stomped around without stepping back to think things through and figure out a different approach to a problem. That lack of thought, which I made up for with aggressive behavior, made me an easy target for the teasing and mean-spirited remarks that were never in short supply.

In fact, I was well into my thirties before I developed the ability to step back and analyze situations that were—or seemed to be—threatening to me. Because I had been living an emotion-driven life for so long, I'd made many mistakes that could easily have been avoided *if* I'd taken time for the slightest amount of reflection. With luck—and my own input—my kids will not make those kinds of mistakes.

Besides, using your head ought to be fun as well as sensible. Why not try some thought drills with your teenager? At the supper table ask your child what impressed him most that day in school—and why. You'll probably get vague, bored responses at first. Make clear that they're unacceptable. Get him to focus on one important thing that stood out during the day. First, it has to be described: something learned in class, or something that happened in gym class, or a conversation with a friend or teacher. Then it has to be explained. *Why* did this particular idea or event stand out? What did it *mean?* Did it change his view about something or make him want to learn more?

Your child needs to learn to reflect on his day, to start thinking about what goes on around him and what he can learn from it. Our brains, which made it possible for us to take over the world from the other animals, don't help much if they aren't used—*constantly*. Encourage your child to become a kind of reporter at school. This thought drill requires observation, memory, description, and analysis. In other words, it requires the mental tools we all need in our adult lives.

When the day's choice is finally explained, you should discuss it. Show that you are interested in his opinion and explain what you like about his choices. You may be surprised, in fact, at what you learn about your teenager's daily experiences and how he is looking at life. His interests will surface and so will his fears. You will have a terrific new way of keeping close tabs on the kind of information your teenager is digesting. After a few days, this will be fun for both of you, if you do it the right way.

Remember, simple is good. Also remember not to criticize your child's choice, even if it sounds dull or dopey to you. It's his life; he's living it. If he can explain his reasons, that's the point of the game.

Here's another easy educational game: Have your child point to a place on a world map or globe. If you can, tell her an interesting story or fact about that place. If you draw a blank, then you can both look up the area in a world almanac—a necessity for any household—and see what you learn. This is the kind of sleuthing that interests some people who collect stamps. Make sure you tell a good story. Use your imagination to make it lively or funny. You may be surprised what images pop up from your reading or news watching or past conversations with traveling friends.

Suddenly a foreign name opens up for your kid an entire part of the world, maybe just because of the sound. Timbuktu, Uzbekistan, Mandalay, the Bay of Fundy, Four Corners, the Khyber Pass, Belize, Lake Titicaca, Goa—the world is chock-full of mysteries. In each of these places and all of the others, people live differently than they do in Levittown, or wherever you are. To add suspense to the game, have your child close her eyes and pick a spot at random. A friend of mine knows a couple who choose their annual vacation destination this way—and they haven't been disappointed yet.

And, since most kids love excitement, how about renting action movies with historical themes? There are hundreds of them that bring alive other times and places, movies like Disney's Revolutionary War flick *Johnny Tremain* and the Civil War epic *Glory*. A good general rule about Hollywood is that the costumes, sets, and backgrounds are likely to be historically accurate, even when the stories and characters stretch the limits of artistic license. Anyway, you aren't preparing your child for a history exam. You are making him or her aware of the world's amazing variety of experiences.

You may have more and much better ideas for engaging your child's mind. The point is, it's your responsibility to teach your children those two important things I've mentioned: to become aware of the world and to think logically.

You can't depend on the schools to teach these things, except for the occasional outstanding, unusually courageous teacher. As institutions of the establishment, schools are designed to teach conformity and the basics. Teachers know that, of course. For the "big picture," you the parent have to make the extra effort. This is a gazillion times more important than yet another soccer game, but it should be fun, and there should be no negatives. One other thing: If you can get your kid interested in chess, the game will improve his mind and concentration.

Finally let's recall the strategy I suggested in regard to dealing with drugs and alcohol: "Our family doesn't do that kind of stuff, we are better," etc. Keep reinforcing that idea during the teen years. Don't let up. From school, the neighborhood, and the tube, you will find numerous new examples of people who mess up their lives because of personal weaknesses. Make these sad stories into examples for your teenagers to avoid. Yes, it is lecturing, but your kids will listen to an interesting lecture on the subject.

And if you are able to turn your lecturing into brainwashing, so much the better. That's good strategy. It will stay with the kid forever.

Still, there are no guarantees. The son of one of the finest guys I know is a heroin addict. This selfish young jerk abandoned his own daughter, so his father is helping to raise her. The dad, who feels terrible about the whole situation, sometimes blames himself for his son's weakness and cruelty. No one else does. We all know that it is entirely the son's fault. He was unreachable.

Some people are born self-destructive. There's nothing anyone can do about it. Some children will fail, no matter what, just as some will succeed when the circumstances of home life are against them. No one knows the answers to these mysteries. That's just life.

✄

As I've said (and my mother said it first), my parents were basically clueless in the child-raising arena, but they did set a good example for me by being consistent. My sister and I knew what to expect and what was expected. I have no complaints. We went to church and to the beach; we were given birthday parties; we had clean clothes and all of the basics.

Since my folks didn't have money, the materialism addiction was never a threat. I never felt envious of what other kids had. I can remember thinking about material things only at Christmas, which seemed to be the point of that particular holiday, at least to us kids. And then there were the times when some of the other guys at my Catholic high school made fun of me for having only two sports jackets—neither of them exactly Armani.

Most of the time, though, I knew I was pretty lucky. I saw that some other kids had drunken, sleazy, or uninterested parents. That was a much rougher go of it than being a two-jacket teenager whose parents didn't understand how to teach life skills.

But the twenty-first century is going to be a greater challenge for teenagers than the 1960s and 1970s. Employment and social life will be much more competitive. Your kids will be judged every time they walk into a room or open their mouths—and some of those judgments may follow them for the rest of their lives.

So here's a brief O'Reilly manual—not complete by any means—to suggest some of the things a parent today has to think about:

TABLE MANNERS. Miss Manners is right. No one wants to eat near a slob, whether she's the top pom-pom girl or he's BMOC. Rudeness spoils the finest meal. Also, it's unfair to your children to let them go out into situations where they will feel embarrassed because they don't know the basic rules of etiquette. Sit them down and explain how to use silverware. Work on eating habits: sitting up straight, chewing like a human not a bison, eating at the pace of the rest of the table, asking rather than grabbing for seconds or condiments. These things matter! I have been at dinners where someone behaved with great courtesy, then made the mistake of folding her napkin at the end of the meal. It was the giveaway that she had not been raised "properly," according to my upscale dinner companions. Suddenly she dropped lower in their eyes. She didn't know that in this social set you are supposed to crumple your napkin. Why does it matter? Is one method better than the other? Not really. But one is the more acceptable, and people will notice.

GROOMING. This isn't easy, especially when we go through a period when "dressing down" is the style of the day. Still, good grooming is essential for success in America. A certain hip casualness in clothing shouldn't prevent anyone from keeping clean and healthy. Children should have straight teeth, even if they're wearing army boots and grunge. They should be taken to a dentist every six months (no exceptions) and to a dermatologist if there's a skin problem. They should be instructed in the use of deodorants, shaving products, and cleansing agents. When they manage to look clean and healthy, tell them so. Also, even though you may be rowing upstream against some mysterious fad, try to teach them the basics of sensible dress. In my teens I often walked out of my house looking like a carnival display: No one told me that stripes and checks clash. Sanitation guys would mock my ridiculous color combinations.

ABILITY TO SPEAK. Use one double negative in a white-collar job interview, and you are toast. (You *might* get away with misusing pronouns, since David Letterman, Ted Kennedy and a lot of other public figures do it all the time, but you really should teach your children not to say "between you and I" or "for he and she." Why? Call up your kid's English teacher or look through a grammar book. It's right there.) As a parent, you should speak well yourself and *then* insist upon proper English from the kids. And cursing is out! I cringe when parents swear in front of their children. This is nuts! That kind of language helps no one in the outside world, unless they're writing Hollywood screenplays or managing a professional sports team. They do not throw the f-word around at Harvard, in case you had to ask. Impose rigorous standards against swearing on your teenagers and on yourself. If the children complain, that's bleeping tough. A well-spoken individual is so rare in America these days that he quickly sets himself apart from the pack. And, please, don't make a fool of yourself by copying your teenagers' use of slang. Let them say "cool," "awesome," and "whatever" to each other, because that's the point! Don't make these words the basis of family conversation between the generations.

COURTESY. Children used to be taught to be polite. Can you imagine having to make that observation? What happened? When did we forget that children *need* to be taught to be polite? Expressing themselves healthily does not include running into people in the mall or slamming doors or ripping things out of the hands of other children. These behaviors are just *wrong.* But if you want to be selfish about it, they are also dangerous to your kid's development. She will lose friends, expect too much of the world, and not understand why she is left out and behind. Courtesy is correct, but it also pays off. If your child is impolite, send her off immediately to courtesy camp. What, there is no such thing? Well, I guess that means *you* will have to teach her how to behave in public places. That includes such things as opening doors for the elderly, giving the right-of-way to people coming out doors, saying "excuse me" if she bumps into someone, and on and on. It's also true that courtesy, as you should teach your child, is a cultural thing. In England, for example, if you accidentally step on someone's foot in a crowd, your victim will automatically say, "Excuse me." And mean it! In the United States young children are usually expected to give their bus or subway seat to an elderly woman; in Italy it's just the reverse. In many parts of the southern U.S., men of all ages say "ma'am" to women of all ages. Try that in Manhattan and a woman might think you're implying that she's over the hill. In other words, courtesy is the custom of the country or the town or the neighborhood. You should learn the rules that apply where you live and pass them on. They may say that courtesy is "contagious," but if your kid seems immune, make sure she catches something she might not like.

SPIRITUALITY. You may not be religious, but it's imperative to teach your child to respect nature. And if you are religious, take responsibility for your child's spiritual life. Don't delegate this important teaching to anyone else entirely, even a rabbi, preacher, imam, or priest. *You* have to provide your child with a moral foundation. Instilling an appreciation for the spiritual side of life will defend your children against the American emphasis on materialism. Devotion to accumulating things rather than to helping others is a mental cage that millions of us have enthusiastically walked into. Ultimately, though, that cage is not a nice place to be. And speaking of "not nice" places, do not try to teach morality by threatening your children with the fires of Hell. Virtue should be its own reward, as the old saying goes. You shouldn't do good because you're afraid of the devil and his pitchfork. Besides, it doesn't work. I had been threatened with eternal damnation so often by the eighth grade that I assumed I was bound to Hell for certain. And why not? It looked just as certain that all of my thug friends would be there, too.

KINDNESS. Do you make the mistake so many parents make these days: worrying all the time about what your children are *doing* but not about what they're *thinking?* The inside of their heads is very important. That's who they are. It's the thinking that controls the doing, right? For example, kindness is so important to living a decent and productive life, you should talk about it often. Perhaps some children are born with a giving personality, but most need to be taught. Why not set up a game that awards points for being kind? Once a week, perhaps on Sunday, ask your kids what act of kindness they performed during the previous seven days. (And be prepared to answer the question yourself!) Discuss what they report, then enter their story into a journal. At the end of the month give them a "kindness treat" or gift. A bribe? Well, sure, but it's a *good* bribe. After all, kindness easily becomes habit-forming—not because of your gifts, but because of the grateful reactions of the recipients of your kid's kindness. (But be prepared for the times when the little old lady or whoever is suspicious of your kid's motives. That's another life lesson right there, unfortunately.) You have to teach kindness because it's probably not on the curriculum in school and it's certainly not being taught on *Melrose Place* or *Dawson's Creek*. And if you're not all that generous yourself shame on you! But teach your teens altruism because you want them to have everything you didn't have!

ᵟ

RIDICULOUS NOTE: Despite the furor of the Lewinsky scandal and other sordid associations, President Clinton was chosen the "most admired man" by Americans questioned in a 1998 Gallup poll. The pope came in *second*.

Ridiculous? Well, umm, yeah. But, in my opinion, this says more about our celebrity-mad culture than about anything else. With the White House backdrop and the helicopter and *Air Force One*, Clinton has a lock on the dazzle. The pontiff's spirituality is nowhere near being such good TV.

That brings us to the next chapter, "The Celebrity Factor."

11. THE CELEBRITY factor

NOTE TO SHARON STONE: Listening to you helps me understand why Americans turn to celebrities for advice. You're all so deep! When special prosecutor Kenneth Starr's investigation produced enough evidence to convince the House of Representatives to impeach Bill Clinton for perjury and obstruction of justice, you opined, "Those Republicans will, I swear to God, drag our nation into the gutter to take President Clinton with them. I just hate it. It's like the movie *Fatal Attraction*. Ken Starr is Glenn Close." That's some original political analysis, Sharon, but I don't quite get it. I'm pretty sure Starr didn't plunge a bunny into boiling water. I think he did read the U.S. Constitution, though.

Fame contributes so little of value, if anything, to our society, but Americans are absolutely out of their minds these days over "celebrities." I mean, it is totally out of control. Millions of us spend a good part of our lives watching and reading about actors, politicians, sports figures, singers, and the rest. Even serial killers make the cut. Some of these celebrities, as far as I can tell, are famous only for *being* celebrities. I don't get it.

We don't really know anything about these people as human beings, but we get emotionally involved with them. They become our imaginary friends. We bring them into our homes via all of the media. We buy products they recommend, and we listen to what they say about the environment or the NRA.

But we really care less about their "thoughts" than about their private lives. Does Cher have a new boyfriend, and how much younger is he? What is going on with Tom Cruise's marriage to Nicole Kidman? Is Neve Campbell *really* happy? Whom did Derek Jeter pick up at China Club last night? How can Kathie Lee Gifford stay with Frank after what he did in that hotel room? I don't know, you don't know, and *she* probably doesn't know. But I don't care!

And not only that. I don't care about Jerry Seinfeld's marriage or what Mariah Carey ate at Balthazar or how Streisand is remodeling or anything at all about Puff Daddy's home in the Hamptons. *I don't care.* Is that anti-American?

It's no exaggeration to say that America has become a country that worships the famous. I guess there are several reasons. The stars look as if they're leading exciting lives, while we snack on junk food and watch them from the couch. We're dull; they're living in the fast lane. We're nodding out after a full day of labor; they're screwing like rabbits. Beautiful hard bodies, sexy clothes, rambling homes with pools fit for a Roman emperor, and fast sports cars to get them from one star-studded party to the next. Celebrities rule! Sunny L.A. days, breezy Manhattan nights, and an around-the-clock spree in South Beach.

Of course, this whole scene is nuts, but it isn't going to change anytime soon. When people like Warren Beatty and Donald Trump can command massive media attention for their ridiculous presidential teases, you know that celebrity frenzy has reached the point of extreme absurdity.

RIDICULOUS NOTE: After weeks of coyness, Warren Beatty finally made a speech about his political ideas before (of course) a crowd of celebrities in Los Angeles. Among other things in a speech that needed a better script, he announced that he is disappointed with the Democratic Party because it has moved to the political center. He described himself as an unrepentant tax-and-spend liberal and claimed that's what America needs in the White House. The crowd applauded wildly. Afterward, their boy was driven home in a limo. "Limousine liberal," in case you weren't around at the time, was the snide term used back in the 1960s for rich left-wingers who gave their money to causes but never really got into the fray and did something politically productive. Warren Beatty, the man who made *Reds*, promotes a socialist philosophy but would last about ten seconds in that kind of society. Hey, Warren, I believe there *are* condos available in Havana.

So what the bleep is going on here? In some circles Oprah Winfrey is considered a political sage; there's even been a kind of boomlet for her potential as a vice presidential candidate. Alec Baldwin got front-page action when he verbally assassinated Kenneth Starr. Cybil Shepherd, when not out on the road pushing her book about her sexual adventures, fancies herself an effective defender of women's rights. Are the Founding Fathers twirling in their graves? No, if alive today, they'd probably want front-row seats at the Grammys.

In my twenty-five years of reporting I've met hundreds of famous people. I think I've given them all a fair shot, but very few were impressive. For one thing, their fame burdens them with a sense of entitlement. They expect people to do things for them. They expect to be deferred to.

CELEBRITY SIGHTING: When I was a local news reporter for CBS's Channel 2 in New York City, I happened to be standing in line one day in the station cafeteria when in walked Morley Safer, one of the stars of the top-rated national show *60 Minutes*. Morley must have been in a hurry because he cut into the line ahead of me and others. Nobody said anything. Except for one solitary individual. Me. (You knew that, of course.) I looked Morley in the eye and let forth with, "There's a line here, sir." Safer duly stepped aside and went to the back of the line, but he was not happy. Oh, yes. This was another great political move for O'Reilly at CBS.

A LATER CELEBRITY SIGHTING: Roger Ailes, my boss at Fox, got married recently, and the endless receiving line was chock-full of famous faces, most of them behaving like normal people. Suddenly Maury Povich and Connie Chung jumped in front of the entire line. Everybody saw it. Instantly I came up with something very loud and very rude to say. But then I didn't say it. My rationalization was that I didn't want to embarrass Ailes, but maybe I had more guts when I was younger.

Trust me. You would not want to hang around with many celebrities unless you find self-absorption and childish impulses fascinating.

Yes, the famous are often under pressures that cause them to behave differently, but that sense of entitlement is a killer. It destroys humor and perspective, and sometimes it can be the death of relationships. It also explains those crazy contracts in which a rock band demands bowls of M&M's in their hotel room, a concert pianist will perform only on Sundays, and a famous TV actor won't go on the set unless a refrigerator nearby is filled with bottles of the fine wine Pouilly-Fuissé kept at a specified temperature.

Here are some short takes I've seen that tell much of the story:

- Baseball star Reggie Jackson walking past some eager young kids in the lobby of Boston's Sheraton Hotel, snarling and refusing to sign their autograph books.

- Marlo Thomas throwing a fit—there's no other expression for it—when I asked whether or not her father's fame had helped her career.

- Tom Selleck's publicist telling me that the star demanded approval of any other guests that appeared after him on my news program. This was after the segment was taped—and after Selleck himself had left the set.

- Sylvester Stallone refusing to allow any spectators watch him being interviewed by me. The room was cleared.

- Sean "Puff Daddy" Combs, who arrived for an interview with an eleven-person entourage, demanding that all questions I asked him be about "the positive aspects of rap."

RIDICULOUS NOTE: When I was putting together a story that featured Roger Moore's work as a goodwill ambassador for UNICEF, the actor refused to visit a group of poor children in Harlem. This was one of the most bizarre celebrity stunts I've ever seen. These disadvantaged kids were attending the Children's Storefront school, which has a great reputation for educational success in challenging circumstances. Moore's interaction with those lively, excited children on national television could have brought in thousands of dollars in donations to support the school. But he would have none of it. His publicist whispered to me that no one could understand 007's refusal. To this day, I get steamed whenever I see the man's face in the movies or on TV. The "ambassador" inspires no feelings of goodwill in me.

All right, a celebrity can have a bad day just like the rest of us, but I think you see my point. When you're surrounded all the time by yes-men and hangers-on, when you're basking in waves of adulation (or so you think), you can lose all perspective.

And Americans are not helping these people by worshiping them. Bad for them, bad for us, and a *total* waste of time. But what can stop the madness?

RIDICULOUS NOTE: Politically correct talk show hostess and tone-deaf singer Rosie O'Donnell seems to believe it is her duty to instruct her fans on the issues. She is so rabidly and sourly in favor of gun control that when the cast of the classic Irving Berlin musical *Annie Get Your Gun* visited her show, she refused to let them sing a song that had any reference to a gun in it. (It is not true, however, that she demanded that the cast be announced as performing in a revival of *Annie Get Your Slingshot*.)

                    ◻

My personal all-time favorite celeb story features blond bombshell Marla Maples and Donald Trump when their famous tabloid romance was at white heat. Marla was friends with a former girlfriend of mine, and these two ladies got the bright idea of going on a double date with "the Donald" and me.

For a lot of reasons, this sounded like a bad idea. First and foremost, unlike most broadcast "personalities" you see on your home screen, I do not like to hang around socially with people I'm likely to report on someday. In that department Maples and Trump were *extremely* likely suspects.

But I was weak and gave in to the ladies. For reasons unknown to me, the "date" chosen was a Paula Abdul concert at the Meadowlands complex west of New York City in New Jersey. After all, as you may know, the average age of the audience members in an Abdul concert is about twelve. Anyway, we drove over in Trump's limo and were waved into a parking lot beneath the Brendan Byrne Arena. We popped out of the car and took an elevator up to a private box to watch the show.

Slightly to my surprise, things were going okay. Trump and I chatted casually about the football season and about his casinos. Our dates talked about their mutual friends and other pleasant subjects. The private box was luxurious. Everyone seemed to be having a relaxed, good time. I wondered why I had resisted coming along.

Onstage, the first act was Color Me Bad, a group who opened with their hit song "I Wanna Sex You Up!" It was downright bizarre when they asked the young kids to sing along, thousands of preteens screaming, "I wanna sex you up . . . Let me sex you up!" You can imagine the faces of some of the parents who had come with their kids. They were aghast. It was an unforgettable moment in concert history.

There was an intermission after the sex guys' act. That's when things began to get interesting in our party.

Trump suggested that we all take a walk around the arena. *What?* If you missed the Marla-Donald story, you're probably still waiting to hear about the sinking of the *Titanic*, the defeat of the Nazis, and a certain blue dress. This was the tabloid story that sold papers and boosted TV ratings for months, and there were thousands of people milling around down there in the arena. They'd all seen the photos, I knew.

So Donald really wanted to *walk around the arena?*

Oh, yeah. He sure did.

I remarked to him that it was probably not a good idea to take such a stroll without massive security—like, to begin with, a battalion of fully armed, battle-tested U.S. Marines with full-metal jackets. Some rudeness might break out, I continued. And what about sexpot Marla in those *six-inch spike heels?*

No problem, Donald said. We would have *Tony and Lou* with us.

Okay, personal bodyguards Tony and Lou were certainly large and testy. But the odds against them were about 15,000 to 2—odds I did not like. But this excursion wasn't my problem, I decided. It was their choice. I'd wait for them to come back.

But my decision made Marla unhappy. For some reason, she insisted that my date and I go out there with them—out there where the mob would instantly recognize the cosmically famous lovebirds. And then my date looked at me with great sadness in her eyes. Why was I doing this to her? The sad eyes got me and I gave in. Taking a deep breath, I stepped out of the luxury box, and our stroll began.

You can picture it, I know. Within ten seconds the hallway of the Brendan Byrne Arena was in screaming, crowding chaos. The excited teenagers, already revved up by Color Me Bad, dropped popcorn boxes, spilled soda, spit beer: The whole thing was nuts. Some people said nice things, and some people were very mean. We all got shoved. Most of the guys, of course, focused on Marla, who was dressed or sewn into a tourniquet-tight black outfit. They stared in a way that is usually seen only in prison. And then there were those who simply screamed the name "Donald" over and over. He loved it.

We only walked around—I mean, fought the tides—for about ten minutes, but it seemed longer than Lewis and Clark's trek on the PBS series. Trump, whose bodyguards somehow kept anyone from actually touching him, couldn't get enough of the scene. Marla looked uneasy but tried to smile. (This was a far cry from her hometown of Dalton, Georgia .) Since I felt as if I was in *The Rocky Horror Picture Show*, I tried to blend into the crowd of extras, keeping as far as possible from the celebrity couple. But our stroll wasn't enough for Trump. He now wanted to watch the rest of the concert from the floor!

So long, luxury box. Standing on the arena floor surrounded by extra security guards, we watched Paula Abdul perform the rest of the concert. As she sang and danced, the crowd kept screaming "Donald!" and "Marla!" Abdul seemed confused by that.

We went backstage after the show to say hello to the star, who could not have been nicer to us, no matter what she thought of the demonstration on the floor. That was the end of the double date. I couldn't wait to get home.

What I'd seen, if I haven't made it clear, was Trump's addiction to fame in full force. Yes, fame can be addicting, and he was hooked. He didn't do anything that terrible, but his actions that night showed me that money and power just aren't enough, once a certain kind of person has tasted fame. He feasted on that nutty adulation. He craved the roar of the crowd, and he got it. But why were the young teenagers going wild at the sight of this balding, paunchy builder?

Well, it's not because he's an entertainer or an athlete or a poet or a statesman. He isn't any of those things. It's certainly not because of his business acumen. Those kids couldn't care less about that kind of thing at their age.

No, Trump was a celebrity to this crowd simply because he was having an affair with a glamorous woman. *That* was all it took to propel him into the public consciousness and give him the fame that he wanted so much.

Is this society crazy? Yes, it is.

RIDICULOUS NOTE: Again and again, the celebrity is unreasonably treated like an expert on everything, but sometimes the shoe might fit, although in strange ways. A reporter for the *Weekly Standard* asked the *very* famous O. J. Simpson for his considered opinion on President Clinton's problems with Paula Jones. His reply revealed the wisdom of a man with experience, I guess: "If it's true what happened to Paula Jones in that room with Clinton, then simply for hitting on a dog like her he should do thirty days. Other than that, I don't think it's anyone's business." Why didn't the White House put Mr. Simpson on the witness list for the Senate trial? And is it true that Johnnie Cochran claims that the quote was put into his former client's mouth by a rogue detective on the Los Angeles police force?

THIS JUST IN: "Men often mistake notoriety for fame, and would rather be remembered for their vices and follies than not to be noticed at all."— President Harry S Truman

There is some good news in the celebrity orbit. I don't want to close this chapter without giving the nod to some very admirable celebrities.

Arthur Hailey, most famous for *Airport* but the author of many other best-selling books, had never met me when I finished my novel *Those Who Trespass*. That didn't keep him from taking the time to read the book and send my publisher an enthusiastic blurb. He got nothing from doing this favor. In addition, he spent time giving me some very good advice about writing, and I mean to use it in my next novel.

There are other good guys in the spotlight:

- You probably know about actress Susan Sarandon's out-spoken left-wing activities. She speaks her mind, like it or not. But you don't know, because she keeps it quiet, about her many charitable and completely unpolitical activities behind the scenes.

- I can tell you that Jimmy Carter can be a difficult person one-on-one, but you know that his continuing work for Habitat for Humanity is magnificent. I wonder if Bill Clinton will be doing this kind of humanitarian work when his term expires. Ronald Reagan didn't. I predict we'll be seeing Clinton at the trough, taking millions for speeches, public appearances, and book contracts.

- Joe Piscopo, the former *Saturday Night Live* star, and basketball great Alonzo Mourning are both deeply, and quietly, involved with helping troubled teenagers.

These celebrities understand what a great opportunity fame gives them to accomplish some good in the world. A famous person can attract attention to a cause or get his friends to perform in charity benefits to raise money. He can work out of the spotlight in a hands-on way that will make a lasting impression.

Only after her senseless death did we learn about many of Princess Diana's secret charitable activities. Publicly, when she shook hands with a victim of AIDS, a new light was shed on this disease. When she was photographed with children who had lost their limbs to land mines, she was criticized for getting involved in a complex political situation that she supposedly could not understand—but she brought attention to the tragedies of those children. We can't demand that our celebrities behave generously, of course, but we should be a lot more discerning about whom we admire.

And that discernment should double when we consider the people who want power over us: the politicians.

12. THE POLITICS factor

TALKING POINT: We have the right to vote. People have died to protect that right. But half or more of us stay home during important elections. When we talk to pollsters, we reveal amazing ignorance about the issues, the candidates, and even the structure of government.

Who represents you in Congress? And is he or she Democrat or Republican? What's his or her stand on abortion, gun control, trade with Communist China, taxes . . . ? You'd be surprised at how many Americans haven't a clue to the answers to questions like these. And if you're surprised, I'm amazed. These people make the laws that define our lives, and they decide how to spend the money collected by a confiscatory tax system.

Well, we're not entirely to blame for this sad state of the Union. Politicians have come close to making themselves obsolete in American life. They're below the radar screen, as far as many voters are concerned. They are looked upon as charlatans, thieves, liars, and exploiters. The most harmless of them are simply clowns. To recall the Reagan ads, it really is "morning in America"—we've waked up to the realization, at last, that we can't stand politicians.

VIEWER TIME-OUT: "Mr. O'Reilly, I hate you. You are a Mr. Know-It-All. If you're such a big shot, why don't you run for president?" (Mary M., Ranshaw, Pennsylvania)

The last eight years have seen a peak in the cycle of corruption. "Business as usual" has become the politics of sleaze. Not since the infamous administration of Warren G. Harding have the White House and its minions been so blatantly corrupt. Bill Clinton supposedly worries about leaving a "legacy," a mark on history. No problem, Bill . . . You and yours have already left a beaut.

How did Clinton pal Webb Hubbell get an $800,000 consulting job between indictmnets? How did Clinton's best friend and erstwhile mortgage guarantor Terry McAuliffe turn a mere $100 into $2.5 million? I mean, how *do* things like that *happen?* Do they happen to you? They certainly never happen to me. They don't happen to you and me because we are not pulling strings in the slimy world of American politics, twenty-first century-style.

Right there, very simply, is why the American people do not like politicians. Regular folks have seen enough to suspect that many elected officials fight their way to win public office for two reasons: either to enrich themselves off the public trough or to bask arrogantly in the power and glory of the statehouse or Capitol Hill.

You don't hear that "public servants" are widely admired or cheered for a commitment to improving the country and their constituents' daily lives. A deep cynicism has descended upon the American people. We believe that too many politicians are self-centered crooks. This cynicism, in the long run, is very dangerous for the ideals that led to the founding of this nation in 1776.

THIS JUST IN: "You have to put in the coins to open the gates," Johnny Chung told me in an interview, comparing the White House to a subway after handing over a check for $50,000 to Maggie Williams, aide to First Lady Hillary Rodham Clinton. Or, as Democratic Congressman Mel Levine said in 1992 when he was defeated for reelection, "[Political] decisions are clearly weighted and influenced . . . by who has contributed to the candidates. The price that the public pays for this process, whether it's in subsidies, taxes, or appropriations, is quite high."

Of course, not every politician focuses on the money, and no party has a monopoly on the bad guys. Still, there is enough muck to taint the whole bunch. Can you say "Dan Rostenkowski"? Can you say "Henry Cisneros"? And how about that federal judge ruling that a sitting president, Mr. Clinton, lied under oath to a federal grand jury? No wonder that the breeze off the Potomac River has such an unpleasant smell.

ロ

There's always been a certain level of corruption in American politics, of course. Aaron Burr is the poster boy for power-mad, ruthless public servants. Outfoxed in his elective ambitions by other politicians, he tried to start his own nation and was tried for treason. So political shenanigans and demagoguery are nothing new.

What *is* new is the staggering hypocrisy and boldness of some elected officials today. They and their spinmeisters turn the truth into an appalling game of "parse the sentence."

RIDICULOUS NOTE: In August 1998 an ABC News poll showed that 37 percent of Americans would oppose the removal of President Clinton from office *even if* it could be proved beyond a shadow of a doubt that he had perjured himself before a federal grand jury while in office.

THIS JUST IN: "Politicians are the same all over. They promise to build a bridge even when there is no river." —Nikita Khrushchev, premier of the Soviet Union, 1957–64

I could list hundreds of examples of political hypocrisy. After all, I deal with them on a daily basis on *The O'Reilly Factor*. But you already know that many of our elected officials and their spinmeisters are corrupt phonies. The important question is why.

The guys who set up the political system in America were deeply distrustful of authority—perfectly understandable, when you consider how Mother England was ripping off the colonists who were over here doing all the work. Parliament taxed the hell out of them but refused to allow them to elect their own parliamentary representatives to stand up for them. (If you really want to learn about naked power grabs, read up on English history. It wasn't quite as genteel as those Victorian soap operas on PBS-TV.) King George III, who was later diagnosed as insane, believed that Americans were barbarians who existed only to be exploited by their betters. He had the same attitude, by the way, toward the Irish and Scots and East Indians and Africans, not to mention his own lower classes being overworked and underpaid in the first factories of the Industrial Revolution. A fun guy, that George. He could tell even Leona Helmsley a thing or two about how to deal with "the little people."

Anyway, when the colonists kicked the red-coated British army out of here, they were determined to establish a *limited* government. They didn't want any more King George types with the power to take advantage of them. Their idea changed the world: Regular folks like farmers, carpenters, and bartenders would be elected for a short time, a term of two years, to represent their neighbors in the House of Representatives. This assembly would have the power to check the activities of Senators—the richer, better educated types who had six-year terms—and the president as well. In short, the House was designed to express the true voice of everyday Americans.

The British tyranny left our Founding Fathers with another resolve: to guarantee the right of the citizens of this new country to arm themselves. That right, of course, is at the root of today's gun control controversy more than two centuries later. The right to bear arms was intended to prevent local government tyranny and to make military coups d'état less likely. Again, our system of government was founded to include a healthy suspicion of authority and superior firepower.

◻

But that was then. Now, American politics has evolved into a position of entitlement, and we've let it happen! No longer does Jared take a coach to D.C. for a couple of years and then return to his plow. Today many politicians are "lifers."

And why not? It can be a very sweet deal. Expenses are covered, the salary is six figures (and can be raised just by voting an increase), you get all kinds of vacation time, many trips to exotic places are free because they're "fact-finding," and a busy staff is there to keep you from being hassled by such ordinary needs as fetching your own lunch.

Some politicians are chasing fame, some take advantage of power-hungry women (and men) who deliver sexual favors, and some amass wealth in a variety of ways by using the contacts they make while in office. If they lose an election, they might make millions by becoming lobbyists, since they know from inside how the system works. And the voters? Many times *your* needs are not even visible on the radar screen.

Wait a minute, you say. Doesn't the voter "hire and fire" elected officials? Well, not in the way the Founding Fathers intended. Today the politicians don't court individuals, because elections are won by voting blocs. If you can get labor to like you, you'll get a lot of votes. In certain parts of the country, pander to the right wing and your campaign will prosper. In other places, just get minority leaders on your side and you're in. When more than half the eligible voters stay at home on Election Day, blocs rule!

Plus, it's not hard to buy your way into office, unless you're Steve Forbes. You can squander your inheritance, if that's an option. More likely, you'll be making backroom deals with kindly rich people and corporations for huge amounts of campaign cash. That money, which Lyndon Johnson called "the mother's milk of politics," can be used for TV and radio ads that clog the airwaves with lies, distortions, and false promises.

That's what the 1996 Clinton/Gore campaign finance scandal was all about. The commander in chief opened up the Oval Office to anyone with a wallet. That's why the Democrats could buy up a massive amount of TV time long before the election. For months the ads frightened the bejesus out of the elderly and some minority groups by warning that the mean Republicans would cut benefits. Unnerved already, the target viewers took one look at dour Bob Dole and thought, Yeah, this guy would do it! Dole, who had not yet discovered Viagra, looked so uptight and constricted that nothing he said could counter the other side's scare tactics.

THIS JUST IN: "Since a politician never believes what he says, he is surprised when others believe him."—Charles de Gaulle, president of France, 1959–69

But for one of the most outrageous examples of using money to spread lies, I go back to my own situation living in Nassau County. All politics is local, right? As I mentioned, the Republican machine in power has bankrupted the county government by loading up the payroll with patronage jobs and paying huge salaries across the board. We have some of the highest taxes in America. Swedish officials vacation in Nassau County because they feel right at home.

The situation deteriorated so badly that the county's bond rating dropped into the junk pile. When that Nassau paper was offered for sale, investors snickered. Even boiler-room guys wouldn't touch it. Desperate, County Executive Tom Gulotta brilliantly came up with yet *another* tax: Anyone selling a home now has to pay the county 1 percent of the sales price.

Of course, this is an outrage. Nassau County officials should be thrown into Boston Harbor. (This is not as rough as it sounds; the water's been cleaned up since the Dukakis days.) You'd think these swine would be so embarrassed by such incompetence that they'd resign in disgrace. But noooo.

Instead of admitting that he was responsible for screwing things up, Gulotta bought $2 million of TV ad time. (Excuse me, Tom. Did you forget that the county is *broke?*) The spots feature this blockhead praising himself for slashing the budget and getting things under control. The word "chutzpah" doesn't even begin to cover it. Finally, the voters of Nassau County woke up and the 1 percent "home" tax was repealed.

$\not\square$

VIEWER TIME-OUT: "O'Reilly, you continue to rehash a bizarre ideology. Public opinion differs from you. You spout off without self-reflection or self-doubt. You don't listen, and you don't learn. I am saying to myself, This guy will never evolve." (Pat C., South Freeport, Maine)

Well, to continue spouting off, I believe that Gulotta and people like him think that they can get away with their shenanigans because many Americans refuse to pay attention to anything that isn't *fun*. We want immediate gratification. We don't want to spend time analyzing local budgets and bond issues. Do you think thousands of Nassau County homeowners show up at public meetings about property taxes? They don't—and we all continue to get screwed. In the Old West County Executive Gulotta would have been staked to an anthill.

I trust I'm not being too subtle here. Politicians take your tax dollars and give them to their friends and patrons. What sense does that make? Well, it works because politicians know that you won't notice that you're being stiffed as long as the malls stay open late and your cable system provides twenty-four-hour sports coverage.

In other words, the political climate in the U.S.A. has changed in favor of the crooks and incompetents. How can you guarantee yourself a future in public service? Be willing to sell out for campaign money. And if you're an especially talented liar, you can go very far. Both major parties would be happy to have you join the hustle. (But get in line quick. It's only the first few who will be allowed on board. Any more than that, and the bandits get nervous.)

Am I being too harsh? Maybe. But after watching the Clintonites operate, after listening to the likes of Newt Gingrich and Ross Perot pander and babble and weasel, and after analyzing the continuing stream of vile and dishonest propaganda from both parties, I feel locked in a bitter closet. I've seen too much. I'm suffering from political post-traumatic stress disorder.

Here's how bad things are. This is a column I wrote in the fall of 1999:

THE GREAT CLINTON LEGACY

Even though he's still got a year left in office, the historical legacy of William Jefferson Clinton is already being felt throughout America. That legacy is one never before seen in the United States because, by his conduct, Mr. Clinton has made it possible for certain American citizens to run for President who could never have done that before. The opportunities for playboys, eccentrics, professional wrestlers, sit-com stars and talk show queens are now virtually unlimited in national politics. Mr. Clinton has paved the way for a carnival of Presidential candidates that would make Federico Fellini jump up and applaud. Let's look at the field.

WARREN BEATTY is a playboy actor who for decades spent vast amounts of his time dating beautiful young women. One former model I know told me that Beatty would call her at three in the morning and ask what she was doing. This demonstrates an inquisitive mind of the highest sort. By his own admission, Mr. Beatty is firmly committed to the political philosophy of taxing the population and spending the money on huge government projects—a philosophy that is heartily embraced in the canyons of Bel-Air.

DONALD TRUMP is a playboy casino owner and luxury apartment builder who wrote in *The Wall Street Journal* that America needs him as President. Mr. Trump pointed to his success in building an ice skating rink in New York's Central Park as an example of his political acumen. The Donald also says he'd like to be "The President" in order to lift "the moral climate" of the country. When asked about his own checkered marital past, Mr. Trump said he had never committed "an infidelity," a statement that sent Ivana Trump and Marla Maples scrambling to find a dictionary.

JESSE VENTURA has his eye on the Presidency in 2004 and is shrewdly building a loyal constituency among atheists and armed militia members. Mr. Ventura is smart enough to avoid commenting on situations like Kosovo, where professional wrestling has never been televised. The Minnesota governor is also banging the drum on drug legalization and labor unions for prostitutes, two cutting-edge issues that threaten to overtake the decline of public education in the national discourse. Keep your eye on the governor.

Candidate Donald Trump has nominated Oprah Winfrey as Vice President, but the talk show hostess is "not interested at this time." However, she is "leaving the door open." This, of course, is terrific news, although I'm not exactly sure why. Word is that Oprah is such a good negotiator that she may be able to continue doing her program *and* be V.P. at the same time. This would be great for President Trump, who could simultaneously discuss policy and his relationships with many beautiful women "on the next Oprah."

CYBILL SHEPHERD has thrown her gown into the ring and is running on a platform that is "supportive to women's rights" and to good time slots for female sit-com stars. She is adamantly opposed to cable and to limelight-hogging co-stars like Bruce Willis. Ms. Shepherd has not yet defined her platform, but her publicist hints it will include installing a hair salon next to the Oval Office.

ROSS PEROT has just about given up his dream of becoming President but is still making charts and graphs showing how much time he spoke on "The Larry King Show" as opposed to how much time Larry spoke. Larry's deficit is tremendous so Perot has come up with a plan that would restore King's dignity while at the same time allowing Perot unlimited appearances to spout his whacked-out philosophies. Perot will unveil the plan when he next appears on the King program.

So, thank you, President Clinton. The way you have conducted yourself as President over the past seven years has changed the Presidential landscape and has made it possible for a different kind of American to seek the highest office in the land. Another proud Clintonian accomplishment, and all I can say is: Monica in 2008!

☐

VIEWER TIME-OUT: "Dear Mr. O'Reilly: A professional journalist never uses the word 'I.' Have you ever counted how many times you do that? No one could ever assert you are professional. You are synonymous with a migraine! Your attacks on Attorney General Reno, Hazel O'Leary, and our First Lady—three enormously intelligent, gifted women—suggest that you are emasculated by strong women. In closing, I would like to say that you perform a great injustice to our First Amendment." (Delphia M., Pittsburgh, Pennsylvania)

To be fair, there are some politicians out there who are sincerely interested in helping people. But how can you tell? As they say in Hollywood and on Madison Avenue, sincerity is such an easy thing to fake.

Our elected officials don't even have to try it on their own. Their spin doctors and image-makers, working on the payroll that we pay for, show them how. Yes, you've hired the likes of Dick Morris, Ed Rollins, Mike Deaver, and Tony Coehlo to coach our leaders in how to seem sincere to us. We're paying to be conned! And, as the Clinton White House has demonstrated time and again, the pros can spin *anything*.

We are living in very dangerous political times.

So what can you do? And why should you care? Good questions both. You should care because, ultimately, the horrible decisions made by our politicians will ricochet and dent your pocketbook. Thanks to a Republican White House and a Democratic Congress, you and I paid billions to bail out the dullards and crooks responsible for the savings and loan mess. Most of the sinkholes dug by both parties are not quite that large, but they do add up—and they keep coming.

RIDICULOUS NOTE: Clinton vetoed a tax cut, claiming it would endanger "saving Social Security," the so-called cornerstone of his historical legacy. Then he signed a budget that spent federal money on projects like the following:

- $230,000 for a study of the sex habits of houseflies.

- $27,000 for a study of why prisoners want to escape.

- $4,000,000 (that's right: six zeros) to distribute info on the correct way to cut toenails. To quote Dave Barry, "I am not making this up."

- $100,000 to find out why Americans don't really like beets

Now, because I am a concerned American, I will give the government the following information for free:

- Houseflies mate when no one is looking.

- Prisoners don't like prison.

- Toenails should be cut with a toenail clipper every week.

- Beets don't taste good.

I've just saved the nation $4,357,000. Easy. Where's my medal, Mr. Clinton?

If you do care about the nonsense, what can you do? Well, you have to pay attention to what's going on at all levels of government, and you have to speak up. Make time to fight a guerrilla war against dishonesty, sleaziness, and incompetence. Write these people letters and e-mails. Telephone their offices.

And don't go it alone. There's political power in numbers. Politicians may be sloppy about spending barrels of money, but they fear negative publicity. Get your friends involved in the action. Form political "watchdog" clubs. Have some fun with the whole thing, because that will help keep you going. Imagine what would happen if everyone in the country got really teed off when some sleazeball pol voted himself a big raise or supported a stupid, wasteful program. For sure, you'd see a much more responsible Congress.

But this is real life, not some feel-good movie. When Mr. (or Mrs. Smith) goes to Washington, the reformer often becomes the "go-along kid." And the voters—charter members of the video-game and sports channel brigade—are never going to participate actively in the political process.

But *you* are different. You have brains and dignity. If you didn't, you wouldn't be reading this book! So you have no excuse not to harass your least favorite, dopiest politicians. Trust me on this: You will feel better after writing a well-thought-out letter to some pol who's screwing up. (Keep it pithy, as I tell viewers who want to write my show. The harder you work to make your point concisely, the more effective it will be.) And keep copies of your correspondence. They will evolve into your own personal historical diary, which will be a lot of fun to read again years from now.

🖵

The politician I most admire is Abraham Lincoln. The reason is simple: A deeply kind human being, he showed his concern for everyday Americans while trying to lead this country through its greatest crisis so far. Failure to act wisely and courageously at the height of the Civil War would have destroyed the nation that was founded at such risk barely a hundred years before.

Even so, Lincoln devoted one day a week to reading mail from the people and answering with notes on the reverse side of the page. Not surprisingly, many letters were written to seek jobs or other favors. The president often tried to help these ordinary people, even though they were strangers to the corridors of power and influence. (He did not simply add their names and addresses to a campaign solicitation list. Today, if you write to the Clinton White House, computerized mailings and dinnertime phone calls will dog you to the grave.)

I have seen a number of these letters from mothers who wanted to visit their wounded sons, from older men who needed work to support their families after all the young relatives had gone to war, and from children worried about their fathers in uniform. Lincoln's replies are amazingly compassionate. He reveals himself as a great man who used determination and humility to save the Union. Neither vain nor vengeful, he had no spin guys or bagmen and took no money. Because he loved his country, he suffered greatly at the loss of life on both sides of the conflict. Despite the tremendous personal stress and the nationwide chaos, Lincoln still helped individuals while working to keep the country whole. Where are today's Honest Abes?

Perhaps we should ask Bob Packwood or Ted Kennedy, or the descendants of Richard Nixon and Spiro Agnew. Politics is now a job, not a service. Some people will do almost anything to keep their jobs. Thus, the political landscape in America has become insulated and self-centered.

THIS JUST IN: "If America ever passes out as a great nation, we ought to put on our tombstone: America died from a delusion she had Moral Leadership." —Will Rogers

BACKUP STATS: As of April 2000, George W. Bush had raised at least $73 million for his run for the presidency. At his first fund-raising event a year before, 150 D.C. lobbyists promised to raise $25,000 apiece. Al Gore, his opponent, could rally only 20 $25,000-a-pop loyalists at his first fundraiser, but he wasn't to be counted out, by any means. Although he had raised only a total of $37 million by April 2000, that topped the entire Clinton/Gore take in 1996 by $9 million. Besides, by that time Bush had spent most of his funds to defeat John McCain. We would all be hearing from both of those boys as the campaign progressed.

Despite the decline in political leadership, however, I continue to believe that there is no greater country than America. But it was ordinary Americans who overcame tremendous hardships to make the United

States the most powerful and well respected nation on earth. If only our politicians reflected the courage and self-sacrifice displayed by our military throughout the twentieth century, we'd really have something.

Unfortunately something happens to many of those who achieve great power. Lyndon Johnson knew that the situation in Vietnam was out of control, but he continued to send young Americans to their deaths for fear of being the first president in U.S. history to lose a war. His ego became more important than the lives of those men and women whose names are now engraved on a black stone wall in Washington. John F. Kennedy, his predecessor, was well aware that his father, Joe, made deals with organized crime, but he never said a word publicly: Mob-controlled union votes put him in office. Richard Nixon knew that his "plumbers" were breaking laws, and he encouraged them. Bill Clinton had to realize that seventy White House visits by low-level businessman Johnny Chung were way beyond unusual (that's a lot of subway rides), but he wanted the money that the guy was bringing to Democrats. The door was always open, and the president didn't care a fig about where the cash was coming from.

In each of those examples, a president put his own desire for power above the well-being of the country. Truth be told, we will never know the true extent of the unprincipled dealing behind the elections of our most powerful politicians. Yes, we need campaign reform in America, but not just in the finance area.

Why not a law against lying in *any* campaign advertisement or literature? If a candidate puts out something that he or she knows to be false, then prosecution should follow in a federal court.

Why not have the FBI establish an election unit to see that campaigns are kept honest both financially and editorially? Too many crooks have bought their way into office. This has got to change. Since the bastards won't police themselves (after all, who is pure enough to cast the first stone?), we should demand that law enforcement police them.

Finally it makes me queasy to see big-time politicians rake in the money after they leave office. Former president Reagan's friends got together and bought him a luxurious house in Bel-Air, the swankiest neighborhood in the Beverly Hills area, when his term ended in 1988. He and Nancy should have bought their own house. They had to know that ex-president Harry Truman returned to his modest family house in Independence, Missouri, where he got up every morning to stoke the basement furnace himself. Ex-president Gerald Ford has made millions by sitting on corporate boards and appearing as a greeter at such momentous events as shopping-center openings. That's only part of the reason a regular guy from Grand Rapids, Michigan, has been able to amass a fortune and secure expensive real estate in Vail and Palm Springs, after spending almost his entire working life in public service. Ex-president Bush was paid so much for a speech in Japan that the yen was probably weakened. The Clintons . . . Well, don't get me started. Let's just sit back and watch the cash roll in.

All politicians should emulate Jimmy Carter and Michael Dukakis. Carter lives in comfort, mostly because of his best-selling books, but he spends much of his time doing charity work. Dukakis, who lives very modestly in a Boston suburb, teaches college. I don't begrudge politicians their books or paid lectures. The marketplace is competitive.

But sucking dollars out of powerful corporations when they've left office sends a terrible message of possible collusion and influence buying. Washington is filled with ex-pols making big dollars off people for whom they rendered favors while in office. There's not a law on the books to halt this revolving door. But the whole thing is flat-out wrong.

Strangely, many Americans aren't outraged by the money bit. Why? Because all they care about is the ideology of their elected officials. If the politician echoes their beliefs about abortion or welfare, gun control or the environment, that's all that matters to them.

LET'S STOW THAT ATTITUDE! We should examine the *person* first, then scrutinize the platform. Don't let ideology blind you to the scams. America desperately needs good, honest people in office, not poll-driven, ruthless automatons who change their positions with the seasons. Read my lips: "These people will say anything." To repeat: Look closely at the person, and be skeptical about the rhetoric.

That's a good rule for every issue, but especially for the hot-button issues: Probably no issue, as I'm about to explain in the next chapter, arouses so much anger and confusion in America today as race.

13. THE RACE factor

NOTE TO AL SHARPTON AND DAVID DUKE, LOUIS FARRAKHAN AND THE GRAND WIZARD OF WHATEVER: You are demagogues who use race as a crutch to bring attention to yourselves. You are deceiving your followers, who should stop paying attention to you. True Americans value fairness and honesty. To them, skin color doesn't matter. But you guys and a lot of others thrive on stirring up racism. That's not American. That's not right.

TALKING POINT: Do I really believe that clear-thinking Americans don't care what color or ethnicity you are? Yes, I do. Clear-thinking Americans care only how you treat them as individuals.

Don't ask me what percentage of Americans is "clear-thinking," however. Racism still exists, as we all know. Not since the 1940s have whites sent postcard pictures of lynchings or so-called Negro barbecues to their friends. Since the 1960s we no longer have legally segregated bathrooms, hotels, and restaurants throughout the South. The legal obstacles set up specifically to prevent black citizens from voting have been struck down at last. More and more blacks are working their way into the middle class. Black elected officials run major cities, police departments, and even a few corporations. Some of the most admired and beloved actors, musicians, and sports figures in America are black.

But while this may be progress, it is not the end of the story yet. We have to keep working on seeing the person, not the skin color. There are racist attitudes still at play out there in America. If not, some of the worst racist demagogues wouldn't be seen so often on the nightly news. And no race has a monopoly on racism.

Whites hating blacks, blacks hating whites—that's only the beginning. Cross the street in some neighborhoods, and you can be beat to a pulp for being East Indian or Mexican or Vietnamese. What's this all about?

As a kid in the 1960s, I encountered white racism, but I could never understand where it was coming from. I mean, my neighborhood in Levittown was *entirely* white. Yet some of my friends ran around saying nasty things about black people. Why did they think these things when we didn't even *know* anyone black?

Well, naturally, I asked them that question. Never got an answer that made any sense. They just shot back something stupid that reflected, I knew, what their stupid parents were saying at home.

But what about Willie Mays, the fantastic New York and San Francisco Giants outfielder? Voted the most valuable National League player in 1954 and 1965, he was my childhood idol. I treasured his autographed photo, and it hangs in my house today. Mays was black, of course, but my friends and I didn't think about that. We all liked him much better than we did Mickey Mantle, the white New York Yankees superstar.

Yet some of the same kids who cheered wildly for Mays said some of the worst things about blacks in general. It made no sense. Now, I know that millions of American kids had to think about these contradictions long before I did, because racial differences were part of everyday life. But we kids in Levittown had no face-to-face experience to draw upon.

Mays is still alive after racking up 660 home runs in his career. Some of the prejudices I learned about as a kid are also alive regrettably.

THIS JUST IN: "It is never too late to give up our prejudices." —Henry David Thoreau, American author of *Walden*

¤

The attitudes of my friends' parents came, I think, from the history of our lily-white town. Levittown was populated in the 1950s mostly by whites who fled Brooklyn after World War II. This sudden exodus was caused by evil real estate agents. They began buying up small apartment houses and moving black families in. This was not an enlightened plan to promote integration and harmony among the races. They knew that many Irish,

Italian, and Jewish families would succumb to prejudice—and to well-placed rumors—by selling their row houses in a panic.

That's how "blockbusting" began. Real estate prices dropped drastically in many working-class sections of Brooklyn. The real estate people, the blockbusters themselves, snapped up the houses cheap. Then they subdivided them, squeezing two black families into a one-family structure. One thing led to another, and the quality of some neighborhoods spiraled downward fast. The agents, now acting as landlords, made a killing on rent but provided little maintenance.

I know what I'm talking about because my family experienced it. My grandfather meticulously maintained his home on West Street in Brooklyn because he owned it. The black families coming into these areas usually could not afford to own. As renters, they reasonably expected their landlords to be responsible for maintenance and repairs. Few of these landlords bothered. Maintenance cuts into profits.

Naturally, many blocks owned by the blockbusters began to deteriorate. Some whites blamed the black renters for this decline, but they were looking only at the surface. The slums had been created by the blockbusters, and they were never really held accountable. Setting one race against another, they used fear and prejudice to make money, not caring that well-kept, peaceful neighborhoods were destroyed.

THIS JUST IN: "We didn't all come over on the same ship, but we're all in the same boat." —Bernard Baruch, U.S. financier and "adviser to presidents"

My parents never said a bad thing about black people, or about any racial group. I realize now what a great gift this attitude was to my sister and me. My grandmother was a very different story: She was terrified of all black people. This was even more irrational than it would usually be, because there was not a single black person living anywhere in her neighborhood. (My grandmother was not an intellectual giant.) And because she was afraid, and fear leads to loathing, she was extremely prejudiced.

At a very early age I figured out that blacks in America had it much rougher than whites. Again, many millions of kids had more opportunity to see this for themselves and begin to understand it sooner than I did, but Levittown was something of an enclave. Still, if the dolts among my companions could be so hateful without a reason, it made sense that the black path had to be difficult. As Bill Cosby said, "If a white man falls off a chair drunk, it's just a drunk. If a Negro does, it's the whole damn Negro race."

I got into a number of fights after telling white guys to shut up about blacks. Now, I'm not patting myself on the back here as some kind of hero. I wasn't defending anyone I knew; I was just teed off, as I am today, at mind-boggling stupidity. I was less courageous than impatient: Dolts get me steamed, whatever the issue.

I still didn't know any blacks. That would not change until I went to college. And the picture there was complicated by changing times and attitudes—not always for the better.

ㅁ

When I played football at Marist College, there were four blacks on the team. The two I got to know pretty well were funny guys, very quick with the snappy one-liners. We had good times, but I could see that they were very conscious of being outnumbered by whites at the school. Also, the other black students pressured them to separate themselves as much as possible. All of the blacks clustered together in the cafeteria and lived together in the dorms. It wasn't exactly Black Power, but it did look like a show of solidarity. After all, when anyone organizes an "Us," then everyone else becomes "Them." This behavior caused occasional friction with some of the white football players, who were the kind of jocks who believed that teammates should stick together off the field as well.

At the same time, it was obvious that the white majority at the college was often self-conscious around our small black minority. This was the height of the 1960s: Many whites wanted to have black friends, just because that was considered cool at the time. Of course, that was a kind of insulting objectification, even if it was well intended. Liking someone because he's black is not as bad as hating him for that reason, but it ignores his individuality just as much. Our black students recognized these overtures of friendship for what they were. They'd spent a lifetime reading the signs.

So the result of all this groupthink on both sides was an embarrassing uneasiness in most black-white social encounters. Militant blacks pressured their peers not to get too close to whites, and self-conscious whites patronized blacks. The best encounters were merely awkward, but the worst could get really tense.

I was very aware of these events and troubled by them. In addition to playing football, I was writing a column for the campus newspaper. I wasn't fully formed as a journalist, but when I look back at some of my writing then, it's surprising how much of the Bill O'Reilly voice of today is already there. (Sort of like how the young Bill Clinton writing that letter to weasel out of the draft sounds pretty much like the President Clinton you heard in the federal grand jury testimony.)

Anyway, the campus rumor mill reported that one white female teacher was so "sensitive" to blacks that any black student who enrolled in her class was guaranteed at least a B+. Actually several of her white colleagues were also known to make it easy for blacks to succeed in their classes, but she had become notorious among white and black students alike.

As it happened, I took her class because of her specialty, which filled out my academic requirements. On the first day, a black guy named Nate sauntered in and sat down right next to me. I knew who he was and he was definitely not a good citizen. In fact, Nate was a campus "badass," well known and in some quarters feared for his intimidating behavior and his trafficking in drugs. He gave me his patented "Nate look," a kind of scowl, and that was the extent of our relationship. Because Nate never reappeared. He cut the entire semester after that first class.

But when grades were handed out at the end of the term, as I heard on the grapevine, Nate had somehow garnered a B from this unusually understanding teacher. I guess he missed the + because he had so openly done *bupkus*. Like many other students who actually turned in the work and showed up for class most of the time, I also got a B from the woman.

Ever the journalist, I sought out Nate to ask him about his rumored grade.

"Shiiittt, that jive-ass course don't mean nothin' to me," he said. "So I got a B . . . You got a problem with that?"

Well, yes, Nate, I did. My next newspaper column explained this situation and suggested that this teacher was guilty of reverse racism. Is the pen still mightier than the sword? You bet. When that column got passed around the dorms, all hell broke loose on campus. This was my first real experience with racial politics—a good preparation for dealing with the likes of Al Sharpton and David Duke—and it was not pleasant.

Attacks on me were personal. While some kids thought I was wrong and others that I was just stupid, there were others who accused me of being racist, just for bringing up the subject. Once that charge is raised, it's a hard one to beat. In fact, in the heat of the incident I was called every racial name in the book, and some the book never heard of. Boy, did I get an education, and it wasn't in the classroom. (Of course, my column not only embarrassed the teacher; it also brought in question every decent grade actually *earned* by a black student in that history class. But that was *her* fault, not mine.)

In the end, though, I won the battle. Too many people on campus knew what was going on. Now that it was out in the open, the teacher could not defend Nate's grade. Quite unrelated to this incident, Nate later dropped out of college. Soon afterward he murdered a policeman.

⌗

Racism is very complicated and constantly evolving. I'm not going to cover the whole subject in this brief chapter, but neither have most of the long and long-winded books written in the last few years. We don't need any more studies or sermons or White House conferences. We need good intentions and common sense.

One thing is certain: Racism in America cuts both ways. Whenever a person of one race factors in skin or ethnicity or religion to make a decision about another human being, the racist card is being played. And it happens all the time.

Take this story. In October 1999 a group of Ku Klux Klan members came to New York City to demonstrate for God only knows what. The excuse doesn't matter. These white racist losers were just after publicity, and, of course, the media gave it to them. After saturation coverage before the event, about six thousand demonstrators showed up to confront the KKK. There were exactly twelve of them on hand. Hundreds of cops had to be assigned to guard this little racist band, and some of the demonstrators attacked the cops. Very nice all around.

A few months earlier the black racist Khalid Muhammed held his annual Million Youth March, also in New York City. And again, the media provided breathless reporting in the days before the event. On the day itself the march was short about 995,000 youths, but few demonstrators showed up to heckle Khalid.

So here's my question: Why didn't the six thousand who protested against the racist KKK also demonstrate against racist Khalid? Racism is racism: Every form of it has to be condemned.

I confronted Congressman Jerrold Nadler of New York with that opinion. Nadler joined the anti-Klan demonstrators but made no public comment about Khalid Muhammed's march.

"Interesting question," he replied.

Yeah, Congressman, it is.

What we need in America, I think, is equal-opportunity demonstrators.

✣

But until that happens, can we just forget the past and get on with the future? You'd have to be illiterate not to know that American Indians and blacks got a really bad deal historically. The Chinese, Mexicans, and, yes, the Irish and Italians weren't met by welcome wagons when they got off the boat, either. Everyone has had to fight for fair treatment, and the fighting is not over yet.

But it doesn't do anyone any good to hang on to resentment of past wrongs. In fact, this is also a racist point of view and will hurt you big-time in America. Whites generally control the power and the economy. That may not be fair, but that's the way it is. To confront the white power structure with historical inequities is a waste of time. They are in the majority, okay? They don't want to hear your complaints about the facts of life. You might be labeled a malcontent, or worse.

No, you are not going to change the history that produced you. Forget it. Enjoy your life, and create a better future for your children than your ancestors could possibly imagine. Help as many people of all races as you can. Be true to yourself, not to some political fad that suffocates your individualism by emphasizing racial, ethnic, or religious background. In short, chuck the racial filter.

THIS JUST IN: "I think we Negro Americans have just as many beautiful people in mind and body, as well as skin, as any other group—and that we have just as many stinkers as any other group." —Thurgood Marshall, U.S. Supreme Court justice

I know some of you are thinking that it's *easy* for a white guy like me to say, "Foget the past injustices." Well, maybe a little easi*er*. But think back to Chapter 1, which was about the class system in America.

Of course, I didn't have it nearly as tough as I would have as a black, Indian, or Hispanic. But believe me, I did lose career opportunities at the network news level because I was not from the upper classes. I'm not imagining this. On a regular basis, well-connected people from wealthy backgrounds were promoted ahead of me, even though they had less talent. What did I do? I got angry—and worked harder than they ever would or could.

That's why I now make more money and have more power than most of those "legacies." And that's why my accomplishments are so satisfying: I overcame the class *dis*advantage. No one can say that I was handed anything because of who my father was. Often, no one can say that the entitled guy lives up to his privileged position. You know, maybe having to work for something is a privilege, too, in the long run.

So join me in looking at classism and racism as challenges to be overcome, not as obstacles to be used as excuses for not doing our best.

Then when you do make it, help others who have had to face the same challenges you met.

And if you can't go along with me, if you still think that skin color matters in understanding another human being or in making a good life for yourself, I'll say a prayer for you. I mean that . . .

Which brings me to the only issue in America that is perhaps touchier than race in some parts of the country: religion.

14. THE
RELIGION factor

TALKING POINT: St. Peter was leading a group of new arrivals on their first tour of Heaven. Suddenly he stopped and put his finger to his mouth. "Shhh," he whispered. "We can't make a sound when we walk by this room. Remember that." When they passed out of hearing range, one of the new souls asked why. "Because," the former fisherman explained, "that room is full of Southern Baptists, and they think they're the only ones up here."

I've found out that any remark I make about religion is likely to make some viewer steaming mad. And the fundamentalists really hate it when I say something like this: The most important thing I can say about religion is that it's a good thing for all of us to have. It doesn't matter what you believe—as long as you believe in *something*.

VIEWER TIME-OUT: "Bill, you poor, misguided fool. If you haven't yet accepted Jesus Christ as your personal savior, even you are going to Hell." (Sheryl L., Buena Park, California)

Well, Sheryl, my religion is Roman Catholicism. I go to church, but I'm an independent thinker. For me, religion is primarily a way to examine my conscience and spend some time thinking about things more important than my own existence.

For a TV guy, this is very hard. Those of us in the media are often self-absorbed hedonists. Jesus would probably have put us TV types right up there with the tax collectors.

But all of us can have spiritual lives without the threat of eternal damnation; however, we have to work at it. I'm reminded of a former girlfriend, the most unspiritual human being I've ever known even though she had been raised as a strict Protestant. She was good-looking but unbelievably self-involved. Far from denying it, she cheerfully admitted that her every waking moment was spent thinking about herself and what she could get in the way of goods and services that particular day.

Amazed by this shallowness, I once asked, "Is there anything you believe in besides having a good time?"

"Why, I believe in nature," she replied.

Quite a commitment of the spirit. By the way, I dated this woman solely because I was attracted to her looks. You're right. That was very shallow of me—and not at all spiritual.

RIDICULOUS NOTE: Margaret Fuller, considered the most intellectual woman in America in the nineteenth century, once exclaimed, "I accept the universe!" Thomas Carlyle, the British writer, muttered back, "She damned well better."

I have always believed that it takes more faith *not* to believe in God than it does to embrace a deity. As just about everyone outside Hollywood knows, there is an order to the universe. The tide comes in, the tide goes out. The sun comes up, the sun goes down (I know, I know, it only looks that way). Seasons change, people do not.

Does science explain these things? Not to me.

Sure, you can tell me that the earth is about 4.5 billion years old and the universe measures 15 to 18 billion light-years across. You can explain—although scientists haven't done so yet—how all of the forces in the universe work together to keep it ticking. But those answers will never satisfy the soul or spirit or whatever it is inside us that keeps asking, Why? and What does it all *mean?*

And then there's the greatest mystery of all: Why do human beings foul up almost everything beyond belief?

Even if there is no God or Heaven or Hell, I still believe religion is a positive force. The time I spend in church thinking about spiritual things is still time very well spent. Hearing people preach about helping others and being honest is refreshing and uplifting. The traditions of Roman

Catholicism are magnificent, especially the Christmas and Easter pageantry that has been in place for almost two millennia. And my religion is comforting, if you factor out some of the ridiculous stuff that sometimes rolls off the tongues of overzealous clerics.

Your religion should be comforting as well, but that's not always the case, I know. Sometimes people use their religion as a weapon to denigrate those who do not share the same faith. This is wrong, and it is dangerous.

☐

In the fall of 1999 we ran a story on *The O'Reilly Factor* about some Southern Baptists who were trying to convert Jews. Predictably some Jews didn't like this activity at all. My guest, a Baptist pastor, insisted that Jews were bound for Hell if they didn't swing on over to the Baptist side. (Catholics were not in such good shape, either.) I pointed out to him that I didn't think Jesus had this attitude when he engaged with all kinds of people back there in Galilee. The preacher rapped out a few New Testament verses in reply and insisted that Hell was a crowded place.

Could be, preacher. Someday we'll all find out.

By the way, this segment generated thousands of pieces of mail, much of it warning that a vengeful God was gunning for me. A pastor in Lakeland, Florida, was more diplomatic:

> Bill, you say you believe a good person can go to Heaven regardless of religious belief. What is a good person? Who decides?

Not me. That's in God's job description.

But another viewer, Keith S. of Tucson, Arizona, had the best answer I received to the Baptist preacher's warnings:

> Hey, Bill, let me get this straight . . . All of the innocent men, women and children of the Jewish faith who died so horribly in the Holocaust are in Hell because they did not accept Jesus as the savior? As Woody Allen once said, "This is worse than California."

THIS JUST IN: "I was just thinking, if it is really religion with these nudist colonies, they sure must turn atheists in the wintertime." —Will Rogers

I've always believed that God is merciful but also has a sense of humor. Sorry if this seems puerile to you, but that's the way I see it. As I'll discuss in the next chapter, I believe that all of us have the power to live successful lives. No matter how much sorrow and hardship we experience, we all have the strength necessary to overcome it.

So I do not believe in an angry God who will punish human beings for having different spiritual beliefs from my fundamentalist Christian pen pals. Yes, I believe very strongly that evil will be punished. But God isn't keeping a list and checking it twice. If you try to be kind, responsible, and honest, good things will likely happen to you—both on this earth and in the hereafter, whatever it is.

VIEWER TIME-OUT: "O'Reilly, how did you miss the truth about Jesus Christ? Doing good will not—I repeat, will not—get you into Heaven." (Kim J., Boise, Idaho)

Well, Kim, my political hero agrees with me. Abraham Lincoln once said, "Whatever you are, be a good one."

THIS JUST IN: "Brother, you say there is but one way to worship and serve the Great Spirit. If there is but one religion, why do you white people differ so much about it? Why do not all agree, as you can all read the book?" —Chief Red Jacket to Christian missionaries, 1805

☐

Think back on your life. Each time things got really, really bad, didn't something happen to turn it all around?

My own life could be pictured like a chart. After every disaster, every unhappiness, something good occurred that allowed me to keep my life flowing in a positive way. Sometimes the good things took their own sweet time, but they always arrived—and usually from right out of nowhere.

We all make mistakes. We all have bad things that happen to us that are completely out of our control. But reflect on this: as in Nature, there is a balance. The positive will neutralize the negative almost every time, unless the person is self-destructive and refuses to accept the good things that come along and the talents he or she is born with.

I know I'm starting to sound like a New Age lemming here, but I do believe in the balance. I also believe in evil.

Over the course of my twenty-five years in journalism I have seen some *really* bad things. The worst involved child abuse. I am one of the few people on earth who interviewed Joel Steinberg. This is the monster who tortured and killed his little daughter in perhaps the most infamous case of child murder New York City has ever seen. The man is a true psychopath. He has no feelings for anyone other than himself. Sitting across from him, I actually felt his evil affecting me. It was all I could do to restrain myself from beating him senseless. Although he'll never get out of prison, I have to believe there's another punishment awaiting Steinberg after he leaves the earth.

Evil is a constant presence throughout the world. I've seen soldiers gun down unarmed civilians in Latin America, Irish terrorists kill and maim their fellow citizens in Belfast with bombs, and heroin addicts with AIDS knowingly share needles with other addicts without telling them about the infection. Evil.

Once, I stood in the cellar of an abandoned Italian church that had been used by Satanists in rituals that included murder. The feeling of evil permeated the room. I had never felt anything like it.

But then I felt it again in Africa at Victoria Falls in Zambia. I stood where human sacrifice was practiced years before by tribes native to the area. Victims were tossed off the cliff into the thundering falls. I got out of there quick.

So I know that true, unrepentant evil exists. And I firmly believe it will be punished, just as good will be rewarded. That is part of the order of the universe, if we only take the time to recognize it.

RIDICULOUS NOTE: But you don't want to imagine evil where it does not exist. The Reverend Joe Chambers, who runs the Paw Creek Ministries in Charlotte, North Carolina, recently warned his flock that Barney the dinosaur is an agent of Satan and Pokémon is also lined up with the devil. The Power Rangers, Pocahontas, and the Cabbage Patch Dolls cannot be trusted, either. The reverend is a tad bit soft on the specifics of how these playthings are leading kids straight to Hell, but I have to admit, Barney has been looking a little shifty lately.

My last word on religion is a practical one based on timeless logic: If you live your life subject to the rules of Judeo-Christian tradition (or Buddhist, Islamic, or another religious tradition), then you will do more good than harm on this earth. You will love your neighbor and help other people out. You will not do things that hurt others or yourself.

So, if everyone was religious, wouldn't the world be a much better place in which to live? Of course it would. And if there is no God at the end of it all, what does it matter? You're in the ground or scattered to the winds. If the deity is a fraud, you won't possibly care. You're gone.

But while you're still here, the real trick is to live a successful, positive life. And so we march on to the next chapter to talk about that most elusive of goals: true success.

15. THE SUCCESS factor

TALKING POINT: There is only one rule of success that really counts in the long run: Success is measured by how many people on this earth *respect* you.

We all know what respect is (though I don't mind hearing Aretha remind me in that song again and again). Respect is the state of being regarded with honor or esteem. All the money and fame and babes in the world can't beat respect. If the majority of the people who really know you respect you, you have achieved success. That's the truth.

But this is not an easy standard. It's not easy to achieve the kind of success and respect I'm talking about. It requires a consistency of behavior that is truly *impressive*. It requires that you treat others in an honest and caring way. When someone else feels that you are not fair, or that you are putting your own welfare ahead of his, you will not be respected.

The first step to gaining respect is pretty difficult: *Always do what you say you are going to do.* When you say that you are going to call someone back, you have to call that person back. When you promise to deliver a favor or perform a service, you must come through.

Have I suddenly started writing in Esperanto here? You look as if I've lost it, because you know from experience that very few Americans adhere to this code these days. Keeping a promise can get to be a pain in the butt.

How many times has someone failed you and said, "But I *meant* to." Meant to, tried to, etc., doesn't cut it. We Americans are always shooting our mouths off about what we are going to do. But how many of us follow through?

Not many, but you can be one of the exceptions to the rule. When you discipline yourself to fulfill every one of your commitments—no matter how insignificant—you will be respected. And if you are able to combine this responsibility with sincere interest in those with whom you interact, well, you will be *revered*.

If this sounds like fairly simple advice, I repeat: It's more difficult than it sounds.

Achieving the kind of success I'm talking about is harder in America than anywhere else because our countrymen adore wealth, power, and fame. These are the enemies of true success and respect: The self-absorption that usually accompanies materialism and fame will destroy any chance of relating well with others. A strong sense of entitlement will not gain you respect. Neither will greed, narcissism, cruelty, manipulation, dishonesty, apathy, callousness, and lack of courtesy.

Some of the celebrities I know and have already talked about are not truly successful, in my definition. They may be among the most famous and powerful people on the planet, but their selfish egotism makes them revolting. They remind me of Ernest Hemingway's line: "Some people, when they hear an echo, think they originated the sound."

This kind of disease doesn't afflict only the superstars. Any material success and career gain can create problems that will overwhelm people in every walk of life. For example, I know many doctors who started out sincerely interested in healing and helping the sick. But then somehow along the way, the Mercedes and the beach house became more important. As the bills for personal expenses and adult toys got bigger, the caring got smaller. Here's a tip: If you walk into a doctor's office and the receptionist asks you about payment before she asks about your medical problem, get the hell out of there. Of course, not all physicians have turned into currency werewolves, but you get my point.

High-paying, high-pressure jobs can change people for the worse. No question about that. If you surrender to that kind of change, forget about it. As the money and prestige come rolling in, you have to make an extra effort to maintain perspective. If you don't, you'll turn into a weasel. Or worse. Remember the guy from *Nightline* I wrote about in Chapter 4? There are millions of guys like that. It's one thing to achieve material success and power in the workplace. Being able to handle it is quite another.

THIS JUST IN: "It's the hardest thing in the world to accept a *little* success and leave it that way." —Marlon Brando

☐

In December 1987 I wrote a piece for *Newsweek* about being a blue-collar guy making good in a white-collar world and about the special problems of that situation. This was during my job as a New York–based correspondent for ABC News. On some weekends I went back to my old Levittown neighborhood to play touch football with some of the guys I'd known growing up.

Here's part of what I wrote:

The drive from my home to my mother's house in Levittown takes about 45 minutes. In the city, I'm in contact with the powerful and prosperous. In the old neighborhood, simplicity rules. The fast lane there can lead to the takeout window at a fast-food place. But for me to feel at ease in both the city and the neighborhood requires more flexibility than I have. I'm amused to see how fashionable it has become for the powerful to exaggerate their humble roots. The truth is that there are vast differences between social classes in America, and attempting to operate in two separate spheres can get complicated.

Returning to the old neighborhood makes me sometimes feel like an outsider—which I now am—someone with money in a prestigious position. People who scolded me 30 years ago for running on their lawns now stop and stare. I am a topic of conversation. I am careful in conversation not to talk about my travels or possessions. Tradition binds me to the neighborhood, but my economic prosperity has stretched the cord. If I let my guard down, unpleasant things can happen.

Recently, I stopped into one of the local saloons and was talking to a woman who has never left the neighborhood. She told me she was applying to night school to get some college credits and then said: "The big problem is I have to write a paper for this one class and I'm not too good at punctuality."

"I think you mean punctuation," I said, immediately wishing I hadn't. She was embarrassed and excused herself a short time later. I felt like a snob.

Even though it isn't easy, I believe I'm benefiting from bouncing between the two classes. I like the perks that money can buy and the stimulation that my job and position provide. But I also enjoy the intimacy that comes from being with people who know me from the ground up. People who accept my emotionalism and direct style, for that is their way as well. People I can talk to without fear that my words will be used against me.

So I am a tweener, and though I bounce between two worlds, I'll always roll towards home base.

I still feel that way today. Material success has brought me a measure of security and comfort. But it has not brought me respect. I have to earn that every day of my life; and it is not easy, because material temptations are everywhere.

♯

Here's something that really surprises me: The more stuff I have, the more stuff I want. And so I looked around and saw that everyone else was the same way. It was not until I had a few things that I noticed how this works. The material stuff is addicting!

Remembering my parents, I try to fight against the "stuff addiction." I drive a "pre-owned" automobile because I got a great deal on it. (It didn't come from my dad's lifelong friend at the used-car lot, but it was the same idea.) I refuse to buy jewelry or trinkets. I don't need expensive toys like Jet Skis or snowblowers. I keep the material things *under control*, and I banish thoughts of them from my brain. Besides, I am very busy. My life doesn't include window-shopping or paging through mail-order catalogs by the pool or jaunts to compact disc stores or Home Depot. These are all invitations to spend money unnecessarily.

And are there many things worse than an out-and-out greedhead? Greed is the destroyer of success. You cannot be successful and greedy at the same time. I'm talking about both material and emotional greed here.

One of my dates (no, I haven't mentioned this one yet) announced to me that she was in favor of "abundance." When I asked her to explain what that meant, she stared at me as if I had just rolled around in peat moss. Her cute nose scrunched up and she said, "Abundance, you know. Lots of *things*. That's what I want."

Okay, at least the woman was honest about it.

But I know what you're thinking. You're thinking, How come O'Reilly kept going out with all these shallow women? Well, I believe I have a good excuse. I was socializing in Manhattan.

(How many book sales did that crack just cost me?)

Anyway, back to the Success Factor: It is achievable. It is right there for you to grab. But you have to want it and want it bad. You have to keep your word and constantly think about the impact you are having on the people with whom you are dealing. You have to *care* about that.

Forget about accumulating power or fame or "abundance." If you like your job, that's the most important thing—not how much money you make.

True success is within us, but it is a slippery branch to grab on to. It has everything to do with fairness and generosity and awareness of the world around you. That's why I kept harping on teaching your children those things in the chapter on the Child Factor. Success is an ongoing project. You never stop earning the respect.

And that brings us to the importance of making and keeping friends. "Keep your friendships in repair," advised Ralph Waldo Emerson. That's still important advice today.

16. THE
FRIENDSHIP `factor`

TALKING POINT: If you have good friends, keep them. If you don't have good friends, get them. True friendship—a rare gift—is never to be taken lightly. Your friends will tell you the truth about yourself—and not charge you $200 an hour. They will tell you the truth, but they will stick by you when the rest of the world turns away.

I know what I'm talking about because I've been lucky enough to keep many of my friends from childhood. I'm talking first grade here. And I'm surprised at how many people I meet who think it's unusual, or even strange, that I'm still in touch with these people. I can't imagine it any other way. We are a living part of each other's life.

For example, I met Greg Heck and John Blasi at St. Brigid's School in 1955. To this day, they still come over to my house to visit (mainly, of course, because they both need constant advice from me in order to operate at anywhere near peak efficiency).

My lifelong friendship with Jeff Cohen and Lou Spoto did not have that kind of academic background. We first met because we lived near each other in Levittown and—why not?—threw rocks at each other. The three of us live in different states now, but we talk every couple of weeks.

But my first memories of friendship go back to when I was age four or something like that. Lenny, Kenny, Genie, and I formed a kind of preschool gang. The four of us ran around our neighborhood completely out of control. We did things that would have shocked the offspring of Attila the Hun. And they would have been better dressed. In my fantasies I imagine flashing some old snapshots of the gang in front of Martha Stewart. She would gag or worse, no question.

I am not exaggerating. Lenny, Kenny, Genie, and Billy were motley fools, a term used here with deadly accuracy. But I've given you the idea already that my parents were very strict, you say. Yeah, and so were my friends' parents. That's why, when we escaped our various houses and the sharp eyes of our parents, we went absolutely nuts. No one was safe around us. Every one of our activities ended in some kind of brawl.

When I look at little kids today, I laugh at the comparison. None of us ever wore bicycle helmets. By age six we were climbing trees without supervision—trees that were *very* tall (and that's not just the way a child remembers it; they *were* tall). We also did stuff like crawl through sewage pipes, light piles of leaves on fire, and hurl snowballs at cars and school buses. We were creative hooligans.

Of course, our parents got wind of some of these antics. I don't remember knowing what the other guys' parents thought of me, but my parents didn't like me hanging around with Lenny and Kenny. They could tolerate Genie, but just barely. Didn't matter. For some reason, I loved those guys. Perhaps because they made me look comparatively sophisticated. Anyway, I've tracked them to this day. Lenny died young from alcoholism. Kenny lives and works in Manhattan. Genie is deeply involved with Scientology. You know where I am. But the three of us still living share something that no one else has. It endures.

So, as you can see, from my earliest days I've made it my mission to keep in touch with friends. As I grew older and got into journalism, the list included people all over the world. I always make the time because each one of these individuals provides me with perspective. Each has known me in a specific stage of my life and can remind me of things I need to remember to keep continuity in my life—where I've been, where I'm going. The only problem with my old friends is that they all want free books.

THIS JUST IN: "One doesn't know, till one is a bit at odds with the world, how much one's friends who believe in one rather generously, mean to one." —D. H. Lawrence

With the obvious exception of my childhood pals, who were thrust upon me by geography, I choose my friends very carefully. And—pay attention here—I make *demands* on them. In some circles this is unheard of, but I insist that my friends be loyal and keep their promises. This is not a one-way street, as I tried to explain in the previous chapter. I work hard to show that I am loyal to my friends, and I keep my promises to them. If they think that I ever let them down, I want to hear about it. And vice versa. Fifty-fifty.

So, with those strict rules of friendship in play, I've lost some good friends along the way. Maybe they thought my expectations were too high. I don't. I expect friends to *be* friends and keep the friendship energy up—even when their circumstances change and their attention goes elsewhere. Some of my old friends wouldn't make the time to keep our friendship alive, and they drifted away. I miss them, even though I'm annoyed by their stupidity.

The sound of wedding bells, of course, is the most common signal that a friendship may be about to break up. My college roommate and I were legendary pals. We loved to play pranks. In 1971 we actually bluffed our way into the afternoon taping of Johnny Carson's *Tonight Show* and played "Stump the Band" with substitute host Joey Bishop. We were not shy. When we lost the game, we demanded a free dinner certificate, anyway. A perspiring Bishop reluctantly gave in and handed over the certificate.

That was only the beginning of the prank. We drove like madmen from the taping in Manhattan back to Marist College in Poughkeepsie, a roughly two-hour drive. We ran around campus betting everyone we saw that we would appear on the Carson show, which would air at 11:30 that evening. The whole campus turned out to watch in the college auditorium. When Bishop told us to stand up, the crowd went into an uproar. We won hundreds of dollars in addition to the dinner extorted from Bishop. You can't make stuff like this up. My roommate and I were immortalized at Marist.

But this lively friendship did not last. He married a controlling woman, who completely shut him down. Now, let me be clear: This situation is *his* fault, not hers. He should have been stronger. In my opinion he lost big-time by surrendering his individuality to an insecure woman.

On this subject there's a Chinese proverb worth remembering, I think: "You can hardly make a friend in a year, but you can lose one in an hour."

I know some people who don't have any friends. Just a spouse and maybe some kids. So everything they do in life is "for the family." I don't trust people like this at all. Anybody who uses "the family" as an excuse to dump friends is, in my opinion, questionable as a fully developed human being.

⌁

Yes, friendships are very fragile, no matter how big and strong and tough you are. Remember Koko the gorilla? He was involved in a study of ape language, and one of the researchers decided to give him a pet kitten. The two animals spent a lot of time together, until one day the kitten ran out into the street and was hit by a car. Koko became depressed and wouldn't eat. I remember when that story came over the wire and how it hit me. Every creature needs friends.

But many Americans think they no longer need their old buds once they acquire a family and a stable lifestyle. Wiser cultures know this is a tremendous mistake. Friends give you a positive outlet, whether you're a man or a woman. Everyone needs a Boys/Girls Night Out. And old friends are important because they are your history; they are part of what you are. You can't grow if you cut yourself off at the root. Friends can help you redefine yourself or help you get through a crisis. Loyal friends will set you straight and lighten you up. If you want to keep your feet on the ground, they are indispensable. That will always be true, no matter how life treats you.

In my travels I've come to believe that there is a huge difference in the meaning of friendship on the East Coast and the West Coast. Of course, I'm speaking generally now, but as a native easterner I marvel at how the word "friendship" is used in Los Angeles, especially. There, friendships come and go at a frightening pace. A "best friend" might be someone you met only three months ago. My East Coast friends who have moved to L.A. are also bewildered. Few have been able to acquire confidants they can really trust.

TALKING POINT: Sorry, Hollywood. Workplace and neighborhood people do not qualify as "best friends" unless you've known them at least three years and they've passed the friendship test—and that means that they've demonstrated loyalty in some way.

Having acquaintances is fine, but you have to know who your true friends are. Only a crisis of some kind will sort that out for sure. Yeah, all the clichés are right. You really never *do* know who's a good friend until the chips are down. When a parent or spouse died, who came through for you? Or when you lost a job, or your kid got in trouble, or you had a bad accident? I bet you were surprised at the ones who failed and the ones who showed up to help.

I've certainly been surprised in this way at certain points in my life. Fewer phrases are more accurate than the expression "fair-weather friend." Today you run into people who say something like, "Well, I was thinking about you, but I just can't stand to be around pain/funerals/hospitals" (or whatever). That's honest. And so is this: If you can't stand the pain, get out of the friendship. You're nothing but dead weight. Did you think that everyone else loves to make hospital visits or go to funerals?

My best friend Joe Spencer was killed in a helicopter crash in 1986. When I spoke at his funeral, I said that Joe, a correspondent for ABC News, had lived his life to the fullest and had accomplished a tremendous amount by age thirty-two. I somehow found the words to describe this guy who had been close to me for eight years. It was not easy. When we worked together as local TV news reporters in Denver, they called us Butch and the Kid after Paul Newman and Robert Redford. Joe was the Kid.

Even now, Joe Spencer is still my friend. And always will be. I have lots of his stuff in my house to remind me of our adventures. We roamed the world together and had a gazillion laughs. I think about him all the time. My life would have been so much poorer if Joe Spencer had not been my friend.

That's the key to friendship. It makes a difference. When you find a true friend, the friendship makes your life so much better. It's a place in the heart that is different from your relationship with a spouse, lover, parents, or children. Friendship is two people who spend time together out of mutual respect and admiration, not out of a sense of obligation. We Americans should take friendship more seriously.

Any success I have in this life has been helped along by my true friends. If they stopped respecting me, I'd know something was going wrong. For a barometric reading of how you are conducting yourself on this planet, take a hard look at what kind of people your friends are and how they respond to you.

Take a good look at your enemies, too. If you don't have enemies, you might not really have friends. My enemies are some of the most dastardly people around. I take comfort in that. Do I hold a grudge? Yeah. That's the other side of staying true to your commitments, I think. I don't wish my enemies ill, but unless they sincerely apologize, I don't forget their transgressions, either.

Summing up, we all *need* good friends. Not people who supply you with cocaine, or tell you only what you want to hear, or are interested in what you *have*. No, you need people who are responsible, loyal, and caring, and who are available and interested in what you are going through. Such people are rare, and like all the rest of us, they will have their own downsides. But if you find a friend who earns your trust, hold on forever. Your life will be richer.

And you'll have someone with whom to share the last three chapters of this book, where I list exactly what is ridiculous, bad, and, yes, *good* in the United States of America. Read on, then dial up your best friend and kick my choices around some. You're going to have scads of ideas of your own for each of the next three chapters.

17. THE
RIDICULOUS `factor`

THIS JUST IN: "Ridiculous: *adj.*, Deserving or inviting ridicule or derisive laughter; absurd, preposterous, laughable . . . Outrageous, scandalous, shameful." —*The New Shorter Oxford English Dictionary*, 1993

I guess that just about covers it. Welcome to the land of no return.

I'm going to talk now about some things that people in earlier times could not have imagined. And about some people whose antics would have got them in major trouble in past centuries. They might even have been exiled off to Australia with the debtors (and that was long before Outback Steakhouses, beach babes, and good tennis courts). They might have been locked in the stocks or submerged on dunking stools by those wacky Puritans. Or they might just have been horsewhipped after the outraged citizenry had had enough.

But our citizenry doesn't get outraged these days. We're a cooler lot. So in the year 2000 all I can do with these scam artists, charlatans, and buffoons is place them on the page of dishonor among the most ridiculous people and things we have to offer in America.

Herewith, then, the most ridiculous among us . . .

◻

PRESIDENT WILLIAM JEFFERSON CLINTON. What a ridiculous waste! Full of promise, intelligence, and charisma, this man will go down in history alongside Warren Harding and Richard Nixon as the most corrupt presidents of the twentieth century. What a legacy for an Arkansas boy with a modest background who made it to the most powerful office in the world. It's not only ridiculous, it's pathetic.

His lying on TV was just the appetizer. In two terms the man created no meaningful legislation, except the Family Leave Act. He was much more effective in subverting the 1996 presidential election by accepting campaign funds from overseas. He also, to give him his due, presided over the greatest looting of military secrets in U.S. history. (In case you weren't paying attention for the past couple of years, the Chinese "did it.") Mr. Clinton's true legacy will become clearer in the next few years, but I promise you he is less likely to become a hero to the American people, when everything is out in the open, than to the Communist Chinese. Forget impeachment. If it were not for the powerful economy, he would have been tarred and feathered long before now.

The much-publicized affair with Monica Lewinsky was trivial (except to Hillary and Chelsea). What was *not* trivial was his lying about the whole thing, which paralyzed the nation's executive and legislative branches for more than a year. This man did tremendous damage to our country, but, I'm sorry to say, many of our fellow citizens were too busy watching *Buffy, the Vampire Slayer* and professional "wrestling" to figure that out. Even so, a Zogby poll taken in January 2000 found that six out of ten Americans feel *ashamed* of their commander in chief.

They should.

He let us down on almost every level. After taking credit for Republican legislative programs that downsized welfare and cut crime rates, he and Congress raised taxes while doing absolutely nothing to deal with the twin vexations of American life today: the health care confusion and the crisis in public education. At the same time, Mr. Clinton allowed Russian thieves to steal American aid money: This was a waste of *billions* of dollars. And U.S. money keeps pouring into foreign lands. The Clinton administration waged a $30-billion-a-year war on drugs that had no coherent strategy—and so, of course, it has had no results. The president has involved us in Haiti and in Somalia. Nothing of lasting value has been accomplished in either place, but billions were thrown at these problem areas.

These are the actions and inactions of a truly ridiculous leader. For that reason, Bill Clinton is sentenced to be the butt of jokes for the rest of his life. This is poetic justice, but I'm still furious: It is not enough justice for this man. We Americans have the right to expect honest, disciplined leadership. We have the right to demand that our tax monies be spent responsibly. And we also deserve a leader who adheres to a decent standard of behavior within the walls of the White House.

No matter what political philosophy you hold, you cannot question that Bill Clinton was awarded the greatest honor in the world—and then he blew it. No pun intended. The next time you see the President, please tell him he is ridiculous—and always will be. I know it, and you know it. Behind that display of self-confidence, he knows it, too. I guarantee you.

◻

ATTORNEY GENERAL JANET RENO. This ridiculous, incompetent woman has been President Clinton's primary "enabler." She clearly obstructed justice in the campaign finance investigation by refusing to appoint a special prosecutor. This decision was made despite the pleas of her top investigator on the case, Charles LaBella, and also the head of the FBI, Louis Freeh. Reno refused even to meet with LaBella to discuss his lengthy report and recommendations on the matter. Instead, she chose to downgrade his concerns, and then she denied him a promised promotion when he went public with his frustrations.

It's true that the American public did not really care about the campaign finance disclosures, but the Department of Justice is not supposed to be poll-driven. When the attorney general of the United States fails to do her sworn duty to uphold the law, that is way beyond ridiculous . . . It is serious. And it gets worse. This woman cut sweet deals with Johnny Chung, Charlie Trie, and others so that they received extremely lenient sentences in exchange for nothing. Nothing! Chung himself told me he was shocked that the department's investigators never followed up on information that he willingly supplied—*without even being asked*. And why didn't they? That's only one of the questions I would like to ask Ms. Reno—*very politely*—except that she refuses to let me interview her, preferring the rough-and-tumble questions Oprah throws at her.

But there's more, much more.

Janet Reno also refused to allow the FBI to wiretap Dr. Wen Ho Lee's computer in the Chinese espionage investigation, despite overwhelming evidence that he was downloading sensitive military information. Lee was subsequently indicted.

She also totally screwed up the Waco case and, according to the former chief of the Drug Enforcement Agency, refused to pursue Mexican drug lords aggressively. And then there's Elian Gonzalez and . . .

These things are ridiculous enough, but the most ridiculous thing of all is that Janet Reno will be allowed to get away with every one of them. That is the justice we can expect from the Clinton Department of Justice. Her tenure as attorney general has been one of the darkest times in the history of American law enforcement.

⚐

The list of the ridiculous only *begins* at the highest levels of government. They are to be found everywhere in our country:

LARRY FLYNT. The only thing more ridiculous than the smutmeister himself is that Hollywood decided to glorify him in a movie as a "defender of free speech rights." This guy has piled up millions by hawking violent, degrading images of women, but somehow he became a hero to the "socially concerned" film community. Well, I'm all for free speech. I'm going to take advantage of it here: Larry Flynt is the *worst* America has to offer. He brings new meaning to the word "degenerate." There is no excuse for this man and his career. "Ridiculous" doesn't even begin to cover it.

CHARLES MANSON. If you're a viewer of my show, you know that I argue against capital punishment. For Charlie, I could make an exception. Is it sane to allow this vile murderer to be sitting around in a fairly comfortable northern California detention facility? What good does he do for society, except give TV interviews to Geraldo? Manson and others like him (thank God, they're few) should be slapped with sentences of hard labor for their crimes. And they should do their time in a federal detention center in Alaska. That just might wipe the stupid and ridiculous grin off this monster's face once and for all.

"SOUTH PARK," THE MOVIE. Hollywood again. This is probably the most ridiculous flick I've ever sat through. If you missed it, try to imagine a song-filled cartoon that features cute little kids cursing in vile and creative ways. I'm not kidding. That's what it is. Some critics called it "brilliant." I call it "subversive," pure and simple. The filmmakers knew, of course, that kids were going to try to see this R-rated movie, but they didn't care. No adult in his right mind would want to see it. Despite the critics and the hype, which included an Oscar nomination for one of its songs, *South Park* didn't make much money. I hope that's because levelheaded people know what's ridiculous and what isn't.

NBA TICKET PRICES. If you live in the American heartland, you're going to have a hard time believing this, but it's the truth: To see an NBA game in New York or Los Angeles, you will have to shell out more than $200 apiece for tickets, parking, and a few eats. And you will not be sitting down in front with Spike Lee or Jack Nicholson. In fact, your seats will not even be good, and you may be in danger of getting altitude sickness. This is bad for the sport, and it is very ridiculous.

SEX TONICS. With the success of the drug Viagra (thank you, Bob Dole), we now have access to scores of potions designed to make you a sex-crazed caveman or cavewoman. The come-on: Just take a little pill or sip a bit of some concoction and—*zooooooooom!*—you turn into Bill Clinton in full grope mode. You can choose prescription, over-the-counter, mail-order, e-mail account, organic product, and so on. Now, if you want to spend your money on this stuff, go ahead—it's none of my business. But I am begging radio people, *Please discontinue your incessant advertising for these sex stimulants.* These ads are ridiculous. I don't want to hear about sex problems at 6:00 A.M. on Tuesday. I don't know who you think your target audience is at that time, but please give me a break. I'm just trying to open my eyes and find out about the weather. I don't need to be running around slugging down sex potions. Am I wrong here?

JERRY SPRINGER. Okay, he's an obvious medalist in the ridiculous category, I admit. But there's no honorable way to leave him off the list: He is the real thing, really ridiculous! When you think about it, he is doing exactly what Larry Flynt does: He debases other people in order to make money. To be fair, Springer does provide more humor than Flynt, but we all know what drives the entertainment. Jerry, it's ridiculous.

ROSIE'S RANTS. Ms. O'Donnell has talent, she works hard, she's gathered a lot of loyal fans. But what's going on with the political stuff? Nobody should begrudge any American the right to an opinion, but, hey, Rosie, come on, let's think out your flaky liberal agenda a little. Are you making sense, or are you spouting propaganda? I mean, a guy named Joseph Goebbels did the same thing on the very far right during World War II. Ms. O'Donnell demonizes anyone she disagrees with, and her musings are not to be questioned. But if you're gonna use your daytime soapbox to advance ideologies, Rosie, can't you at least allow someone with some knowledge to *question* you about it? (And I don't mean Tom Selleck.) I respect anyone with a well-thought-out opinion, but pure propaganda on national TV needs to be labeled for what it is. There are usually two sides to every issue. It is ridiculous to present only *your* side.

KATE MOSS, CALISTA FLOCKHART, AND THE REST OF THE SKULL-AND-BONES CREW. "Ridiculous" doesn't even begin to describe these matchsticks with blow-dried hair. What's even more ridiculous is that some young girls imitate them, often to the endangerment of their health. Life-threatening conditions like anorexia nervosa and bulimia are reinforced or even inspired by these high-paid wraiths. Besides, why do these ladies want to be so emaciated in the first place? Most guys don't like this look. They want *substance*, if you know what I mean. And people who do not eat properly are prone to serious physical and emotional side effects. I am sending Kate and Calista giant porterhouse steaks, along with a short note gently suggesting that they are being ridiculous.

PAMELA ANDERSON. *Too* much substance, if you know what I mean. This woman used to be really pretty and had a killer body that didn't need any enhancements or surgical interventions. Now she looks as if she was chiseled out of stone by a sculptor with Larry Flynt's artistic sensibilities. I guess some guys like this look and will still fantasize about a date with the renovated Pam. But I know that what she has done to herself is ridiculous. Besides, fellas, consider this: There's a real possibility that you might chip a tooth.

AL SHARPTON AND DAVID DUKE. They've got some fierce competition out there, but these two are the most ridiculous racial demagogues in the entire U.S.A. If God has a sense of humor, as I believe he does, they will be sharing a sauna in the netherworld. With one thermostat.

SOCIAL PROMOTIONS. So here's the deal with this ridiculous "educational strategy." The schools can't or don't teach some kids anything, but, according to the law, the kids have to go to school, even if they're a pain in the rear end. If school authorities insist that they either learn something or be held back, the kids will be around that much longer. So, to get rid of them as quickly as possible, teachers promote them through the system and allow them to graduate with a high school diploma. I've seen kids holding a diploma they couldn't even read. This is just great, isn't it? So now these kids are released into the world not knowing how to make change. That's why you see electronic cash registers that have pictures of products instead of numbers on the buttons. Worse, these kids have been taught one lesson very well in their twelve years of so-called schooling: They are not going to be held accountable for failure. When you have a lot of people believing that, you're in real trouble. Did you wonder why the U.S.A. has more people in prison than any other free nation in the world?

SAN FRANCISCO. Unmatched in physical beauty—even Gorbachev said it was his favorite American city!—this place has been screwed up by some of its ridiculous citizenry. In a misguided attempt at being compassionate, local politicians set up the most generous welfare system in California. Are we talking widows and orphans getting relief? Naw. What's happened is that every hophead and juicehead for miles around has rolled into town. Been walking near Union Square lately? It feels like Bombay. Aggressive panhandlers are everywhere; drunks and dope addicts are nodding out in doorways in full daylight. This is just great for your kids, who expected trolley cars and Fisherman's Wharf and great views of the bay and its surrounding mountains. But the locals don't seem concerned. In the midst of this downtown chaos, Mayor Willie Brown got reelected. You've probably seen him on your home TV screen, because he makes for good video. This is the guy who proposed giving panhandlers portable credit card machines so that people could donate with plastic. This is the guy whose chief of staff held an orgy at a city party, and guess who showed up? Why, hello, Mayor Brown! Brown is also the guy who believes that addicts have more rights than working Americans. The ridiculous city of San Francisco considers itself a town apart from the rest of America. Well, at least they're right on that.

SKIN PIERCING. While tattoos are silly enough, piercing is ridiculous. Do I have to explain why? There is absolutely no need to be pierced. Okay, it might send a message of nonconformity that will appeal to some elements of society, but it is destructive to your personal image in straight society. So, if you can sing like Sheryl Crow or paint like Picasso, by all means adorn your body with trinkets. You'll never have to ace a job interview. But if you have to make a living based on your wits, education, and intelligence, do not pierce! If you do, you'll drastically cut your income and life options. Listen up here: I *know* who is doing the hiring in America. They *don't like body piercing!* Okay? Puncturing your skin with pins, needles, or whatever is ridiculous. (As for tattoos, talk to a skin specialist. Ask how long it takes the pretty colors to run together into one dark purplish mess.)

TV WEATHERPEOPLE. Help me out here . . . Am I crazy? Isn't it ridiculous to have three minutes of weather "reporting" during a newscast? These people are usually likable, and they seem to know a lot about air masses and reservoir levels. But I don't need that stuff on every broadcast! Just put the weather for the next three days up there on the screen—days four and five have diminishing reliability returns—and shut up, please. Does anyone in the continental United States care about the Canadian clipper that may or may not materialize around Manitoba? Do we really need to hear about a low-pressure system that is terrorizing Sioux Falls, South Dakota? *Not unless we live in Sioux Falls!* Get it? Take these nice weatherpeople off the tube and find them some useful work. They may not really be ridiculous themselves, but they're doing a ridiculous job now.

GAYS IN THE ST. PATRICK'S DAY PARADE. This totally ridiculous "issue" comes up every year in New York City. Now, believe me when I tell you that the parade is taken seriously. There are more Irish Americans in the city than there are in Dublin. The parade is—depending upon your point of view—an annual rite of celebration, a drunken party, or an excuse to skip school and work, but everyone agrees it's "a great day for the Irish!" A large part of the city closes down for much of the day. Traditionally the parade honors St. Patrick. That's Patrick the *saint*, who spread the word of God in Erin more than fifteen hundred years ago. The parade marches up Fifth Avenue past St. Patrick's Cathedral, the largest Roman Catholic cathedral in America. The cardinal of the diocese of New York comes out on the church steps to observe the festivities. Get the picture? Add the various civic groups that march to show their respect to Patrick and the traditions of the Irish. Schools march, clubs march, politicians march. But none of these marchers carry signs announcing their sexual preferences. Since the first parade, which may have occurred before 1779, no group has ever participated carrying a sign that read, "The Foot Fetish Club from Canarsie." Nor have the crowds ever been treated to "The Staten Island Chapter of Wife Swappers, Ltd." Forget about "The Levittown S&M Senior Citizens Brigade." Nope, nothing like that. Ever. So it is clearly *inappropriate* for gays to march under a banner stating their sexual preference. That's just not in the context of the theme of the parade. Arguing otherwise is ridiculous!

CLICHÉS. My ears hurt. My mind wanders. Sorry, but I cannot pay attention to the people—and they're everywhere!—who are destroying the English language because they're too lazy to pause for a second, *think* what they really mean, and then choose words that are not being said over and over and over again. You're an individual. You are supposed to have original thoughts. It's ridiculous to fall back on words and phrases like "awesome," "you know," "like," "get a life," "get over it," the f-word, "absolutely," "deal with it," "exactly," and the rest of the pedestrian jargon that has stifled sensible conversation in America for the past decade. (Sports figures are just about the worst offenders, at least on TV. These guys make megabucks but seem to know only three or four phrases that cover the thrill of victory, the agony of defeat, *and* the incessant demands for new contracts.) Now, it's true that we've always had dopey phrases in our culture. And sometimes it's fun to use them tongue in cheek, when we're just playing around. But today the numbing repetition of mindless words and phrases is actually hindering people from *thinking about what they are saying*. We have an entire generation of students who believe that overusing such common terms is erudite and insightful. I know; I talk with them when I give speeches at colleges. This blather is ridiculous, of course, and also annoying. Let's drop the clichés. You don't need to "get a life"—you need to get a *dictionary*.

SEAN "PUFF DADDY" COMBS. Ridiculous, yes, but not a stupid man. He's clever enough to amass a fortune with NVT (that's "no visible talent"). But what is going on with this guy? He makes his millions and millions from catering to antisocial tastes with mind-numbing rap music, then he runs out to the Hamptons to party with the likes of Martha Stewart and Donald Trump. Meanwhile, he is living with some woman with whom he has two young children, but he's also running around in public with diva Jennifer Lopez. This is worse than ridiculous, because it is all being closely watched, naturally, by young kids all over America who think Puff Daddy is swift. Nice message you're sending, Puff guy. And, incredibly, you've got the establishment on board with you. After Combs and two "bodyguards" attacked and severely injured a rival record executive, the judge sentenced the Puffster to attend a single session of an "anger management class." The compassionate jurist also ruled that the conviction would not appear on Combs's permanent record. Nice sentence, if you can get it. And an effective deterrent! A few months later the Puff monster was arrested in connection with a nasty shooting incident in a Manhattan nightclub. So all in all this guy is bad news—and completely ridiculous. I hope he marries Martha Stewart. What were you thinking, Jennifer?

☐

Then there's the *tax code*.

I don't need to tell you, This is the most ridiculous thing in America today. Of course, that's been true for a long time. It was the great physicist Albert Einstein who said, "The hardest thing in the world to understand is the income tax." Well, the reason it's so complicated, Al, is that politicians want to (1) tax the hell out of you and (2) give the government an unfair chance to beat your brains out in court if you take it that far. Most Americans, because taxes are too complicated and often hidden, have no idea how much money they fork over. In New York State they come close to literally sucking your blood, since they tax it. Can you believe this? If a doctor suggests that you get a blood test for the good of your health, the state taxes the test. Wherever you live, chances are that you are paying tax on every important thing in your life: food, clothing, fuel, heat, home, car, savings, inheritance, travel, and on and on. This is truly sinful. America was not founded in order to keep you from holding on to your hard-earned money. The tax code and the philosophy behind it are simply out of control.

Politicians will argue—as many have on my program—that the government needs your money to operate properly. This is a lie. There is more than enough tax revenue available today to pay for the armed forces, roads, police, and other vital services without looting the take-home pay of working Americans. No, the reason our taxes are so punitive is right there in front of you: obvious and arrogant wastefulness in government-run programs. Forget the $400 toilet seats in the Pentagon budget— peanuts. The real killing waste is in programs that simply do not work.

I've already talked about the $30 billion the Clinton administration wastes every year on the so-called drug war. The program is a horrific failure, but they won't consider alternatives like coerced drug rehabilitation and mandatory drug testing for welfare recipients. Enough. Wipe out this annual $30 billion loss by ending the program.

Clinton's people have also spent $200 billion in his two terms to improve public education in America. Guess what? It has *not* improved.

Standardized test scores are flat. And that's true even though the tests have been dumbed down, while the dimmest students are exempt from taking them. Of course, it doesn't help the situation that many American schools are physically falling apart *despite* the massive spending at both the federal and the local levels. If you're a homeowner, you're probably paying a sizable school tax, even if you have no kids in school. Yet, your money has not prevented most of public education from being in disarray.

Why? Because the federal government cannot control what happens in local schools. Only local people can make a difference. So what are the feds doing? Throwing money at the problem instead of doing what could bring improvement: I mean, holding teachers accountable and enforcing strict discipline in the classroom and all over the school grounds. Bulletin: These things are *free*. As a former high school teacher, I can tell you that more tax money is wasted on foolish school programs and lunatic theory than on just about anything else in America.

I could give you hundreds of examples of ridiculous government waste, but that would take a whole other book. Right now, I have enough on my hands trying to write this one. But you can trust me on this: The tax situation in this country is brutal, including the fact that your elected representatives and their opponents are using entitlements to buy votes. That includes Social Security, Medicare, and Medicaid. Listen very carefully when the pols talk about these hot-button programs. Are they making sense, or are they pandering? *You* have to decide. The bottom line is that few government programs are run effectively or with discipline. What we call "waste" or "pork" is *reelection insurance* to our leaders. Besides, the prevailing wisdom is that there will always be more tax money coming in, so don't sweat it. Is it time for another tea party like the one given in honor of King George III in Boston Harbor? I'll meet you at the water's edge near the Big Dig.

☐

Finally in the realm of the ridiculous, the *most* ridiculous part of our American system is this: Different rules apply to the rich guys. It's not supposed to be that way, right? Our country was designed to be "for the people." *The* people, not the *rich* people.

But in today's America there are two kinds of justice: One for the rich like O. J. Simpson and Claus von Bulow and JonBenet Ramsay's parents, and the other for poverty-stricken thugs who get socked with tough sentences. Yes, money buys too much in America, including things that should never be for sale. So it can sabotage our system of justice by buying clever attorneys who know how to confuse, manipulate, and intimidate juries. As the campaign fund-raising scandals blatantly demonstrated, cash can also buy you access to a president. It certainly influences Congress, thus preventing any real reform. It also discourages our elected officials from acting with fiscal responsibility when spending public monies. It corrupts law enforcement from sea to shining sea, from the big cities to the smallest villages.

Want to take on the system and run for office yourself? Great idea. But if you don't have the money in your war chest, you haven't a prayer of winning. How democratic is that? The national preoccupation with money has damaged our society in deep-rooted ways.

There are solutions, but it will take discipline to make them work. Reform should start with the press. Rather than ridiculously glorify the Donald Trumps and Ted Turners, journalists in all media should go back to working-class sensibilities and values. If reporters would regularly expose the corruption that is all around us—but which they take for granted as part of the normal way of doing things in politics and business—then it would become much harder to play the money game.

Why doesn't that happen? Well, as I mentioned in my chapter about the Media Factor, it's because the press is mostly owned these days by people who are very rich themselves. They sign the reporters' paychecks. But they also make money only when you buy their newspapers or watch their news programs. If you support honest reporting, things might start to change.

To sum up, we have a ridiculous blind spot in America: the power and glorification of money. It's holding us all back. It's ridiculous, and it's related to some of the worst things I talk about next in the Bad Factor.

18. THE
BAD factor

When I use the word "bad," I mean "awful." "Bad" is so annoying that you want to club it with a baseball bat and bury it forever. But that's not possible. The bad in America is with us wherever we go. Whatever we do, it still raises its ugly head. We can't escape, no matter how hard we try. In our times, technology makes the bad worse, because it cannot distinguish between bad and good. It just spreads it all around, wildly. That is the moral weakness of technology.

For some reason, millions of us embrace the bad. I know because, at times, I am one of them. My excuse? I find bad things funny. But that is merely an excuse, and I'm not proud that I pay good money to see bad movies and eat bad food and read bad books. On the other hand, sometimes I just get hoodwinked. And often I am too lazy to seek out the good stuff—it's usually more difficult to work my way through and/or it costs more. That's the difference between a cheap mass-market paperback thriller and a new hardcover book about history or politics.

There are so many bad things in America I'm only going to give a sampling.

📺

ANY U.S. AIRLINE. Okay, it's a little bit worse for me because of my height. Still, anyone who boards an airplane in America these days is bound to feel like a POW along the River Kwai. Same food: meager and foul-tasting. Same accommodations: cramped and dirty. Same attendants: surly and (generally speaking) apathetic. All that's missing is David Niven to buck up our spirits and recommend a stiff upper lip. Maybe if we all board the plane whistling the theme of that movie, he'll show up and rescue us. Actually I don't think we're going to get through to the airline personnel by doing that or anything else. Standards began collapsing when Jimmy Carter deregulated the airlines. It seemed like a good idea at the time: Let market forces rule the skies. In practice, it has led to decreased service to many midsized and small markets. And flying anywhere is a painful experience to anyone over five six. Seats were downsized along with the IQ levels of the average employee, because salaries were cut. The entire system has since become a chaotic mess. Now Congress is threatening to get involved. That means the mess will probably get even worse. But somebody has to do *something*. I can ignore the food. I can survive the flight attendants who behave like indifferent toll collectors. But for the sake of *humanity*, the airlines ought to have enough people on staff to check in the flight without forcing passengers to wait an hour or more on line. And for heaven's sake, they ought to take a row or two of seats out of the cabin. That way, people like me won't have to practice involuntary yoga, and all of us can breathe more of the polluted, recycled airline air. Did you hear much outrage when a passenger was charged recently with trying to strangle a gate agent? I don't think so. It's bad on the ground and in the skies, and they are still not listening to us. I don't know what it's going to take.

RICE CAKES. Bad. No matter what you put on them, you are still eating dust. Plaster. Cardboard. Loam. There is no excuse for eating rice cakes at any time. Something very odd happened here. These objects were obviously manufactured for some other purpose, unknown to me, and were somehow mistakenly labeled and sold as food.

SPORT UTILITY VEHICLES. If you don't believe these monstrosities are big trouble and bad in every way, just look at some of the Americans who drive them. These people think they're riding stallions or something. Their eyes gleam at the power rumbling beneath them. They tailgate viciously, speed in all kinds of weather, and generally zip around as if they're invincible. When they race up near my Yugo, I tremble in fear. If I ever get rear-ended by one of these gas-guzzlers, I'll *land* in Yugoslavia. All right, you would never drive a Yugo, but these SUVs are a scourge and a menace to any sensibly sized, sensibly priced, economically fueled car. You find a parking place but when you return to your car, you're squeezed between two SUVs. It is *impossible* to see possible traffic or pedestrians as you back out. It's worse on the road. The women who drive them are especially crazed. The SUV is their great equalizer on the road. As her little kids freeze in terror, Mom weaves in and out of traffic, flipping the bird to anyone who doesn't like it. (Maybe now we know the answer to Sigmund Freud's famous question, "What do women want?") SUVs should be immediately outlawed. But they won't be. I may have to buy a Bradley fighting vehicle and exact my just revenge.

ROSEANNE. I don't care how many people watched it faithfully, her sitcom was *bad*. Her trash-mouth character didn't "represent" working-class America; it was a put-down. Her recent talk show was not just bad, it was *incredibly* bad. How this woman became rich and famous is a mystery that ranks right up there with the lost continent of Atlantis. This no-talent was once in a movie with Meryl Streep and Bruce Willis called *She-Devil*. Rent it, if you dare, and your VCR will refuse to function. Roseanne even managed to make Streep look bad on-screen, which is just about impossible. I hope Roseanne realizes how lucky she is. She keeps getting paid good money for bad performances . . . again and again and again. At least, so I hear. You won't find me anywhere near anything she does. Ever.

NFL GEAR. Troglodytes would refuse to wear this tacky garb. Wander into a prehistoric cave decked out in the ugly Cincinnati Bengals jersey, and you'd be beaten within an inch of your life. What do these National Football League marketing people think of us? Their garish cap, jackets, and double-knit jerseys are eye pollution. Clawing panthers? Purple Vikings? It would not be hard to come up with classy, tasteful designs that would be fun without making the wearer look foolish. The *worst* is the uniform of the Denver Broncos, evidently designed by a Mongolian nomad who knew nothing about Colorado or the franchise and was working off a hangover from fermented yak butter. Are there no mirrors in Colorado?

STEAK TARTARE. Did we have to do something very bad to the Tartars? And just what is this? Raw meat, right? Well, actually, it's raw minced beefsteak. But that's just the beginning. It's then mixed with onion, seasonings, and, to continue the theme, raw eggs. I don't want to eat it. I don't want to watch anyone else eat it. But if you like it, enjoy. With a side order of rice cakes.

LEONARDO DICAPRIO. (Skip this one if you're a fifteen-year-old girl.) This guy was so bad in *Titanic* that I was rooting for the iceberg. It's not bad enough that he's in the most-hyped movie of the decade. He's also in our face all the time with his personal escapades. He flits around New York and L.A. with a gang of hooligans, running up huge bar tabs and getting his name in the gossip columns. (And don't blame the gossip columnists. Do you think they get every one of their items from old-fashioned shoe-leather journalism? Naw. A lot of that stuff you see is paid for by restaurants or stars through their publicity reps.) Anyway, all of the publicity makes you wonder all the more what the guy has *really* done. He's bad. And his recent movies have sunk faster than the famed ocean liner. Also his interview with President Clinton on the environment proudly upheld Leo's bad status.

ONION-FLAVORED POTATO CHIPS. Not as bad as tomato juice flavored with clam juice? I think so. If you want to offend every human being you meet for the next forty-eight hours, then munch a few of these foul chips. You could aim a flamethrower into your mouth and still not exorcise the taste. Is there a reason to eat these things? No. They are bad for you. And they are also bad for the plants and humans you breathe on after eating these vile things.

WARREN BEATTY. This actor—once handsome but now as thick and jowly as Nixon—is a kind of senior citizens' DiCaprio. Yes, he's done some good work, such as *Bonnie and Clyde*. But seriously . . . *Dick Tracy?* What was *that* all about? And *Reds?* Communism is *swell?* Easy to say when you're living in Bel-Air or Malibu. The best thing about Beatty is his sister, Shirley MacLaine. The second best is his wife, Annette Bening. I just don't see what the Academy of Arts and Sciences sees, since they voted him a Lifetime Achievement Award. Did that include *Bulworth?* It was bad, and he was worse. He did achieve some dates with Madonna, but she ridiculed him so badly in a documentary that it couldn't have been worth it. I thought he'd lose his lunch right there on the screen. I'd give him a chance to respond on my show, but Warren probably needs at least three days to set up his lighting.

ABORTION. This is bad not just for the fetus but for all Americans. I'm not preaching here, but the destructiveness of the procedure does cheapen life. That's inevitable. We should all calm down and reevaluate the entire debate. It doesn't help to say that abortion is a lesser evil than interfering with a woman's right to control her own body. I understand that. It doesn't help to argue about exactly when life begins. No one knows. But

Americans should abhor abortion, not champion it. Everything should be done to avoid it. It's brutal. Brutality is always bad. And let's drop the spin words "pro-life" and "pro-choice." Let's go back to the basic problem and come up with answers that are not as violent as the act of abortion or as the actions of some demented antiabortion activists.

BARBRA STREISAND (AS AN ACTRESS). Can't knock her singing, except for some misguided screeches, but as for her acting, *please*. Did anyone see *Yentl*? Then tell me why that picture was made, except as a weird ego trip for the star. Who was the target audience? Robert Redford can be very convincing as an actor, but he flopped at convincing me that he was actually going after Barbra in *The Way We Were*. Okay, so he played a novelist, but that doesn't necessarily make him bonkers. Come on. How about *The Mirror Has Two Faces*? Did you see that? Nobody did, except me. And I had to because I was doing a newspaper column on Streisand. Barbra herself didn't even see the movie. She knew she was bad and stayed home.

DONALD TRUMP. What's up with the hair, Donald? Things are *bad* up there. He tried a scalp reduction operation a few years ago, but that wasn't a huge success, they say. Maybe that's why he's so mean-spirited. Not long ago, he tried to throw some little old lady off her property in Atlantic City. Bad. But she was a tough bird who had run an Italian restaurant for years, and she fought back with lawyers. She won, but it cost her. This is the guy who said he would be good for the country as our next president. How so? Would we all be forced to live in his condos? Trump is rich, which is supposedly good in America, but the man is bad, and he knows it.

PHONE SOLICITORS. The worst! This has to be the most terrible job in America, but that's no excuse. This is a full-employment economy. No one has to participate in this bad activity. How can you face yourself if you spend your work shift annoying people in their homes, often at dinnertime, by trying to sell them things they don't want—and using bad grammar while you're at it? These people are as bad as their jobs, I believe. They should be ashamed, but they're not. That makes them not only bad but stupid as well.

WAYNE NEWTON. Speaking of little old ladies, quite a few of them like Wayne. Ask them to explain it and all they can say is, "Well, he looks nice." That's a matter of opinion, and it isn't mine. When I saw him perform live in concert, I thought that calling the whole show bad was being too generous. He opened with an Elvis tune. If the King really were still alive, we'd know it: He'd have come out of hiding and jammed a blue suede shoe down Wayne's gullet.

JESSE HELMS. This guy is old, and he hates Wayne Newton. But that doesn't count for much since he hates just about everything and everybody and is still holding a grudge over the Civil War (sorry, Jesse . . . the War of Northern Aggression). He symbolizes the worst in American politics, aside from being Big Tobacco's fiercest champion. The good voters of North Carolina deserve better, but Jesse's divisive, take-no-prisoners campaigns bring out the crazies and scare off potential opponents. He's a bad thinker, legislator, and storyteller. When people call him a staunch conservative, they mean, "unable to hear anything anyone else is saying." Bad, bad, bad.

TED KENNEDY. The poster boy for a bad physique, he has explained to reporters, "It's the sauce, boys." This rich guy has somehow acquired a reputation as a devoted champion of the poor and downtrodden, but he has never associated much with any person fitting that description. In his somewhat younger years he was the top bad boy on Capitol Hill for a long time, mostly because he never met a waitress he didn't try to shag. No longer a boy by any definition, he's still bad, no matter how he tries to hide it. This is a karma thing with Kennedy, and you know what I'm talking about.

TATTOOS. You want to look like Dennis Rodman? Tattoos are a kind of label, but they don't say what the wearers think they say. They don't say, "I'm hip and cool and unique and pushing the envelope." No. They say, "Beneath these silly pictures and slogans on my skin, I'm a dunce." With a tattoo you are never going to make it in the white-collar world of America. That's your choice, of course. I leave you to it. But a tattoo is a bad thing if you care about your earning power.

MICHAEL JACKSON/JESSE JACKSON. Not related, but both bad. Michael was born with incredible talent and worked hard to develop it, but his personal life has turned him into an international pariah, and deservedly so. Did he have a strange childhood, and does he have serious psychological problems now? Sure, but he's an adult in terms of years, and it's time to work it out. Michael, you have no one to blame but yourself for your stunts today. Your weird public behavior and odd relationships offstage cannot be excused. (An exception: What goes on between him and that monkey is his own business.) Your flat-out bad actions have wrecked your career in America. Again, we might be seeing karma in motion: What goes around, comes around.

And what about Jesse Jackson? Well, he's *still* around . . . the reverend who's a millionaire even though he's never had a job in the private sector except some weekly CNN show that's really bad and doesn't pay well. His latest book took a lot of gall. It's called *It's About the Money*. Yeah, it *is* . . . in your case, Reverend. But how'd you get all that money? Who gave it to you? What's the deal behind it all? This guy has "bad" written all over him—and not by a ghostwriter.

CHINESE FOOD IN AMERICA. I know, I know. Since "everybody" likes the stuff, it's un-American to say that it's bad. But it is! The Chinese don't eat MSG in China. They don't eat "foo-young," or whatever they're serving down at the corner restaurant. I've never trusted the "Chinese food" you get in this country because it's so gooey I can't tell what's in there. Whatever it is, I strongly suspect, has got to be bad. And it's even worse if you make the mistake of ordering takeout. The goo becomes congealed. And there's always something missing. Those little boxes look as if they have live goldfish in them. And everything looks and smells the same. Bad.

MARTHA STEWART. You knew she'd rank among the winners here. A first-rate con artist who fights with nearly everyone in her quest for fame and riches, Ms. Stewart has created a fantasy about herself and about "the good life" that is bad for common sense and bad for your pocketbook. (Check out the price for a quart of her house paint.) While she masquerades as a paragon of good taste, she has turned herself into a snooty, condescending mogul of trivia. The woman has convinced millions that she is Harriet Nelson for the twenty-first century, but she isn't. Harriet's TV image was about values and caring. Martha's is about material things and showing off and prettifying your table settings instead of being aware of the world outside your house. Harriet was good. Martha is bad. I mean, she leaves a bad taste. (Hold the applause, if you can.)

MONICA LEWINSKY. Okay, I've made the point elsewhere, so I'll be brief. The princess of bad attitude, Ms. Lewinsky continues to win sympathy from some Americans. That's bad. She ought to get a job and keep her mouth shut (again, hold the applause) in all situations. If she takes responsibility for her life and stops the whining, I'll never mention her again. Except possibly in something like the next chapter.

SUSHI. No way. The dictionary definition of "sushi" is "raw fish that has been handled by sixteen people before it gets to me." It's not hard to figure out what that means. Bad.

CHARLES GRODIN (AS TALK SHOW HOST). A really good actor, Mr. Grodin was such a bad talk show host that NBC sacked him. Is this a case of an airhead actor needing a script to come across well? Whatever, no one ever knew what he was trying to say on the air. Huh? Whazzat? When the man sat there talking at the camera, I couldn't for the life of me get the gist of his diatribes. He liked Clinton, but why? He seemed to like Letterman, too, but he was always mad at him for some unexplained reason. It took a lot of work to watch Grodin. You weren't waiting for the other shoe to drop; you were waiting for *any* shoe to drop. That's not good for a talk show host. That's bad.

DAYTIME TV. Firemen on twenty-four-hour alert have to watch this stuff. Think about that next time they ask for a raise. ER personnel have it playing in the background. You might want to page your own doctor quick. From Springer (see above) and Montel to Jenny and Sally to the soaps and the judges to the girl-chat programs, daytime TV is worse than a desert. Deserts are usually quiet. You do not want to find yourself hooked on this swill. In my opinion, daytime TV is the true reason U.S. unemployment is so low. I mean, would you rather watch a cooking show or sling hash at a diner? Easy question.

JOHNNIE COCHRAN. Does anyone believe that Cochran, who's obviously pretty slick, thinks that O. J. Simpson is innocent? Does *anyone* believe that? (Except those morality-challenged students at Howard University who applauded the murderer's acquittal on national television. The rest of us have better sense.) All right, so how can this guy run around talking about "justice" when he helped spring a killer? I know that everyone is legally entitled to a fair trial, but "fair trial" does not mean playing the race card. Cochran did that big-time with a naive and minimally educated jury—and it worked. But this victory seems to be very good for his pocketbook. That was bad, Johnnie. We haven't forgotten your role in the Simpson fiasco, and we're not going to. Whenever you get up on the next soapbox, everything you say about "justice" will be taken in context of your cynical perversion of justice in that L.A. courtroom. Does the name "Nicole" ring a bell, Counselor?

SEX TALK RADIO. "Hey, Tom Leykis? . . . It's Larry from Cleveland. Yeah, I got a problem with this chick. She won't put out even though I bought her a dinner. She's got a great bod, but she won't do the deed. What should I do now . . ." I've got some very useful advice for Larry, but he won't like it. And there's nothing to say about such programs except they're indescribably bad. So I'm not going to describe them.

HOWARD STERN. Fifteen years ago I loved this guy, who had been a classmate of mine at Boston University. I admired his daring on the radio and his irreverent antiauthority brand of humor. But then Howard became obsessed with lesbians. Now, many men have fantasies about ladies "mingling." That's not unusual. But to talk about it every day of the week for four hours beginning at 6:00 A.M. is in the same league as those sex potions. Howard, it's 6:20! Give the lesbians a break. And the audience, too. Stern's schtick is getting tired and, unfortunately, bad.

◻

As I said earlier, I would have to leave a lot of bad people and things out of this chapter. No time. No space. And you know that some new culprits will arrive on the scene between the time I write these pages and this book gets into your hands. Don't worry. I'm keeping track of the Bad Factor every night on *The O'Reilly Factor*.

There will always be so much bad stuff that no one can list it all. So if I've left out any of your favorite bad things and bad people, maybe next time.

But we can't end on that note. There are plenty of good things in America. And you know what? The list is even longer, so I will be leaving out even more. In the next chapter I'm going to list a few personal favorites. But I hope that's just a way of reminding you of your own.

19. THE GOOD factor

For the rest of the book, let's be totally positive. And why not? There are more good things in America than anywhere else on earth. I can only list a fraction of them. And there's not much to say about them, because you'll recognize right away what I mean.

If you're afraid I'm going to start sounding like Up with People or something, skip this chapter. The next chapter, which is very short, is the last important thing I have to say. But if you'd like to join me in thinking about some of the good things and people that enrich our lives in America, here goes . . .

✍

Let's forget the bad and ridiculous people by honoring the good people. No nation on earth has produced so many original personalities as we have—and still do.

I'm listing just a few of the Americans I admire:

BILL COSBY. Maybe he comes across as a little bitter sometimes, but he is honestly funny. In fact, I prefer him when, as in his earlier solo stuff, he doesn't get cloying in situation-comedy style. Even now, though, he is capable of keenly insightful jokes that can be devastating. Kindly Dr. Huxtable has a very sharp mental scalpel. And through his positive image on TV Cosby has presented an admirable role model.

BILL MURRAY. With good material Murray is the funniest human being in the country. Even with bad material he's always watchable. He's got that great gift of making you think that only you and he are in on the joke—

even though tens of millions of other people are watching and get the same feeling.

MIKE MYERS. The ultimate funny yuppie, Myers is the most creative performer I've ever seen. How did this Canadian get our culture down pat? In person he makes you wonder if he might really be out of his mind, though he is very much a gentleman, and he certainly deserves the big bucks for the two Austin Powers flicks. Some of his cleverest characters are in the *SNL* skits, and even though Myers did a cloying Oscars interview with Barbara Walters, he's still damned good!

PAUL NEWMAN. This seventy-five-year-old sex symbol made a pact with the devil. I know it! He can still steal the screen from any young actors, men or women, by just raising an eyebrow. But it's one thing to maintain a magnetic screen presence into senior citizenhood. Much more important, Newman raises millions for ailing children. Warren Beatty talks big. Paul Newman walks big.

CHARLTON HESTON. He's underrated as an actor. His conservative politics probably keeps some critics and other people from appreciating his great talent, but he commands the screen no matter how hokey the flick. A director friend once shot a sixty-second public service spot with this very professional actor at Heston's Hollywood home. Heston looked at the script for the first time, walked once around his pool, then sat down before the cameras. "Would you like to take time to memorize your lines and rehearse, Mr. Heston?" my friend asked. "Son," said the actor, "I've been doing this for a while. Just roll the cameras." The take was letter-perfect. During some of the recent uproar about his work for the National Rifle Association, Heston was satirized in an Op-Ed piece by Gary Krist for the *New York Times*. Heston tracked down the writer's home telephone number and called to say, "That was very funny. It's good to have some humor injected into this thing." Good. Sane. A gentleman.

LUTHER VANDROSS. His early stuff was the best, to my ears. Now he has a tendency to "Barry White" the romantic ballads, and that's not fair to his own originality. Still, his music is almost perfect. It holds up well after many airings. And I say that "Here and Now."

SANTA CLAUS. Originally Dutch, he was brought over as a folk tradition by the folks who settled the present-day New York area, calling it New Amsterdam. When that colony collapsed and the English moved in, they took over Santa Claus, too. Now we Americans own the rights. He is a great role model for kids, so keep the faith going as long as you can. They will thank you for it when they're adults. Everyone remembers when they discovered that Santa Claus might not exist. Can't prove it to me.

ARETHA FRANKLIN. According to published reports, the woman can be quite a behavioral problem. Okay, I'll steer clear of her, but her recordings will stay with me forever. She's laid down no better single than "Chain of Fools."

GENE HACKMAN. The best character actor alive, he and his agent had to fight hard to get him the lead in *The French Connection*. But that hit movie is unimaginable without him. He never overdoes a role, even though he's been signed to do some intense villains and maniacs. Check out his Lex Luthor in the *Superman* movies for a different side, a comic brilliance that is quite a surprise after so much serious stuff.

DENNIS THE MENACE AND THE PEANUTS GANG. All put together, these are the greatest kids on the planet. They were my childhood role models, along with Eddie Haskell. Make of that whatever you will.

THE HARDY BOYS. I'm talking about the original, the authentic brothers in the Dixon books, not the bland Frank and Joe in Disney's TV series. And I don't much like the new Hardy Boys paperback books being written by a slew of writers today—too much violence and realism, too much sophistication. No, if you have young boys, make sure they go back to the originals.

JANET JACKSON. Don't know why, but I like her. It's time for her brother Michael to be installed in Madame Tussaud's Wax Museum. I mean *now*. But Janet is a lively performer who seems to understand the meaning of the word "melody." This, of course, separates her from most of the other top rock performers of the day.

STEVEN SPIELBERG. With his technical expertise and superb visual sense, he is a great moviemaker. Sometimes his movies try too hard to make a political statement, maybe, but every one of them has been interesting. That's something you can't say about the work of another great filmmaker, Francis Ford Coppola. And Spielberg is always trying something new. At his best, he comes up with deep insights into the human condition.

TOM HANKS. This great actor is also a hysterical comedian—an extremely rare combination, although too many actors and comedians today don't realize it. He's also rumored to be a nice guy, but I don't know that from my own experience. I first noticed him in the TV series *Bosom Buddies*, in which for some reason he ran around every week dressed like a girl. Even then, you could see that he had star power. By the way, his costar in the show was Peter Scolari of *The Bob Newhart Show*. When Regis asks, you will know.

ROBIN WILLIAMS. I mean, Robin Williams the comedian. Not R.W. the actor. Especially when he goes for the heartstrings, he tries too hard and he's not convincing. But he was terrifically funny in *Good Morning, Vietnam*; *Mrs. Doubtfire*; and *The Birdcage*. These were cartoon characters, but it worked. Williams is unusually smart, bringing in several levels of humor at once and juggling words like crazy, but sometimes the wit is lost in the swirl of his hyperdelivery.

JONATHAN WINTERS. Williams's acknowledged role model, Winters is one of the funniest men who ever lived. He has been very underappreciated in America because it's so hard to harness his wild genius in the usual TV and movie formats. If you've never heard them, try his comedy albums. They are the best of all time, and that includes the albums of Mel Brooks, Carl Reiner, Richard Pryor, and George Carlin (and I believe they'd all agree with me).

SAM DONALDSON. You have to know something about backstage TV to understand how good Sam is. He's a risk-taker in an industry dominated by phonies and charlatans and yes-persons. And he's never boring. Even if you think he can be obnoxious, I think you have to agree that he has proved over and over that he has guts. That is rare in TV news. (Of course, I guess another exception, if you believe ABC-TV, is hard-hitting Earth Day correspondent Leonardo DiCaprio.)

CHARLES RANGEL. The congressman from Harlem may be to the left of Karl Marx, but he will show up anywhere to defend his positions, and he does so with good humor. I always enjoy sparring with him, and I find that he is always worth listening to. Why? Because he is a hardscrabble guy who actually cares about his constituents. If we had more elected officials like him, from left to center to right of the political spectrum, this would be more like the country designed by our Founding Fathers. There's nothing wrong with having opposite points of view. What's wrong is corruption or incompetence.

DORIS DAY. For my eyes, she is quite simply the prettiest, most all-

American actress ever. She is also a comedian with a deft touch. It's become chic or something to laugh at just about anything about the 1950s, and that includes such Doris Day classics as *Pillow Talk*. Well, go out and rent one of her hits, and you might be surprised. They've gotten better with age. In her personal life Ms. Day apparently had a great many disappointments, but she does not whine publicly, and she has devoted herself to doing great work with abused animals. In case you have no idea *who* I'm talking about, the closest thing we have to Doris Day on today's screens is Debra Messing, star of TV's *Will and Grace*. I hope she learns from her predecessor how to have a memorable career and a dignified public image.

MIKE WALLACE. If you're still the best interviewer in the television business at age eighty-two (and also a noted figure on the New York City celebrity circuit), you're doing something way right. Wallace is deeply ensconced in the establishment, and so the portrait of him in the film *The Insider* is mostly accurate. Still, he demonstrates that it's possible to get better with age. Maybe that's because he's still just about as competitive as when he started out.

PAUL HARVEY. Even further into his eighties than Wallace, he is as good on radio as Mike is on television. In fact, I consider Harvey to be the best radio man ever. In person he is much more soft-spoken than you expect and almost frail. But when that studio light turns on, this pro booms out his stories and opinions in a voice that still gets people thinking all over America.

DAVE BARRY. He is the funniest writer in America, and it has nothing to do with his haircut. Barry's yuppie frame of reference, which you might think has already been covered by others, is staggeringly original and *funny*. And I am not making this up.

ELVIS PRESLEY. Despite the outfits from Hell—those capes and sequins!—there's never been a better onstage performer, at least not in my lifetime. Even if he was usually in a haze, he somehow knew exactly how to engage the crowd on every song. He made Frank Sinatra look like Frosty the Snowman.

ANN-MARGRET. She was reputed to be a close friend of Elvis. Whether that's true or not, she is perhaps the sexiest woman in the country. (Sorry, Ms. Reno.) If you haven't seen her in *Viva Las Vegas*, you must do so immediately. As I recall, Ms. Margret didn't need silicone-enhanced boobs or lip implants or fake cheekbones. She still sends Pamela Anderson to the back of the line.

STEVE ALLEN. This totally original comic mind is the godfather of talk TV. Aside from some of his dopey songs and half-baked political ideas, he was great hosting *The Tonight Show*. With his topical humor he opened the way to the equally brilliant Johnny Carson and the less brilliant Jay Leno.

ELAINE MAY. It's simple: She's the funniest woman in America. She and Mike Nichols burst on the scene with their comic skits in the late 1950s. No one had ever hit the nation's funny bone in quite that way—it was dry wit that had people rolling in the aisles. If you have no idea who she is, check out the movie *The Birdcage* with Robin Williams and Nathan Lane. Nichols directed, and she wrote the screenplay.

MICHAEL JORDAN. Okay, he didn't make the grade in minor league baseball, and his enthusiastic golf outings leave him pretty much in the duffer class. But the greatest basketball player of all time is also the best athlete I've ever seen play in any sport.

ROBERT KENNEDY, SR. He was the toughest politician I ever saw. He said that he never forgot a friend or an enemy, and I believe him. He took on the Mob and the corrupt unions. Biographers say he was "ruthless," but there's no question that Bobby Kennedy was also ruthlessly *effective*. He did what all politicians should be doing: He tried to right wrongs. How his brother Teddy came from the same family beats the hell out of me.

WILLIE MAYS. His stats are legendary, but there was more to Mays than the numbers. The whole package—man and talent—made him the best baseball player I've ever seen.

CLINT EASTWOOD. I've mentioned our encounter in "The Celebrity Factor," and you know that he's been my role model on bad days. He was the shrewdest actor/director I've ever met. If he went downhill after *Unforgiven*, give the guy credit. After all, he dug pools for a living before becoming the biggest movie star in the world. There's never been anything fancy about Eastwood. He just understood screen presence and timing. He's made some of the most entertaining movies ever, at least for the men in the audience.

PETE HAMILL. I've never read a better columnist and print journalist. He's honest and unafraid. He knows that this country is based upon the hard work of blue-collar Americans. Hamill remains a role model for me to this very day.

WILLIAM SAFIRE. The smartest newspaper columnist I've ever read has also got to be one of the hardest working. Agree with him or not, you can see that he always does his homework before spouting his opinion. He does not rest on his laurels.

MIKE ROYKO. Based in Chicago, he didn't get as much attention, maybe, as the journalists in New York and Washington, but he was the toughest newspaper columnist I ever read. His death left a huge vacuum in journalism but was a relief for some of the scoundrels who inhabit the Windy City.

PETER GENT. This former Dallas Cowboys football player wrote the finest sports novel ever, *North Dallas Forty*. Don't rely on the movie. Find the book and read it.

MICHAEL CRICHTON AND TOM CLANCY. Crichton's *Rising Sun* and Clancy's *Red Storm Rising* are the two most entertaining American novels I've come across. Maybe something about the word "rising" does it for me, but both men know how to keep a story rocketing along. They also pack their novels with fascinating facts about how the real world works.

"THE STAND," BY STEPHEN KING. There's no better piece of science fiction—in or out of print. That includes Jules Verne and Isaac Asimov.

"SHIBUMI," BY TREVANIAN. This is by far the most gripping thriller I've ever read. I don't know how he does it. From writing my own novel, I've learned that it's not as easy as it looks.

"THE LEGEND OF SLEEPY HOLLOW," BY WASHINGTON IRVING. Call it fantasy, horror story, literary folk tale, whatever you want, it's the best. Do *not* see director Tim Burton's ridiculous movie of the same name starring Johnny Depp. Unless you just want to see how brilliant storytelling can be turned into childish nonsense.

THE DOORS. Okay, I'm sorry about Jim Morrison. I can't defend his outrages or his self-destruction. Another waste of talent and promise. I wish all of these guys had more sense about their personal lives. But in the end, all I care about is their music: They were the best hard rock group ever.

THE BEACH BOYS. Forget the sentimental, confused TV "docudrama," or whatever it was. These guys are responsible for the most fun songs ever. That's all I need to know about them.

EARTH, WIND AND FIRE. Tops in the R&B category. By the way, if you think you don't like R&B, try them as an introduction. Same for the Doors, if you think you don't like hard rock. You might be surprised. When someone's the best—in *anything*—it's worth your time.

☐

Okay, you've heard me out on some of the good people I know something about. They give me pleasure, sanity, entertainment in a world that can be crazy and disappointing some days. They remind me of the good things in American life.

And there are many good things . . .

For example, we take for granted the amazing convenience that is available to practically all of us, especially in the matter of feeding our faces. We don't have the best food in the world, because we race around like lemmings, but we do have the most variety. In many parts of the country restaurants and grocery stores are open around the clock. And we have the best *junk food* on the planet, including Breyer's ice cream, Nathan's hot dogs, Pizza Hut deep dish, and Snapple orange drink. Don't tell your nutritionist (or any of your kids going through a health food phase), but I have to tell you that purely from the standpoint of taste, you can't beat this stuff.

In addition to convenience we have the widest variety of diversions. Even if you're a miserable grouch who hates everything, you can find some diverting entertainment. The listings for live music, sports, traveling shows, fairs, rodeos, exhibitions, lectures, and all the rest in even a medium-sized town are usually amazing throughout the year. Or you can click through hundreds of cable TV channels. (Yeah, I made fun of them in an earlier chapter, but if you have special interests and you read the schedule carefully, you're likely to find something good every night of the week. Sports, history, nature, drama—it's all there.) If you've joined the twenty-first century, you're hooked up to the Internet—a continually growing international resource of information and conversation. There's stuff on the computer I haven't even figured out yet, but it's making the world a more interesting place. And there's your local library, where every kind of book imaginable is *free*. Try getting that kind of info in Cuba. You'll be cutting sugarcane for the rest of your life.

And aside from watching sports live or on TV, this country is chock-full of people who like to keep playing until they drop. You are bound to be near some kind of league doing something. Anyone can bowl. Soft-ball teams are available for all age groups and talent levels. There are pickup games of basketball and baseball in most parks. Health clubs are everywhere, so it's easy to find an affordable place to swim, jog, lift weights, or simply baste in the sauna pretending to be Finnish.

I mean, only a moron can be bored in this country. Take a trip to Bel-gium and then tell me America isn't the land of diversion and entertain-ment. Soon, if the experts are right, the technology of "virtual reality" will allow you to experience just about *everything* without having to leave your house. Twenty-four hours a day of this would *not* be a good idea, of course: Leaving the house and getting out into the real world is what life is all about. But occasionally, when you're tired some day, the virtual option can provide an interesting break, right? Hello, Halle Berry—is that really you inside the virtual reality gizmo?

And speaking of options, we have religious options, style options, lifestyle options, vacation options, transportation options, and on and on. Americans have more options in more areas than anyone else alive. The Swiss? I believe fondue, Alps, and yodeling just about covers it. Talk radio in Lucerne? No way. Professional wrestling in the shadow of the Matter-horn? Doesn't happen. The NFL? Can't get it, Klaus. Back to the slopes with your toboggan, guy.

Maybe it's jingoistic, but I thank God that I was born here in America—even though it was in New York City! My parents brought my sister and me into a world of plenty, even if our seats weren't all that great—but that was just the luck of the draw. I could just as easily have been conceived in Islamabad. In that case, I'd be much more familiar with the habits of a cobra, maybe, but I would have missed out on Howdy Doody, the Mouseketeers, and *The Untouchables*. I wouldn't have played Little League baseball and high school ice hockey, or had my first slow dance to the hit single "Hey, Paula!"

But what better tells the story about America than the movies we love? I can't end a chapter about the Good Factor without listing my favorites. After all, despite Fellini and Kurosawa and David Lean and a few French-men whose names I forget, American movies are still the best in the world. It all started here in 1896, when Thomas Edison's assistant W. K. I. Dickson came up with the first camera/projector system that actually worked. A little more than a decade later Cecil B. DeMille and other directors were at work in Hollywood. And look how they churn them out today!

Expensive blockbusters don't mean quality, of course. Modern film in America has declined at about the same rate as the national educational system. Thank God the good movies of the past are available on cassette, CD, and cable. Here's what I like, and why:

THE GODFATHER, PARTS I AND II. For my money, these are the best films ever made. Both (unlike the jumbled *Godfather, Part III*) are rich in almost every way: superb acting, brilliantly written scripts, and fantastic production values. Besides, a film is destined for historical importance when it contains the immortal line "Leave the gun. Take the cannolis."

CASABLANCA. The famous story goes that they had almost finished filming this classic before they could decide how to end it. No wonder, because no viewer ever wants it to end. You can see it ten times and then come back again. Made on the cheap, the film captures the menace of the conquering Nazis in an exotic Moroccan setting. Humphrey Bogart (of course), Peter Lorre, and Claude Rains turn in great performances that are also unforgettable acting lessons, but somebody forgot to wake up Ingrid Bergman. She's beautiful, but only semiconscious.

DRACULA. Of all the attempts, the best take on Bram Stoker's novel is the one starring Bela Lugosi. It has the best line, and he delivers it perfectly: "I never drink . . . wine."

THE WIZARD OF OZ. Judy Garland's a little old (they had to bind her sizable seventeen-year-old's breasts) and the special effects aren't much better than you get at Photo Mat, but no one's ever complained. The thing works. It's the best kids' movie of all time. There's no better witch anywhere than Margaret Hamilton. You hate her. You love her. The best line: "O-leeee-o, o-leeee-o."

THE PRODUCERS. Quite simply the funniest movie ever made, it is also one of the smartest. Zero Mostel, Gene Wilder and Mel Brooks collaborated on this caper movie with its notorious musical *Springtime for Hitler*. (Yeah, this kind of joke and most of the movie require a frame of reference that may be lacking in the audiences for *American Pie*.) Because the script's so witty and the three stars are obviously improvising like crazy, you have to see the flick at least three times to catch all of the fun.

SCHINDLER'S LIST. You will feel that you are actually in a concentration camp. This terrifying but inspiring story is a tremendous achievement; it will stay with you forever. Unlike a later film also directed by Steven Spielberg, *Saving Private Ryan*, the film understates its violence, making it possible for a larger audience to see it.

THE EXORCIST. Max von Sydow, the great Swedish actor, is unforgettable in this film, which is both scary as hell and historically accurate. The best line: "I usta be a good Catlic, Father."

THE SHOOTIST. John Wayne's last film is the best western I've ever seen. One of the classic acting moments of all time is the first meeting between the Duke and Richard Boone. If you ever doubted Wayne's savvy as an actor, you have to see him in this movie. Sure, he had more presence than almost anyone, but he also had the talent to go along with it.

DR. NO. The first James Bond film may be the best. For the first time, we saw Sean Connery, who gives one of the most dominating film performances ever. For my money, he still owns the role. He could play it in a wheelchair in his eighties, and I'd believe it. And then there's Ursula Andress! She is very *convincing*, largely because she has only six words of dialogue and lets her bikini do the rest of the talking.

THE BRIDGE ON THE RIVER KWAI. In my book (no pun intended) this is the best war film ever made. Alec Guinness is spectacular. Jack Hawkins and William Holden aren't slouches. Like *Schindler's List*, this is also great moviemaking that puts you believably inside a concentration camp, this time along with POWs. The best scene: captured soldiers tortured by being forced to stand in the hot sun.

A SHOT IN THE DARK. Peter Sellers was great almost all of the time, but this is his funniest movie of all—and that includes the Pink Panther flicks and *Dr. Strangelove*. With Sellers you got unbelievable comic timing along with perfectly coordinated facial expressions. (You also got gastric distress working with this difficult actor, they say. When he had a heart attack on the set of a Billy Wilder film, the director said, "Heart attack? You have to have a heart to have an attack.") Don't even blink your eyes, or you'll miss the full impact of Sellers's genius.

SOME LIKE IT HOT. You certainly know about this one: Marilyn Monroe, Jack Lemmon, and Tony Curtis, with the boys running away from gangsters by disguising themselves as members of an all-girl band. Even Curtis is good in this very funny, very clever romp. Marilyn is her legendary self, but her eyes are unusually clear, for once.

SATURDAY NIGHT FEVER. I've already told you about my own disco fever. This movie perfectly captures a Brooklyn subculture of the 1970s that had echoes in towns all across the country. Look beyond the disco madness and you'll see some of the best character acting ever. Best line: "Don't hit the hair. I spend alotta time on the hair and you go and hit it." And Travolta? He does the role so accurately that we all thought that's all he could do, because he was just being himself. He's been proving us wrong in a huge range of parts ever since.

THE BIRDS. Even people who never saw it think they saw it. The film is part of our culture and part of our language. Hitchcock scared the pants off us with some of nature's most harmless creatures. Check out Tippi Hedren: She *really* looks frightened. (And that's before she had Don Johnson for a son-in-law.) Rod Taylor just looks confused. It's the birds who look as if they're having a real blast.

BONNIE AND CLYDE. This is pure hokum and pure entertainment. Gene Hackman, who made my list of good people earlier in the chapter, is terrific as Buck Barrow. Even my pal Warren Beatty is good in this one. For once, he actually seems to be playing a character.

Well, that's enough. If I've missed your favorites, don't write me a nasty letter. But I would like you to write me on another subject, as I explain in the next chapter.

20. THE
GRATITUDE `factor`

TALKING POINT: Thanks for reading this book. I'm grateful.

Time is tight for just about everybody these days, and you're probably bombarded by all kinds of information and opinion. So thanks for taking the time.

Because I appreciate your interest, I look forward to your feedback. You can write to me:

BILL O'REILLY

FOX NEWS CHANNEL

1211 AVENUE OF THE AMERICAS

NEW YORK, NY 10036

Or you can e-mail me at *Oreilly@FoxNews.com*.

First of all, I really want to know whether or not you found this book worthwhile. I intend to keep on writing in this format, but if I can help it, I don't want to waste anyone's time. Second, I want to know exactly what you liked and what you didn't like. If I've been unclear or incomplete or dead wrong, in your view, I want to know about it.

Your comments might raise the kind of issues that I need to address down the road on the air or in my weekly column for *APBNews.com* or in the next book. I want my viewers and readers to be an active part of my ongoing discussion of what's good, bad and ridiculous about our great country.

And if this book enhanced your life in any way, I'd *certainly* like to know about it.

THIS JUST IN: "Ingratitude is always a form of weakness. I have never known a man of real ability to be ungrateful." —Johann Wolfgang von Goethe

What I most wanted this book to accomplish was to instill in you a belief that you can realize your dreams and goals. As I've emphasized throughout, that takes discipline and determination—at least, to do it honestly—but it also takes an awareness of the big picture in today's America.

The formula is simple: Face the truth, then make the best of it. I hope this book has closed that deal. When you find yourself challenged by a tense situation, factor in the message of this book. Understand the game . . . and you will win—*if* you work your tail off and stay honest.

What I'm talking about here is your Personal Factor.

Use it.

And as you do, I wish you the very best. After all, that's the least I can do for someone who has honored me by reading this book.